EXPLICIT UTOPIAS

EXPLICIT UTOPIAS

*Rewriting the Sexual
in Women's Pornography*

AMALIA ZIV

Published by State University of New York Press, Albany

© 2015 State University of New York

All rights reserved

Printed in the United States of America

No part of this book may be used or reproduced in any manner whatsoever without written permission. No part of this book may be stored in a retrieval system or transmitted in any form or by any means including electronic, electrostatic, magnetic tape, mechanical, photocopying, recording, or otherwise without the prior permission in writing of the publisher.

For information, contact State University of New York Press, Albany, NY
www.sunypress.edu

Production, Jenn Bennett
Marketing, Anne M. Valentine

Library of Congress Cataloging-in-Publication Data

Ziv, Amalia.
 Explicit utopias : rewriting the sexual in women's pornography / Amalia Ziv.
    pages cm
 Includes bibliographical references and index.
 ISBN 978-1-4384-5709-3 (hardcover : alk. paper)
 ISBN 978-1-4384-5708-6 (paperback : alk. paper) — ISBN 978-1-4384-5710-9 (e-book) 1. Pornography—Social aspects. 2. Feminism. 3. Feminist theory. I. Title.
 HQ471.Z58 2015
 306.77—dc23
                                                    2014031755

10 9 8 7 6 5 4 3 2 1

For my parents, Tova and Gideon Ziv

Contents

	List of Illustrations	ix
	Acknowledgments	xi
	Introduction: Pornography, Subjectivity, and the Reinscription of Fantasy	1
ONE	Between Sexual Commodities and Sexual Subjects: The Feminist Pornography Debate Revisited	25
TWO	The Phantasmatic Gay Man: Cross-Identification in Women's Pornography	71
THREE	Refiguring Penetration	101
FOUR	The Phallus and Its Vicissitudes	139
FIVE	Sexuality beyond Gender: Gender Performativity in Lesbian Pornography	171
SIX	Female Sexual Subjectivity in a Queer World	197
	Coda: Pornographic Pedagogy, Explicit Utopias, and the Future of Female Sexual Subjectivity	227
	Notes	233
	Works Cited	275
	Index	293

Illustrations

3.1. The "mega-gasm." Still from *The Sluts and Goddesses Video Workshop*.   136

4.1. Butch striptease. Still from *Clips*.   160

4.2. The femme phallus and the female cum shot. Still from *Clips*.   164

6.1. Receptivity as hypermasculine. Still from *Alley of the Tranny Boys*.   208

6.2. Deterritorializing the vagina. Still from *Sexing the Transman XXX*.   211

6.3. The transmasculine continuum. Still from *Alley of the Tranny Boys*.   213

Acknowledgments

Many people have contributed to the formation of this book in various stages of its evolution.

The impetus for this project dates as far back as my graduate studies at Brown University, where I became preoccupied with the question of female sexual subjectivity in pornography and began to explore it in courses I took with Carolyn Dean and Henry Abelove. Carolyn Dean's class The History of Pornography was especially formative and laid out the foundations of my knowledge and thinking on the subject. I am indebted too to Hannan Hever, who agreed to advise a dissertation on this topic at Tel-Aviv University and helped me structure the project. Special thanks go to Mandy Merck, who generously shared with me her knowledge and scholarship and commented on drafts of an early version of this work. David Halperin, whose work has been a constant source of inspiration and a model of scholarly rigor, and whose support and encouragement throughout my academic path I have deeply cherished, helped me think through some key issues, offered exacting criticisms, and made valuable bibliographic suggestions. Gayle Rubin not only shared with me some of her thoughts on lesbians' adoption of aspects of the gay male sex culture and suggested important references but also showed extreme kindness in sending me hard-to-obtain texts. Lynne Segal provided very valuable feedback and important pointers for bringing the manuscript up to date. Sarah Schulman engaged with the text in a collegial spirit, offering both competing perspectives and encouragement. I would also like to thank the two anonymous readers for State University of New York Press, who offered exacting criticisms and useful suggestions for revision. I am grateful to my editor, Beth Bouloukos, for her belief in this book project and for efficiently shepherding it through the long and winding road to publication. Finally, my colleague Catherine Rottenberg provided much needed support, advice, and practical assistance in bringing this project to completion, and I am grateful for her friendship and collegiality. I am indebted to all these people for their various contributions to this book, while assuming sole responsibility for its failings.

I am also thankful to Ingrid Ryberg for very kindly allowing me to use a still from her short film "Phone Fuck" that forms part of the *Dirty Diaries* project (Mia Engberg, 2009) on the cover of this book. Annie Sprinkle, Nan Kinney, and Buck Angel graciously gave permission to reproduce images from their films, as did Jae Carranza on behalf of the estate of the late Christopher Lee. I am obliged to all of them.

This is the place to acknowledge also the intellectual and moral support of my friends and colleagues both at Tel-Aviv University and Ben-Gurion University: Orly Lubin with her characteristic generosity has provided continual encouragement, mentoring, and assistance; Aeyal Gross is a partner in an ongoing intellectual dialog as well as in academic activism; Dafna Hirsch and Merav Amir could always be relied upon to provide perceptive criticism. I thank them all, as well as the other members past and present of the TAU forum for LGBT studies and queer theory for their camaraderie. I also thank my newer friends and colleagues at BGU for their friendship, support, and encouragement: Henriette Dahan Kalev, Niza Yanay, Amnon Raz Krakotzkin, Maya Lavie Ajayi, and of course Catherine Rottenberg.

Special gratitude is owed to my students past and present, whose interest keeps reviving my own passion for what I teach. This book is particularly indebted to the students of my seminar on pornography, who could always be depended on to bring me up to date on developments in the field. Throughout the years, I have presented sections of this book in numerous academic conferences and seminars, as well as in nonacademic forums—far too many to acknowledge here —and I am thankful to all those who engaged with my ideas and whose comments, questions, and challenges contributed to my thinking on these subjects.

Last but not least, I thank my partner Sharron Hass for putting up with this project, nearly as long as our relationship, throughout its various incarnations.

During this book's final stages of production my father, Gideon Ziv, passed away. I cannot begin to list the numerous ways in which he had shaped my intellectual formation. It is from him that I acquired the passion for literature as a site of both knowledge and adventure, as well as the fascination with the transgressive. Had he lived to see this book, I believe he would have greeted it with amused satisfaction.

An earlier Hebrew version of chapter 1 appeared in the journal *Teoria Vebikoret* (Theory and Criticism). The reading of the Beauty trilogy in chapter 2 draws on my article "The Pervert's Progress," published in *Feminist Review* 46 (Spring 1994), and part of the analysis in chapter 6 draws on the article "Girl Meets Boy: Cross-gender Queer Sex and the Promise of Pornography," published in *Sexualities* 17:7 (2014). I am grateful to the editors for their support of my work. Some materials from this book also appeared in a much more condensed form in my Hebrew book, *Sexual Thoughts* (2013).

Introduction

Pornography, Subjectivity, and the Reinscription of Fantasy

> Pornography is the graphic sexually explicit subordination of women through pictures and/or words.
> —Catharine MacKinnon, *Only Words*

> It is precisely within this traditionally male genre [pornography] that the idea of re-vision is most compelling: "survival" here means transforming oneself from sexual object to sexual subject of representation.
> —Linda Williams, *Hard Core: Power, Pleasure, and the "Frenzy of the Visible"*

The preceding quotes are taken from the two sides of the feminist pornography debate, a debate that emerged in the late 1970s, reached its peak in the 1980s, largely subsided by the middle of the 1990s, and has reignited in a somewhat different register in the last few years. These two quotes reflect in miniature some of the characteristics of the two positions in the debate. The first, by legal scholar Catharine MacKinnon, one of the leaders of the feminist antiporn camp, provides a definition; its language is authoritative, it claims to offer both a description and an analysis of the phenomenon in question, and its major concern is the subordination of women. The second, by prominent film scholar Linda Williams, whose work on pornography aligns her with the anti-antiporn stance, is much more tentatively phrased and future oriented and balances the concern over the sexual objectification of women in pornography with women's potential to transform the pornographic genre and thereby achieve sexual subjectivity. The two quotes also reflect diverging agendas: while the former is meant to serve as a legal definition for a project of legal restriction of pornography, the latter delineates a strategy of creative intervention in the field of sexual representation.

As noted, we are now witnessing a resurgence of the debate that had polarized North American feminism in the 1980s albeit in somewhat different terms. The first round of what was known as the feminist sex wars had largely run its course by the mid- or late 1990s. The heated popular dispute subsided first, and in academia, as often happens in intellectual debates, the questions at the heart of the debate rather than being settled simply lost gradually their generative power. The outcomes were inconclusive: in academia the anti-antiporn position has on the whole won the day, though this is not equally true for all disciplines and in all countries (in Scandinavia, for instance, academic feminism seems mostly to subscribe to the antiporn stance); yet for the general public, the antiporn position is usually taken to represent *the feminist position* on pornography. As for women in general, present-day antiporn feminists, such as journalist Pamela Paul, complain that due to the massive "pornification" of popular culture, women on the whole have come to accept pornography as normal and inevitable and in an effort to be open-minded and sexy are increasingly consuming it themselves, a fact borne out by numerous surveys.[1]

Feminist opposition to pornography has resurfaced in the last decade allegedly in response to changed cultural conditions, notably the unlimited accessibility of porn brought about by the internet; the pornification of culture, that is, the enhanced social acceptability of porn and the integration of codes, styles, and attitudes derived from porn into various aspects of popular culture; and finally the more extreme and misogynous character of hardcore porn. Interestingly, the new antiporn literature hardly references its predecessors of the 1980s and 1990s and emphasizes the unparalleled nature of the present cultural moment: the unprecedented visibility and accessibility of pornography and what is described as its seamless integration into pop culture.[2] However, what presents itself as a revelation of and response to an unknown and alarming reality[3] often repeats observations and analyses that have already been made in response to an earlier state of the field (i.e., the explosion of the adult video industry in the 1980s). While contemporary antiporn feminists seem to distance themselves, perhaps intentionally, from their precursors, maybe due to the latter's "militant" image,[4] many of their distinctions, concerns, and arguments reiterate those of "first-generation" antiporners and are subject to similar critiques. In view of this rekindling of feminist interest in and concern over pornography, it is worthwhile to go back in depth to the feminist pornography debate, as I do in chapter 1, and identify the main concerns, presuppositions, and modes of argumentation of the two camps.

Further, from a transnational perspective, it is important to remember that the timeline I have charted applies mainly to North American and British feminism and not necessarily to other national contexts; in Israeli feminism, for example, a context with which I am particularly familiar, a debate over pornography first arose only in the early 2000s. Hence, rather than follow a single trajectory, the debate plays itself out in different ways and according to different chronologies in various feminist movements around the world. My own experience of teaching academic courses on pornography for over a decade indicates that the antiporn position has considerable purchase on young women troubled by the increased misogyny of mainstream porn and its growing influence on popular culture, while on the other hand, some of their coevals, especially those who partake in queer or other oppositional subcultures, engage in consumption (and sometimes production) of alternative porn and affirm its political significance. In other words, the conflicting perspectives and concerns of antiporn and pro-sex feminism are being rehearsed by younger generations of feminists, even if with less vehemence and less mutual antagonism.

Concurrently with the pornography debate, and both influenced by its terms and influencing them in return, the 1980s saw the emergence of a new trend—again mostly in the United States but also in the United Kingdom and elsewhere—of women creating sexual representations and appropriating the discourse of pornography. This trend is distinct from women's previous limited participation in the pornography industry, in that the representations attempt to reflect women's point of view (i.e., women's sexual interests) and are geared toward a female audience or a mixed one, rather than toward a predominantly male audience. They aim to provide an alternative to mainstream pornography and exist either on the margins of the industry or as independent subcultural products (as with lesbian porn or fan porn). This wave of pornographic production by women went hand in hand with, and at times overlapped, women artists' growing preoccupation with the body and with sexuality, a preoccupation that had its roots already in the 1970s feminist art movement.[5] In the adult video industry, the 1980s saw the emergence of two women-owned and -run companies: Femme Productions, established in 1984 by former porn star Candida Royalle, which targeted a heterosexual female audience and set out to create porn from a woman's point of view; and Fatale Video, established in 1985 by Nan Kinney and Debby Sundahl, which produced lesbian porn. In the 1990s Fatale was joined by Annie Sprinkle and Maria Beatty, and later by Shar Rednour and Jackie Strano who founded S.I.R. Productions. In the 1980s and 1990s there sprang up a number of lesbian sex magazines, the most prominent of which, *On Our Backs*, first appeared in 1985 and finally ceased publication in 2006. Pornographic fiction by women, both lesbian and heterosexual, usually in the form of anthologies such as *Herotica*, *Best Women's Erotica*, or *Best Lesbian Erotica* and published by feminist and LGBT presses like Cleis or Alyson Books, became available not only in women's and gay bookstores but in wider distribution as well and has influenced contemporary women's writing in a way that effected a blurring of the line between belles lettres and erotica.[6] The internet revolution of the 1990s has significantly facilitated women's access to pornographic production and consumption and provided new formats and new modes of presentation and distribution, whether in the form of sex blogs, women-owned pornographic websites, or websites of independent, amateur, or queer porn;[7] it also created new possibilities for interaction and exchange through and around porn.

Pornographic production by women expanded in the 2000s with the emergence of several filmmakers both in the United States and Europe who "specifically identified themselves and/or their work as feminist" (Penley et al. 11). These include Shine Louise Houston and Tristan Taormino in the United States, Erika Lust in Spain, Anna Span and Petra Joy in the United Kingdom, Emilie Jouvet in France, and Mia Engberg in Sweden.[8] And though it effected a problematization of the very category of women's pornography and brought about its frequent displacement by the category of queer porn, FTM porn—which appeared in the late 1990s, developed in the 2000s (most notably with the work of FTM porn star and director Buck Angel), and draws on both lesbian and gay male porn—bears close affinity to some of the representational and political agendas of feminist porn by women. The crystallization of what might be regarded as a feminist porn *movement* gained momentum with the launch in 2006 of the Feminist Porn Awards, which as Penley et al. note, "simultaneously assumed and announced a viewership, an authorship, an industry, and a collective consciousness" (12).

In a recent dissertation Ingrid Ryberg notes a current "transnational wave of interest in pornography as a potentially vital vehicle for queer, feminist and lesbian activist struggles for sexual, cultural and political empowerment" (14). She sees this interest as crystallized in the form of a transnational queer, feminist, and lesbian porn film culture whose manifestations include extensive production of films, performance and production collectives and networks, events such as film festivals and symposiums, the presence of which is also online.[9] Ryberg dates this wave from the mid-2000s, but she later goes on to trace its origins in the emergence of commercial women's porn in the early 1980s as part of sex-radical activism in the context of the feminist sex wars and views the current film culture as incorporating the legacy of the 1980s debates (16–17). I believe that while a certain stepping-up of pornographic production and porn "activism" is certainly in evidence in the last few years, the wave of politically inflected pornographic production by women has been continuous since the 1980s, with some figures like director Maria Beatty or performer and director Annie Sprinkle as ongoing participants since the early 1990s and companies like Femme Productions and Fatale Video still in business. I am therefore more in sympathy with the description offered by the editors of *The Feminist Porn Book* of "a forty-year-long movement of thinkers, viewers, and makers, grounded in their desire to use pornography to explore new sexualities in representation" (Penley et al. 13). Their definition of feminist porn cuts across many genres—"porn for women," "couples porn," lesbian porn, and educational porn—and incorporates elements of experimental film and performance art; it includes both independent productions and films produced within the porn industry. What unites this heterogeneous body of works is the fact that all these works consider sexual representation as "a site for resistance, intervention, and change" (10).

As Lynn Comella rightly points out, one important factor that contributed to the emergence of such alternative pornographic production was the feminist sex-positive retail context that developed in the 1980s. Women's sex stores, such as Good Vibrations or Babes in Toyland, were not only the first to carry alternative porn by women but also indicated the demand for such pornography, helped create an audience for it, and provided a valuable "feedback loop."[10] As Comella asserts, "[F]eminist cultural production, including pornography, involves much more than just making texts, it also involves making sex-positive contexts and creating favorable conditions of reception" (86).

As the formulation that ties together "thinkers, viewers, and makers" implies, the editors of *The Feminist Porn Book* posit an organic link between feminist scholarship on pornography from a pro-sex anticensorship perspective and the creation of pornographic representations that reflect a feminist sensibility. Feminist porn is for them both "a genre and a political vision" (18), and the political vision is one that underlies and motivates both porn scholarship and porn production. I believe that indeed, whether it is understood in terms of a movement, a wave, or some other term, pornographic production by women since the 1980s should be regarded as the representational counterpart of the theoretical critique of the antiporn position, since it is premised on the assumption that far from being inextricably bound to male power and the subordination of women, pornographic discourse is recuperable for women and for a feminist agenda. Feminist critiques of the antiporn stance have often made the claim that pornography is amenable to resignification and may constitute a representational resource *for* women, but this claim has rarely been backed by analyses of alternative pornographic representations by women.[11] This precisely is what the present book sets out to do, since to answer the antiporn challenge more fully it is necessary not only to point out pornography's potential for resignification but also to examine those representational practices that set out to exploit this potential.

Springing from the pornography debate, the central question of this book is whether pornography—regarded by antiporn feminists as the mainstay of patriarchal ideology and notorious for defining women as sexual objects—can provide an arena for the construction or renegotiation of female sexual subjectivity. I will address this question by looking at the various ways in which pornographic prose fiction by women tackles the problem of female sexual subjectivity. Existing analyses of alternative or marginal pornography deal mostly with visual representations—particularly video but also photographs, graphics, and performance[12]—and so far very little attention has been devoted to literary pornography, which in the case of women constitutes the bulk of pornographic production.[13] Requiring no technological skill and little or no financial investment, involving the least risk of censorship, and affording anonymity, textual pornography has been the most accessible pornographic format for women. However, this may be changing due to the advances of the last few years in computer and communication technology, such as digital cameras, webcams, and file-sharing platforms, which have greatly facilitated the production and circulation of erotic images and videos, resulting in women's greater participation as amateur and independent visual pornographers.

Recent scholarship on pornography has tended to focus on the internet, charting this rapidly changing and expanding field, and analyzing the new modes of engagement it fosters. In the current historical context, in which the internet is indeed the major platform for pornography, the choice to center my attention on literary texts may seem somewhat retrograde and calls for explanation. First, it is motivated by my training as a literary scholar. Second, as I noted, this is an area of pornographic production that has been relatively neglected, probably due to the growing association since the mid-twentieth century of pornography with the visual. Literary pornography also offers the significant advantage of sidestepping the ethical concerns that inevitably come up in relation to most photographic or moving-image pornography, that is, the question of exploitation and abuse of models and performers. Thus, if the antipornography argument claims that pornography harms women both in its production and through the effects of its consumption, and that these two types of harm are interconnected, focusing on literary pornography enables a separation of these two claims by avoiding the production process as a site of possible harm. In this way, the inquiry can center solely on textual analysis of the representations in question without having to account for their conditions of production.[14] Moreover, a focus on prose fiction is particularly suited to my preoccupation with the problem of sexual subjectivity. Much more than film, literature provides easy entry into the psyche of characters, lending itself to far more elaborate and nuanced explorations of the subjective experience of sexual desire and sexual interaction. The literary medium is able therefore to bring out women's sexual agency even in narratives that, had they been transposed into film, might elicit readings of female characters as passive, objectified, and exploited. Even when a character does not overtly initiate and direct sexual interactions, when the text lends us access to her consciousness, it can highlight mental attitudes of seeking and welcoming sexual experiences, the conscious choice to engage, an orientation to pleasure, and the empowering effects of sex.

As evident from the very formulation of my project, its premises and concerns are anchored in the anti-antiporn position, with its focus on the problematics of female sexual subjectivity and its belief in both the possibility and the importance of the appropriation of pornographic discourse by women (a belief that itself rests on the premise that discourses do not maintain a fixed relation to power, what Foucault terms "the tactical polyvalence of discourse" [100]). Moreover, it assumes that, as a genre, pornography may even be particularly conducive to the construction of female sexual subjectivity, since its inherent antirealistic tendency affords the projection of fictional worlds in which gender, power, and desire are differently aligned.

Steven Marcus has argued that the literary genre that pornographic fiction most resembles is that of utopian fantasy and coined the term "pornotopia" to capture the utopian quality of pornography (268). By the utopian dimension of pornography he refers to the fact that pornographic fiction tends to take place in a place that is a non-place and a time outside of time. As opposed to realistic fiction, the narrative's spatial and temporal coordinates are immaterial. Pornography is utopian in its construction of a total and hermetic universe, in which there is no "out there" (273). Marcus notes pornography's "relentless circumscription of reality," which entails on the one hand its exclusion of everything that is not sexual and on the other hand its capacity to ingest all of reality by sexualizing it (277). Finally and most obviously, pornography is utopian in its depiction of a sexual world of grace, a reality of sexual plenitude and abundance, in which there is never a shortage of desirable partners and everyone is always ready and willing.

Marcus's characterizations apply best to the classic eighteenth- and nineteenth-century pornographic novels he had in mind, and they do not fit contemporary women's or queer erotica as well. While there certainly are contemporary pornographic texts that lean on the genres of fantasy (e.g., Anne Rice's fairytale porn that is discussed in chapter 2), or science fiction (e.g., some of Pat Califia's science-fiction porn stories located in a dystopic future), more often contemporary women's erotica situates its narratives in everyday reality and, as Susie Bright notes, tends to integrate details of daily life and, furthermore, takes account of the limitations and risks that beset the erotic lives of its protagonists (xii). When it comes to lesbian or queer erotica, the sexual encounters depicted are usually set within an identifiable sexual culture whose codes, values, and styles they invoke. However, even such more realistically grounded fiction, and even fiction that explores the more complicated feelings associated with the experience of sexuality, retains the basic wish-fulfillment quality of pornography: sex does take place, even in unlikely circumstances and in the face of obstacles, and is always satisfying.

Yet the wish-fulfillment quality of feminist and queer porn relates not merely to the sexual consummation itself but, more significantly, to the worlds envisioned by these texts. The term "utopia" in the title of this book refers then to the use that alternative porn makes of the fundamental utopian tendency of pornography to project "new and better pleasures, other ways of being in the world, and ultimately new worlds," to use José Esteban Muñoz's words in his call for queer utopianism (1). I invoke the term "utopia" less rigorously than Muñoz, without committing to the philosophical tradition of utopian thinking and also without committing to the project of "critical utopianism" that Muñoz outlines. Nevertheless, I find the notion of "concrete utopias" that he borrows from Ernst Bloch useful for characterizing the kind of world-making that alternative pornographic fictions engage in. Muñoz describes concrete utopias as "relational to historically situated struggles, a collectivity that is actual or potential," a description that is particularly apt for feminist and queer pornography that often grows out of subcultural contexts and reflects political concerns (3).

Alternative porn delineates potentialities in the realm of gender and sexuality—potentialities that emerge out of current conditions and relations but are not yet present in actuality—lending them the performative force of fiction. Whereas Muñoz focuses his gaze on queer cultural and aesthetic artifacts that belong to the historical moment before and around Stonewall and teases out the potentialities embedded in them, I look at pornographic texts from the last two decades of the twentieth century, treating them not as relics of a bygone past but rather as products of cultural processes that are still ongoing. In addition, while Muñoz makes a point of refraining from what Eve Sedgwick has termed "paranoid reading," my critical gaze is considerably more suspicious than his. I do select the texts I focus on for what I identify as their utopian potential, but I am also on the lookout for those places where they fail to transcend the dominant imaginary. It bears emphasizing that in pointing out the utopian aspect of alternative pornographic texts I do not employ the term "utopia" in its traditional sense as the depiction of an imagined ideal society but, following Muñoz, see these texts as "concrete utopias," that is, local instances that offer glimpses of or point toward a vision of a more ideal reality. Such texts do not project sexual realities of an entirely different order but rather employ existing cultural and ideological materials in innovative ways to portray women as sexual subjects.

My main working hypothesis is that fantasy is not irrevocably determined by the forces of dominant culture but is subject to reinscription, and that precisely such processes of reinscription are taking place in alternative pornographic discourses, especially those by women and queers. I see these discourses as collectively and semi-consciously engaged in the cultural labor of fashioning new phantasmatic options,[15] which in turn construct new forms of subjectivity and transform social reality; hence, I believe that the reinscription of sexual fantasy deserves the status of political strategy.[16]

As should become evident, the goal of this book is not merely to make an intervention in the feminist debate on pornography. A further motivation is grounded in the belief that representational practice—especially those representational practices that emerge in subcultural spaces—is often ahead of theory.[17] Hence, an examination of the strategies employed by women in their appropriation of the discourse of pornography can both shed light on the difficulties that feminist thought encounters in trying to theorize female sexual subjectivity and help overcome them.

There are three categories central to my discussion that, though by no means unproblematic, I have employed so far without addressing my usage of them. These are: pornography, sexual subjectivity, and fantasy. I now devote a short discussion to each of these categories in order to clarify the sense in which I employ them.

Pornography

For reasons that will immediately become evident, I find it impossible to provide a positive, authoritative "definition" of pornography; further, I believe that the quest for such a definition is a futile and misguided one. Therefore, instead of a definition, I offer a brief historical account of the emergence of pornography as a representational category and its subsequent vicissitudes, an account from which some distinctive features can be extrapolated.

Pornography is a distinctly modern phenomenon. As Lynn Hunt asserts, "Although desire, sensuality, eroticism and even the explicit depiction of sexual organs can be found in many, if not all, times and places, pornography as a legal and artistic category seems to be an especially Western idea with a specific chronology and geography" (10). As a separate category for sexual representations, pornography emerged in Europe around the late eighteenth and early nineteenth centuries, with its roots going back to the Renaissance. Its emergence is linked to an array of social, economic, and technological developments, the principal of which are the rise and spread of print culture, urbanization and the rise of the middle class, free thinking and the attack on absolutist power, the splitting off of the public and private spheres, and the emergence of sexuality as a discrete realm of experience and an object of scientific knowledge and social control.

Before the nineteenth century, pornography was usually indistinguishable from satire, and the tradition of bawdy satire reached its peak in the decades preceding the French Revolution, when anticlerical and anti-aristocratic pornography served as an important tool of social criticism. The emergence of pornography as a "serious" (i.e., nonhumorous) and specialized genre, a genre centered on the objective of inducing sexual arousal, parallels the emergence of a rational discourse on sex documented by Michel Foucault and may be regarded as its counterpart or underside. The same incitement to turn sex into discourse, whose operation Foucault diagnoses in the new "confessional" sciences of psychiatry, pedagogy, criminology, and public hygiene, is at work in pornography, guided by the same motivation to unveil the hidden truth of sex.

An association that has permanently tinged the "meaning" of pornography is the one with radical thought. Already in the sixteenth century, Pietro Aretino, the earliest-known author in the modern pornographic tradition, associated his pornographic sonnets and dialogues with an attack on hypocrisy and the deliberate violation of moral taboos (Hunt 25). And in the eighteenth century, the emergence of the pornographic novel was the product of the "practical application in literature of libertine ideas about sex" (Wagner 214). The influence of libertine philosophy, which combined atheism with strict materialism, is particularly manifest in the work of the Marquis de Sade, whose writing has a strong didactic thrust.

As Hunt observes, "Pornography has always been defined in part by the efforts undertaken to regulate it" (Hunt 11). While up to the end of the eighteenth century, legal control of pornography was conducted from religious and political motives, in the nineteenth century, as pornography lost its political connotations and became a purely commercial genre, regulation began to be undertaken in the name of decency, giving birth to the modern obscenity laws. This regulation reflected a concern among upper-class men about the democratization of culture, a concern that arose as the circle of literacy expanded to include the lower classes and women. As Walter Kendrick shows, a major object of concern was presented by classical literature and art, which were consequently expurgated or reclassified and assigned to "secret museums." To a large extent, it was the very efforts of restriction and prohibition—rather than a coherence of the field itself—that defined, and still defines, pornography as a category of representations. Lacking fixed referential boundaries, the term "pornography" may be taken to signify the very contest over its meaning. In Kendrick's words: "'Pornography' names an argument, not a thing" (31). Already in the mid-nineteenth century, discussions of pornography evinced a fundamental uncertainty concerning what it is that defines the genre: explicit subject matter, lewd authorial intention, or lascivious effect on the audience; and these three options have established the parameters of the ongoing definitional battle that characterizes pornography.

In the twentieth century, the most important and contested distinction came to be the one between pornography and art. In response to the modernist challenge, which linked artistic innovation and sexual freedom, and following a series of obscenity trials over modernist literary works, the obscene was defined in opposition to true artistic merit. This distinction is obviously linked to the one between high culture and popular culture and to the struggle to shore up the former against the menace of the latter. The intellectual debate on pornography before feminism appeared on the scene featured, on the one hand, the liberal and Marxist critiques of pornography—the first regarding it as a threat to individuality and imaginative freedom, and the second seeing in it an escapist resolution of the problems and frustrations of the working class—and, on the other hand, the libertarian or avant-garde defense of pornography. The massive growth of the porn industry in the sixties and seventies was grounded, as Andrew Ross shows, in the libertarian ideology of the sexual revolution—from its arty and elitist version manifested in *Playboy* magazine to its more populist and democratic versions found in the less sophisticated porn magazines (172–174)—while the defense of "high" pornography offered by Susan Sontag in 1969 harks back to the modernist ethos of transgression. In the last two decades of the twentieth century, the feminist critique of pornography, which will be discussed extensively in the first chapter, has radically changed the terms of the debate, moving the discussion to an entirely different terrain.

My understanding of pornography is, then, a historicized one. I regard pornography as a historically specific category, namely, Western and modern, not a timeless one. A historicized understanding of pornography also entails not treating it as monolithic and immutable but recognizing that the social context, generic conventions, and ideological functions of pornography have undergone significant changes in the past three hundred years and will most probably undergo further transformations. As we have seen, the history of pornography indicates that from the outset pornography has been a legal category, a category of restricted and proscribed representations; the very construction of a separate category for sexual representations resulted from the need to regulate their circulation. The history of pornography also demonstrates that the very definitional boundaries of this category have always been subject to contestation and debate. This implies, first, that feminist attempts at legal restriction of pornography cannot entirely dissociate themselves from the long history—as old as pornography itself—of censorship and regulation. It also implies that any attempt to fix the "meaning" of pornography in a formal definition both fails to take account of the inherently contested character of this category and inevitably forms an intervention in the debate over pornography as a social phenomenon.

For these reasons I will refrain from any attempt to define "pornography," and apart from noting the general attributes that have characterized the category of pornography from its inception and largely continue to characterize it—mechanical reproduction, mass distribution, commodity status, transgressive affinities, will to truth—I will make do with a very loose and tentative working definition that classifies as pornography any sexually explicit representation intended to induce arousal. I will also avoid distinguishing between "pornography" and "erotica" and use the two terms interchangeably. As many critics have noted, rather than reflecting an actual generic distinction, this division is usually merely the manifestation of an ideological bias; sexual representations that one enjoys or approves of are accorded the honorary designation "erotica," while others are labeled "pornography."[18] Alternatively, the distinction may reflect class characteristics, with expensive or highbrow representations labeled erotica while cruder ones fall into the category of pornography.[19] My refusal to subscribe to this differentiation reflects, then, a refusal to distinguish between "good pornography" and "bad pornography," or rather, a refusal to disguise ideological judgments as seemingly objective categories.

Female Sexual Subjectivity

As noted earlier, the notion of female sexual subjectivity is at the center of this book. This might seem somewhat odd, not to say retrograde, in light of the fact that in contemporary theoretical discourse "the subject"—and even "the female subject"—is usually invoked only to be repudiated and done away with.[20] "The sexual subject" does figure legitimately in psychoanalytic discourse, yet the notion of sexual subjectivity that I employ is a markedly nonpsychoanalytic one. I should clarify from the outset that this notion is invoked not as a given but rather as a problem. In other words, in stating that women as a group seek to acquire sexual subjectivity or to inscribe themselves as sexual subjects, I do not propose that there is such a "thing" as sexual subjectivity, that is, that the term "sexual subjectivity" refers to an actual positive property of persons that one can either have or lack. Rather, I understand the notion of sexual subjectivity as a discursive construction but one that is not any less "real" for that. To borrow David Halperin's formulation regarding the categories of homo- and heterosexuality, inasmuch as people understand themselves through the notion of sexual subjectivity, this notion is thereby "objectivated" (Halperin 43).[21]

My notion of sexual subjectivity is mostly indebted to Michel Foucault's discussion of sexuality. As Foucault has demonstrated in volume 1 of *The History of Sexuality*, "sex" plays a central role in the construction of modern subjectivity. The discursive regime of sexuality dominating modern Western society constitutes sex as the core of the subject, its innermost truth, and a source of invaluable knowledge to be pursued and unveiled. Consequently, the modern subject is engaged in the infinite task of searching out and telling the truth of [his] sex.[22] Yet, as feminist critics have noted, Foucault's subject is predominantly male. In the modern sphere of sexuality, woman is constructed not as a subject but as a secret or riddle, in very similar terms to the way sex itself is constructed (Martin, "Feminism" 13–14). Women either embody sex[23] or are seen as asexual, but they can never be sexual subjects in the way men are. Foucault, in his discussion, emphasizes the ways in which the deployment of sexuality increases the hold of institutionalized power on the individual, or in other words, the dual role of sexuality as a mechanism of subjection/subjectivation. Yet this stress on the sexual subject as produced by power and dominated through his sexuality deflects attention from sexual subjectivity as a privilege from which women are to a large extent debarred.

This latter aspect is borne out by Esther Newton's analysis of the problematic situation of first-wave feminists in the early twentieth century. As Newton points out, since according to Victorian ideology, bourgeois women had no sexual identity to express, "women of the second generation [of "New Women"] who wished to join the modernist discourse and be twentieth-century adults had to radically reconceive themselves" ("Mannish Lesbian" 285). The pivotal role assigned to sex in the paradigm of modern subjectivity, together with the partial exclusion of women from the sphere of sexuality and their portrayal as lacking autonomous desire and sexual agency, combine to form what I refer to as the problem of female sexual subjectivity. As Newton's account indicates, this problem already preoccupied—though more on the plane of lived experience than on the conceptual level—early feminists, and it continues to pose a challenge both for women as individuals and for feminist thought.

But what does the problem consist of? In what sense is sexual subjectivity inaccessible to women or incompatible with femininity? One type of answer can be deduced from Étienne Balibar's account of the emergence of the category of the subject. Balibar regards the notion of subjectivity as the philosophical counterpart of political citizenship and claims that the "invention" of subjectivity was historically dependent on the achievement of free citizenship, that is, the abolition of subjection (Balibar 11–12). To follow this line of thought, sexual subjectivity is the correlative of sexual citizenship, and as long as women do not enjoy full sexual citizenship they cannot conceive themselves as sexual subjects.[24] This is no doubt true, but while this type of account stresses the material basis of "sexual subjectivity," it still does not problematize the notion itself. Just as the notion of subjectivity contains a particular vision of humanity (one that is derived, according to Balibar, from political citizenship), so the notion of sexual subjectivity contains *a particular vision of sexuality*. A different (though complementary) explanation of women's exclusion from sexual subjectivity would then be that the very paradigm of sexual subjectivity has been shaped according to the norms of heterosexual masculinity, so that the problem is actually that of ascribing women sexual subjectivity *within that paradigm*.

Trying to unpack the notion of sexual subjectivity (again, in a nonpsychoanalytic sense), it could be taken to denote the following constituents: 1. sexual identity—sexuality being central to one's self-definition or sense of self; having and being aware of distinct sexual tastes or desires and regarding them as defining characteristics of oneself; 2. desire—experiencing oneself as a desiring subject and as one whose desires are not merely reactive but self-originated; 3. agency—possessing sexual agency, that is, a capacity not only to identify one's desires but also to act upon them.

The problems for women arise around the dominant constructions of sexual desire and sexual agency, which are congruent with normative conceptions of male sexuality but conflict with those of female sexuality. Desire is normally understood as desire *for an object* (rather than desire for a setting, or a script, or autoerotic desire), desire to *possess* the object (rather than to be possessed), and to *act upon* the object (rather than to be acted upon). Agency is identified with the active pole in the active/passive or active/receptive divide (receptivity being usually conflated with passivity). If fucking is regarded as the ultimate expression of sexual agency, to fuck is usually conceived as a transitive, unilateral action, a transitivity of which women can only be the object, not the subject. Another obstacle for conceiving women as sexual subjects is the perceived contradiction between subjectivity and the disruption of bodily boundaries, that is, sexual penetration. And in the symbolic realm, the overdetermined relation of the phallus, as *the* signifier of subjectivity, to male anatomy presents a further difficulty. When I look at the construction of female sexual subjectivity in pornographic fiction by women, I will focus on how such works of fiction tackle these hurdles and what strategies they devise to overcome them.

Fantasy

The notion of fantasy has figured in feminist discussions of pornography in two major ways: the opposition fantasy/reality and the opposition authentic fantasy versus commercial fantasy. Most pro-sex/anticensorship feminists have insisted that pornographic representations should be understood in terms of fantasy, and that to censor them is to attempt to curb and regulate fantasy; antiporn feminists, on the other hand, have vehemently rejected such an understanding of pornography and argued that pornographic representations cannot be accorded the status of fantasy since they are "real" in three related senses: first, they are a record of real acts; this assertion relates of course to photographic and filmic pornography and relies on a representational realism that, as Judith Butler notes, conflates the signified with the referent. Second, the mode of consumption of these representations (i.e., masturbation) involves a bodily engagement that produces real corporeal pleasure. Third, by affecting its consumers, pornography turns itself into reality, that is, it shapes the real world in its image.[25] While some later feminist opponents of pornography have reluctantly acknowledged the phantasmatic dimension of pornographic representations, they insist on the difference between individual and mass-produced fantasy, affirming the wholesomeness of the former and the malignance of the latter. Thus, for example, Pamela Paul states:"There's a distinction between free-flow fantasy and porn-induced fantasy. Fantasy is an individual's prerogative; pornography is an industry prescriptive. . . . Fantasy is private; pornography is mediated. Fantasy is natural; pornography is artificial and commercialized" (141). And Gail Dines refused to dignify pornography with the term "fantasy" altogether on the ground that it is a formulaic industrial cultural product (83–84). I will revisit the "realism" and the authentic-versus-industrial arguments in the next chapter. For now, however, I would like to stress that it is important to maintain a distinction between private intrapsychic fantasies and cultural representations; but it is also important to acknowledge and trace out their interrelations, which is what I would like to do in the rest of this section.

My discussion of pornography is grounded in an understanding of pornographic representations as "public forms of fantasy," to borrow Elizabeth Cowie's term.[26] The notion of fantasy I rely on is the one offered by Laplanche and Pontalis both in "Fantasy and the Origins of

Sexuality" and in the entry "phantasy" in *The Language of Psychoanalysis*. In these texts, Laplanche and Pontalis posit fantasy as central to the very definition of sexuality: "The 'origin' of auto-eroticism would therefore be the moment when sexuality, disengaged from any natural object, moves into the field of fantasy and by that very fact becomes sexuality" ("Fantasy" 25). They define fantasy as the "setting" (mise-en-scène) or setting-out of desire, and they insist that the central element of the fantasy is not the object of desire but the script or scenario, and that the subject is always present in the scene, even if in a "desubjectivized form" ("Fantasy" 26). Following Freud, they also stress the analogy and continuity between the different levels or modes of fantasy: conscious (i.e., daydreams), subliminal, and unconscious ("Phantasy" 316–17).

If, to paraphrase Laplanche and Pontalis, we can define fantasy as an internal representation, Cowie, relying on Freud's own linking of fiction and daydream,[27] performs the obverse move by defining representations as "public forms of fantasy":

> The same content, the same activation can be revealed in imaginary formations or daydreams and psychopathological structures as diverse as those described by Freud, such as hysteria, delusional paranoia, etc., and in public forms of fantasy such as film and the novel. ("Fantasia" 156)

In other words, if sexual fantasies (probably falling under Freud's definition of "daydream") are a kind of interactive movie we play in our head, pornographic films or stories are fantasies that have been fixed and reified, turned into objects in the cultural field. The relations between these two types of fantasies should be understood as bilateral: on the one hand, pornographic representations can be read as manifestations either of private fantasies—those of the author (as Freud suggests in regard to novels) or of some collective imaginary; on the other hand, such representations in turn structure and nourish individual fantasy. As Cowie notes: "Just as we draw on events of the day to produce our own [fantasy scenarios], so we can adopt and adapt the ready-made scenarios of fiction, as if their contingent material had been our own" ("Fantasia" 165). Teresa de Lauretis even incorporates this work of adaptation into the very definition of fantasy. "Fantasy," she states, "is the psychic mechanism that structures subjectivity by reworking or translating social representations into subjective representations" ("Popular Culture" 307).

Reading pornographic representations as public forms of fantasy, we can understand them as engaged in scripting and setting out the spectator's or reader's desire, or at least attempting to address and construct the reader/spectator as the subject of their fantasy.[28] Since fantasy, as Laplanche and Pontalis assert, structures subjectivity ("Phantasy" 317), and since public fantasies shape and nourish individual fantasy, the field of sexual representation is a deeply political one. As with other types of representations, the settings and scripts of pornographic representations are provided to a large degree by the culture that gives them rise. Mainstream pornography sets out desire according to dominant sexual and gender norms. On the other hand, as interventions in the field of fantasy, alternative sexual representations (often drawing on marginal sexual subcultures) can remold subjectivity and reshape sexual practice as well as individual and group identity.[29] Accordingly, I will be looking at alternative pornographic texts as (semi-conscious) political interventions, which may be evaluated in terms of their contribution to a reinscription of the sexual imaginary, that is, as providing "phantasmatic strategies" for countering the dominant constructions of sexuality. As Judith Butler reminds us, fantasy, in the sense of the capacity to postulate a future that is not yet, "has been crucial to the feminist task of (re)thinking futurity" ("Force of Fantasy" 487). While the applicability of the notion of fantasy to pornography has been one of the contested issues in the feminist porn debate, what has largely gone unremarked is pornography's potential to serve as a site of *feminist* fantasy, a site for imagining gendered and sexual realities that are not yet in existence (or only very partially so) and affirming their possibility and desirability; in other words, what has gone unremarked is pornography's potential to serve as a site of feminist utopia.

Corpus and Structure

When I classify the kind of pornographic texts I am interested in as "alternative pornography" this calls for some clarification, since the distinction between mainstream and alternative in pornography is not necessarily a clear one and the line may be drawn differently from different perspectives. The rise and growing prevalence of amateur porn, and the pornography industry's partial absorption of amateur porn as one of its categories, has blurred the amateur/professional division and substituted a whole spectrum of gradations for a clear-cut distinction (see Paasonen and Jacobs). Moreover, especially when it comes to pornography on the internet, the line between "the industry" and independent porn may be difficult to draw. The borders of the pornography industry are no longer easy to chart, many small entrepreneurs have entered the scene, and both amateur and professionally produced representations circulate both for pay and free of charge. And in terms of content, within the industry itself, the ethos that Linda Williams has dubbed "different strokes for different folks" has led to an infinite proliferation of categories, some of which can certainly be classified as "alternative" compared to the more standard fare. When I speak of alternative porn I am referring mostly to the gender and sexual ideology of representations and less to their conditions of production and modes of circulation (though amateurism and being produced and circulated for motives other than financial profit may also characterize the types of representations I am dealing with).

The corpus I draw on includes texts that, I believe, offer representations of female sexuality or suggest for women phantasmatic identifications that are radically new and thus open up grounds for new conceptualizations of female sexual subjectivity. As the purpose of the readings is to point out new representational options that hold theoretical interest, the choice of texts is guided by the theoretical concerns reflected in them and does not attempt to represent the entire range of contemporary female-authored pornography. The temporal and geographic boundaries of the corpus (American and British texts of the 1980s and 1990s) are determined, therefore, by the texts' participation in the new wave or new discursive configuration of women's pornography. I did not extend this corpus temporally into the twenty-first century, except for a couple of forays in the case of transgender porn, because I am more interested in looking at the earlier pioneering texts, those within the more immediate orbit of the sex wars, which had to work out innovative solutions to the problem of constructing women as sexual subjects with fewer precedents to follow.

Circumscribing the temporal boundaries of the corpus in this way is somewhat arbitrary since, as I have noted, many sociocultural processes that began in the 1980s and 1990s extend into the twenty-first century. The feminist porn movement that emerged in the 1980s grew and expanded in the 2000s. "Queer" as an identity category seemingly oblivious to gender that arose in the late 1980s with "Queer Nation" and gained momentum in the 1990s still functions as a meaningful term of identification for many women attracted to women; though "queer" nowadays is found more often than not in the combination "genderqueer," which denotes gender nonconformity and extends the refusal of identity categories signaled by "queer" from the realm of sexuality to the realm of gender, a development that itself derives from and responds to the transgender movement that formed in the latter half of the 1990s.[30] Nevertheless, despite the continuous nature of many of the processes that shaped the cultural and political contexts out of which grew many of the texts in my corpus, there are indeed some notable shifts that distinguish the time period of the 1980s and 1990s from the present cultural and political moment. In the LGBT community, gay and lesbian identities are increasingly depoliticized and defined in terms of the neoliberal discourse of "lifestyle" focused on consumerism.[31] As sexuality is privatized and shorn of political implications, pornography is increasingly perceived merely as a consumer good. Thus, while compared to the 1980s, there exists today a wider variety of more accessible and more professionally produced lesbian porn, there is no longer a sense of pornography as part of sex-radical activism except in genderqueer or queer anarchist contexts, or else in more peripheral national contexts. Similarly, while there is a marked increase in sexually explicit representations both targeted to heterosexual women and produced by them, arguably much of the production and consumption of such representations is grounded in a postfeminist discourse of personal empowerment that regards sexual pleasure as a form of capitalist consumer entitlement and cuts off sexuality from the realm of the political.[32] In the 1980s and much of the 1990s, on the other hand, the production and consumption of pornography by women tended to be conceived as an explicitly political enterprise defined not only in terms of women's right to sexual entertainment and pleasure but also in terms of reenvisioning gender constructs in the sphere of sexuality.

Since the focus of the book is on the various phantasmatic strategies that pornographic works employ to construct women as sexual subjects and overcome the cultural obstacles for conceiving them as such, its organizing principle is thematic. Chapters are not organized around divisions or groupings inherent to the pornographic field itself, for example, along the lines of genre, mode of circulation, or chronology; rather each chapter revolves around a key theoretical issue, and the discussion of the pornographic texts is accompanied by—and set against—critical assessments of pertinent feminist or queer theoretical models.

As a point of departure for my inquiry, the first chapter goes back to the feminist pornography debate. The chapter offers an analytical summary that brings into focus the key differences between the rival positions: a concern with harm to women versus a concern with women's sexual subjectivity, a focus on mainstream porn versus a focus on marginal representations, and conflicting understandings of the relations between discourse and power.

The second chapter looks at women's phantasmatic identifications with gay male sexuality in and around pornography as a kind of meta-strategy at work in many pornographic works by women. I discuss two distinct instances of such identification—male homoerotic fantasies in pornography by women (Anne Rice's *Beauty* trilogy provides the prime example) and the modeling of lesbian porn after gay male porn—concluding with a consideration of queer theorizations of cross-identification that underscores the political contingencies of this notion.

The third and fourth chapters examine the problems posed by the dominant conception of sexual penetration and the notion of the phallus for the articulation of female sexual subjectivity and look at ways in which women's pornography has dealt with these problems. Chapter 3 observes how the prevailing cultural notion of penetration as antithetical to subjectivity is reproduced within feminist and queer discourses and examines pornographic stories and other sexually explicit texts by women that contest the equation of sexual receptivity with subordination and annihilation of selfhood, resignifying penetration in ways not yet available to feminist theory. In chapter 4 I address the overdetermined relation of the phallus as a signifier of subjectivity and agency to male anatomy. The chapter follows some of the vicissitudes of the Lacanian notion of the phallus in feminist theory and examines the ways in which the phallus is redeployed in lesbian pornography, mostly through its figurative representation, the dildo. My main text for this is an episode from *Clips*, one of the classics of lesbian video porn.

The fifth chapter examines the notion of gender performativity and its manifestations in pornographic texts as a way around the problem of female sexual subjectivity. I explore the links between the notion of gender performativity and the queer subcultural discourse of genderbending and examine the eroticization of genderbending in lesbian pornography. Special attention is paid to s/m fiction, underscoring the performative character of s/m and its relations to gender play and gender-crossing. I conclude with a reading of Carol Queen's erotic novel *The Leather Daddy and the Femme* that reveals a vision of sexuality as a means of transcending gender divisions and boundaries. This vision and the phantasmatic recourse to gay male sexuality are both problematized in chapter 6, which examines how some of the phantasmatic strategies identified in the previous chapters have continued to play out in the context of both the growing currency of "queer" as an ostensibly "gender-blind" identity category and the rise of the transgender movement. The investment in gay male sexuality is tracked to its manifestations both in the topos of cross-gender queer sex and in FTM porn. While I underscore the high degree of intertextuality between lesbian, queer, and transgender porn, I argue that both FTM porn and the topos of cross-gender queer sex indicate the limitations of the appropriation of the gay male sexual imaginary for the project of articulating female sexual subjectivity.

The coda opens with notes on screening porn in academic settings and other formal public contexts. Invoking the utopian aspect of alternative porn, I offer some observations about the ways in which alternative pornographic representations affect their viewers and how their effect is shaped by the conditions of reception. I conclude both affirming and qualifying the promise of pornography for a project of cultural transformation.

ONE

Between Sexual Commodities and Sexual Subjects

The Feminist Pornography Debate Revisited

Since the late 1970s, North American feminists have been engaged in a prolonged and heated debate on pornography that has reverberated throughout Western feminism. This debate has been the center of what is known as "the feminist sex wars," a series of disputes over the politics of sexuality concerned with a nexus of issues surrounding female sexuality, representation, and sexual expression. For about a decade, the issue of lesbian sadomasochism was also a prominent site of contention, quite interwoven with the question of pornography. However, while this remained more of an internal feminist controversy that eventually died out, the issue of pornography has achieved greater salience as a feminist question and continued to generate ardent debate, largely due to the fact that the efforts of the antipornography movement have been directed outward in an attempt to mobilize public opinion and introduce new legislation.

A Brief History of the Debate

The antiporn movement was launched with the founding of Women Against Violence in Pornography and the Media (WAVPM) in San Francisco in 1976, and Women Against Pornography (WAP) in New

York in 1979. Other early landmarks include the publication of Andrea Dworkin's *Pornography: Men Possessing Women*, also in 1979, and the anthology *Take Back the Night* in 1980.[1] The antiporn campaign evolved out of earlier campaigns against violence against women and in particular against rape. As Lesley Stern points out, the work on rape and sexual violence raised the question of how the social climate responsible for sexual violence against women is created, and the answers tended to focus increasingly on the media and particularly on pornography (43–46). Opposition to the antiporn stance was first voiced by pro-sex feminists outside the feminist press, in articles by Ellen Willis in the *Village Voice* (1979) and Pat Califia in the *Advocate* (1980). The lesbian s/m group Samois was the first feminist organization to oppose the antiporn campaign. The year 1981 saw the publication of the *Heresies* sex issue, and the critique of the antiporn stance began to crystallize at the 1982 Barnard College Conference on Women and Sexuality, which also provided the scene for the first major confrontation between the two camps. The critique of antiporn politics was formulated in two collections of essays, *Powers of Desire* published in 1983 and *Pleasure and Danger* published in 1984.

A major landmark in the pornography debate is the drafting of the Minneapolis and Indianapolis antiporn ordinances by author Andrea Dworkin and lawyer Catharine MacKinnon, who subsequently came to be regarded as the leaders of the antiporn movement. The ordinances were a unique attempt to introduce legislation that defines pornography in terms of its harm to women and that makes that harm actionable. The ordinances define pornography as a practice of sex discrimination, violating women's civil rights and opposed to gender equality. The ordinances allow women who allege harm by pornography, either individually or as members of a group, to sue civilly and obtain financial relief for the injury. The four activities the ordinances make actionable are: coercion into pornography, the forcing of pornography on a person, assault caused by pornography, and trafficking in pornography.

The ordinances, introduced in Minneapolis in 1983 and in Indianapolis in 1984, did not come into effect, as the Minneapolis ordinance was vetoed by the city mayor, and the Supreme Court eventually declared the Indianapolis ordinance unconstitutional. They did, however, manage both to make an impact on public opinion and galvanize feminist opposition, leading, for instance, to the formation of FACT (Feminist Anti-Censorship Taskforce), which joined the legal battle against the Indianapolis ordinance and opposed attempts to introduce versions of it in other cities. Thus, in terms of the feminist movement, the ordinances resulted in an increased polarization over the issue of pornography. The ordinances and the antiporn movement in general also exercised an effect on government policy. The Meese Commission on Pornography, appointed by the Reagan administration in 1985, endorsed Dworkin and MacKinnon's ordinances in its report (published in 1986). Further, much of the rhetoric and strategies employed at the commission's hearings were derived from the feminist antiporn movement, including testimonies by victims of pornography (provided by WAP) and slide shows (Califia, "See No Evil" 130–131).[2]

While the political and juridical battles over the ordinances ended by 1986, the pornography debate did not subside but seems rather to have shifted location (maintaining, however, many of its original protagonists) to the academic arena, as feminist scholars were increasingly driven to address the theoretical-political challenge posed by Dworkin and MacKinnon's position on pornography. Much feminist art and media practice in the eighties and nineties was also influenced by the terms of the debate and constitutes both direct interventions in it and subject matter for further critical interventions.

While the first round of the feminist sex wars had largely run its course by the mid- or late 1990s, the debate has reignited in a somewhat different form in the first decade of the twenty-first century with the resurfacing of a feminist critique of pornography. This critique emerged in response to what has been termed the "pornification" of culture—the enhanced visibility, accessibility, and social acceptability of pornography—and "the seeping of pornographic practices, styles, and experiences into the mainstream" (Smith and Attwood, 42). The harbingers were journalist Pamela Paul with her book *Pornified* and journalist Ariel Levy with her book *Female Chauvinist Pigs*, both of which came out in 2005 and introduced the notion of a "pornified" culture (or "raunch culture" in Levy's term). These were joined by media scholar Gail Dines, who became the leading academic spokesperson of the new antiporn movement. In 2007 Dines launched the organization Stop Porn Culture, and her book *Pornland* appeared in 2010.[3] These writings form part of a new wave of public concern over the sexualization of women's bodies, especially of girls, and over children's exposure to online pornography. This concern is reflected in numerous policy reports, for example, the American Psychological Association's report on the sexualization of girls (2007), the report of the Australian Senate Committee on the sexualization of children, and the UK Home Office sexualization of young people review (2010), as well as legislative initiatives both in Australia and the United Kingdom to criminalize extreme pornography or introduce mandatory internet filtering.

On the other side of the feminist divide, there has been a notable increase in pornographic production by women since the beginning of the twenty-first century, as well as an accumulation of feminist scholarship on pornography from a pro-sex perspective: scholarship that focuses on feminist pornography and explores new venues for pornographic production by women (Jacobsen 2007; Sabo 2011; Taormino et al. 2013), studies women as porn consumers (Smith 2007), or examines the sexualization of culture from a perspective that does not necessarily see it as a problem but rather acknowledges both its oppressive and its emancipatory effects on women (Attwood 2009).

The present chapter does not aim to provide a historical overview of the feminist pornography debate.[4] Rather, it offers a selective critical summary of the rival positions. This summary relates mostly to writings from the 1980s and 1990s, while the last section of this chapter will take a look at present-day antiporn feminist writings, compare them to their predecessors, and attempt to trace out the current lines of disagreement between the camps. Since both camps have consisted of numerous voices, any reconstruction of a single coherent antiporn or anti-antiporn position would of necessity be a misrepresentation. In order to avoid such false synthesis and yet not undertake a comprehensive survey of the range of positions within each camp, a survey that would be beyond the scope of this chapter, my strategy will be the following: In presenting the antiporn position, I will restrict myself mostly to the writings of Catharine MacKinnon. In this I follow an already established tendency in discussions of the antiporn position,[5] which seems justified in as much as Dworkin and MacKinnon have set themselves up as the definitive spokeswomen of the antiporn movement.[6] Further, while MacKinnon relies heavily on Andrea Dworkin's work, she seems to offer the most structured and theoretically sophisticated version of the antiporn argument.[7] In addition, since a significant part of the anti-antiporn engagement has been with MacKinnon's work, reproducing this bias makes sense in terms of the exposition of the debate.

When it comes to representing the anti-antiporn position, exposition becomes more complicated, since the opposition to the antiporn movement never coalesced into a movement with definite spokeswomen and can better be described as a set of critiques and oppositional discourses that sprang up at various sites. The different names that have been given to this opposition—anti-antiporn, anticensorship, pro-sex—are indicative of the different stresses laid by various responses to the antiporn challenge.[8] Moreover, it is important to remember that the pornography debate is a nonsymmetrical one, in that the anti-antiporn position was formed in response to the challenge posed by the antiporn movement and had no prior autonomous existence. It is therefore reactive by nature and consists to a large extent of critiques of antiporn arguments and strategies rather than positive formulations concerning women's relation to pornography.[9]

It is interesting to note that while the anti-antiporn camp engages closely with antiporn arguments, the antiporn camp devotes very little attention to anti-antiporn critiques and positions itself primarily vis-à-vis the liberal view on pornography and freedom of speech. This is probably due to the fact that the efforts of the antiporn camp are directed toward the general public with the aim of changing public opinion on pornography as a ground for introducing restrictive legislation. This "outward" focus not only diverts attention from inside critiques but also makes it worthwhile to downplay the scope of internal opposition. Catharine MacKinnon consistently represents her position as *the* feminist stance on pornography, and, based on her writings, an uninformed reader could never realize that there exists a substantial feminist opposition to this position. Two rare allusions to this opposition are a short lecture entitled "On Collaboration," where she conducts a polemic against feminist lawyers who oppose her ordinance, and a two-paragraph discussion of the *Diary*[10] of the Barnard conference in *Toward a Feminist Theory of the State* (135–136).[11] Her brief and reductive summary of her opponents' position stands in marked contrast to their elaborate engagements with hers.[12]

In view of these asymmetries of the debate, the exposition of the anti-antiporn position will be organized around lines of argument rather than around key figures, and an attempt will be made to distinguish between its negative and positive components, that is, between the critiques of the antiporn position and the arguments for the potential value of pornography for women. The former will be incorporated into my own analysis of the faults of the antiporn position, while the latter will be presented separately, as the anti-antiporn position strictly speaking (and consequently, its exposition will be much shorter than that of the antiporn position). One can further distinguish between two major loci of opposition to the antiporn movement, one being feminist sex-radical activists and the other feminist academics, with a certain degree of overlap between the two. These two loci of opposition loosely correspond to two varieties of the "positive" argument—the libertarian strand and the discursive strand—which the discussion of the anti-antiporn position will distinguish and characterize.

The Antiporn Argument: MacKinnon's Critique of Pornography

The revolutionary significance of the antiporn argument lies in its very claiming of pornography as a feminist issue, thus expropriating "the question of pornography" from its traditional frames of reference: the policing of sexual representations in the interest of public morality (pornography as that which "depraves and corrupts") and the contested boundary between art and pornography. This claiming of pornography by feminism is based on the substitution of a new definition of pornography for existing ones—for MacKinnon, pornography is no longer a genre of sexual representations distinguished by their explicitness, their lack of redeeming social value, or their intention or capacity to arouse prurient interest; rather, it is defined as "the graphic sexually explicit subordination of women through pictures and/or words."[13] The strategic move performed by this definition is double: first, pornography is seen as not about sex but about women; second, pornography is defined not as a category of representations but as practice. The first move dislodges pornography from the realm of morality, in which obscenity law is grounded, and establishes it as a matter of gender politics. The second move attempts to bypass questions of free speech and the legal protection of pornography under the First Amendment by removing pornography from the realm of "speech" in the legal sense and conceiving it as practice, and more specifically, as a practice of gender inequality.

In defining pornography as concerned with women and not simply with sex, MacKinnon foregrounds the fact that pornographic representations are predominantly representations of women and calls attention to the tacit equation of women and sex underlying them, as well as to the broad cultural and legal acceptance of this equation implied by the invisibility of this gender bias. But MacKinnon goes considerably further than that. For her, the equation of women and sex and the representation of women as subordinate and inferior are not simply givens of patriarchal culture inherited by pornography. MacKinnon sees pornography as a central discourse of male domination, which does not merely reflect gender hierarchy but has a pivotal role in its construction and reproduction.

Pornography defines women as inferior and subordinate and defines their subordination as sexual. The effectiveness of pornography as a political practice lies precisely in this sexualization, in the linking of female subordination to male sexual pleasure; and conversely, the erotic effect of pornography hinges upon its depiction of women as subordinate. Pornography is not erotic as a representation of sex and oppressive to women as a product of a patriarchal culture: its meaning and function are the eroticization of gender hierarchy, of female subordination, vulnerability, and accessibility. "The question for pornography," says MacKinnon, "is what eroticism is distinct from the subordination of women" (*Theory of the State* 211).

This understanding of pornography as not only an expression of dominant gender ideology but one of its major apparatuses is at odds, of course, with the traditional view of pornography as a marginal and subversive discourse, inherently opposed to institutional power and therefore in need of protection from government censorship. This seemingly subversive relation of pornography to dominant morality is regarded by MacKinnon as a ruse masking its actual function and increasing its appeal, and the battles over the definition and policing of pornography are at most "a fight among men over the terms of access to women" (*Theory of the State* 203).

Pornography as Harm

The central claim of the antipornography camp, and the claim on which relies MacKinnon's call for legal restrictions on pornography, is that pornography substantially and concretely harms women. There are several levels of harm that MacKinnon points to, though, significantly, she herself tends not to distinguish between them but rather to stress their interconnectedness. And the rhetorical force of her argument relies on the accumulation of different forms and instances of harm that resonate and amplify one another, eventually creating an overwhelming sense of the scope and pervasiveness of the harm.

Production-Related Harm

The first level of harm, and probably the most concrete and ethically compelling one, is the harm to the women involved in the production of pornography. The claims of harm are founded on two sources: testimonies by the pornography models themselves[14] and a "documentary" reading of the representations corroborated by such reports. Discussing mainly cinematic and photographic pornography, which constitutes the bulk of the porn industry, MacKinnon refuses to regard it as merely representations or images, or in the legal terminology "speech," and treats these representations rather as the record of actual acts performed in the real world. She calls attention to the fact that everything, or nearly everything, we *see* in pornography has actually taken place—or in her words, has actually been *done to* real women—in order to create these representations:[15] "In pornography, the penis is shown ramming up into the woman over and over; this is because it actually was rammed into the woman over and over" (*Only Words* 18). In the case of violent representations, this means that the represented violence corresponds to actual violence: "In mainstream media, violence is done through special effects; in pornography, women shown being beaten and tortured report being beaten and tortured" (*Only Words* 18–19).[16] The paradigmatic case for this view of pornography as the documentation of real violence is that of snuff films, films documenting rape and murder. The existence of real snuff films, as opposed to films that pretend to such documentary status, is considered dubious by many writers on pornography (Williams, *Hard Core* 189–194, 227; Easton 19), but it is treated as fact by Dworkin and MacKinnon, who often allude to snuff as the extreme end of a continuum that reveals the nature of the genre as a whole.[17]

Even in the case of nonviolent pornography, there is a pervasive implication in MacKinnon's writings that pornography models are victims,[18] that for women, participation in pornography is by definition harming. This is conveyed grammatically by her persistent use of either the passive mode or the object position in the sentence when describing women's participation in pornography (these two types of usage are exemplified in the two previous quotations). In MacKinnon's depictions of pornography, sex is always inflicted on women, women are "violated," "possessed," "exposed," "used," done to.[19] And this negation of grammatical agency appears to reflect a sense that for women participation in pornography in fact cannot be seen to express agency, that it is intrinsically opposed to agency. MacKinnon seems to assume that participation in pornography is, at the very least, degrading for women.[20] And while she opposes "the assumption of consent that follows women into pornography" (*Feminism Unmodified* 180), the opposite assumption is implicitly at work in her texts.

A major production-related harm highlighted in Dworkin and MacKinnon's work is coercion into pornography. MacKinnon cites testimonies by women who were forced through violence and threats to perform in pornography, the most well-known example being that of Linda Marchiano, known as "Linda Lovelace" from *Deep Throat*.[21] Even when there is no physical coercion directly involved, MacKinnon points to the economic disadvantage of women as a group and to the particular vulnerability and lack of options that tend to characterize women who perform in pornography:

> Empirically, all pornography is made under conditions of inequality based on sex, overwhelmingly by poor, desperate, homeless, pimped women who were sexually abused as children. These conditions ... are what it takes to make women do what is in even the pornography that shows no overt violence. (*Only Words* 14)

The picture that emerges from MacKinnon's writings is one in which lack of resources and a history of sexual abuse converge to drive women into prostitution and pornography, a choice that therefore cannot be construed as a choice in any meaningful sense. The sense MacKinnon conveys is that of an overdetermined trajectory, a "cycle of abuse" in which incest, rape, prostitution, and pornography are interconnected, all converging to divest their victim of agency. Thus, while legally such women are still considered free agents, MacKinnon effectively claims that they, and in fact all women, deserve the same protection as minors:

> Some of the same reasons children are granted some specific legal avenues for redress—relative lack of power, inability to

command respect for their consent and self-determination, in some cases less physical strength or lowered legitimacy in using it, specific credibility problems, and lack of access to resources for meaningful self-expression—also hold true for the social position of women compared to men. (*Feminism Unmodified* 181)

In the context of production-related harm, there is another level of harm to the women involved in pornography, harm done not in the process of production itself but rather resulting from the very existence, circulation, and mode of reception of the representations. One such harm identified by MacKinnon is the silencing of the women involved in pornography, their divestment of credibility (*Feminism Unmodified* 180–182; *Only Words* 3–5). MacKinnon describes the process whereby pornography models are disbelieved when they claim they are victims of coercion, because the representations are taken as evidence of their consent, enjoyment, or even desire; further, by providing evidence of what was done to them, the representations appear to reflect on their very *nature* as the sort of women to whom such things are done or who let such things be done to them. MacKinnon condenses this problem in a striking image: "Even if she can form words, who listens to a woman with a penis in her mouth?" (*Feminism Unmodified* 193). She also cites evidence for instances in which the pornographic pictures themselves function as a means of extortion to coerce the women and particularly the children in them into prostitution or prevent them from leaving it. Thus, claims MacKinnon, the pornography, legally regarded as the pornographer's speech, functions to foreclose or discredit the speech of the women in it, since it provides an authoritative frame for construing their experience, a frame which discredits their own construal of it or even prevents them from forming it.

A related harm emerges when pornography is conceived not only as a record of acts but as an act in and of itself, an understanding suggested by MacKinnon when she defines pornography as "a technologically sophisticated traffic in women" (*Only Words* 7). For MacKinnon, it is not only the images of the women that are sold, bought, possessed, and used but also the women themselves. According to this view, the representation is not an object ontologically distinct from the woman in it but rather a medium of traffic: "It is a constitutional right to traffic in our flesh, so long as it is done through pictures and words" (*Feminism

Unmodified 213). Correspondingly, the consumption of the representations is conceived as a reenactment of the events they record. Thus, discussing the harm suffered by Linda Marchiano, MacKinnon states: "No amount of saying anything remedies what is being *done* to her in theaters and on home videos all over the world, where she is repeatedly raped for public entertainment and public profit" (*Feminism Unmodified* 182). The equation of pornography and prostitution is justified by pointing out the lived connection between the two for many women who are involved in both and who arrive at one through the other. The equation also rests on the fact that the two involve the same acts, with the reproducibility and iterability of the photographic and filmic image seen as furthering the exploitation of the represented woman, who is sold over and over or abused over and over. (Accordingly, the pornographers are for MacKinnon either "perpetrators" or "pimps.") And while in the case of women like Linda Marchiano who were coerced into making pornography, there is no doubt that the ongoing existence and consumption of the representation does aggravate the damage done to them, there seems to be a sense in which MacKinnon regards sexual representation itself as a form of violation: "Women are there to be violated and possessed, men to violate and possess us, either on screen *or by camera or pen* on behalf of the consumer" (*Feminism Unmodified* 172, emphasis mine).[22]

Consumption-Related Harm

The second level of harm discussed by MacKinnon is the harm suffered by women through men's consumption of pornography. Here one can distinguish between two types of claims: claims about localized and concrete harms, where one can trace some kind of causal relation between pornography and particular harms suffered by particular women, and a more general claim about pornography's detrimental effect on the status of women as a social group.

To the former category belong the claims that pornography is forced on women in the workplace, the home, and the public sphere; that neighborhoods where pornography is concentrated through zoning policies are unsafe for women; that pornography is used to "season" women and children to prostitution; that pornography teaches men desires and acts that are violent or obnoxious to women and legitimates them in demanding women to perform or take part in such acts; that pornography provides inspiration for acts of rape and abuse; and, based on some experimental data, that pornography makes men more prone to violence against women and to rape or, at the very least, induces attitudes of hostility toward women and tolerance to rape (*Feminism Unmodified* 183–189).

While all the foregoing are empirical claims, relying either on reports by women or on the largely contested and often pronounced inconclusive "effects" research,[23] MacKinnon's more general claim relies not on empirical evidence but on cultural analysis. Of all the types of harm she discusses, this is the broadest, most pervasive harm, because it effects women in general, and therefore it is also the harm that provides the most substantial ground for her call for legal measures against pornography. The claim is that pornography not only reflects the social hierarchy between the sexes but constructs it, not only expresses men's ideas of women but determines what women can be. In short, MacKinnon rejects a simplistic model of representation as an expression of consciousness or a reflection of social reality and suggests an understanding of pornography as a discourse that constructs subjectivities and shapes social reality. MacKinnon's account of the way in which pornography affects women's lives is summed up in the following quote: "Men treat women as whom they see women as being. Pornography constructs who that is. Men's power over women means that the way men see women defines who women can be. Pornography is that way" (*Theory of the State* 196). In other words, pornography shapes men's view of and attitudes toward women, and men's domination of society means that "women live in the world pornography creates" (204).

On a closer look, one can see that throughout her writings, MacKinnon theorizes the effectivity or the harm of pornography according to a number of different—and partly incompatible—models, which she uses interchangeably. These are social construction, ideology, behavioral conditioning, and linguistic performativity.

Social Construction. MacKinnon often employs the language of social construction to describe pornography's mode of effectivity.[24] However, she also departs from a social construction model, as exemplified for instance in Foucault's *History of Sexuality*, in three significant ways: she does specify an identifiable agent "who does the constructing," that is, she regards construction as the act of a subject or a group of subjects: men; she equates construction with determination in that she sees pornography as exhaustively constitutive of gender and sexuality; and she assumes a fixed relation between discourse and power: pornography for her is inextricably bound to male domination and cannot in any way be severed from it or serve to undermine it.[25]

Ideology. The view of pornography as inherently linked to male power suggests an understanding of it in terms of ideology. MacKinnon explicitly bases her analysis of gender oppression on the Marxist model, replacing the capital-labor relation with the male-female relation and positing sexuality in the feminist paradigm as the equivalent of work in the Marxist paradigm.[26] Thus, as the organization of labor defines the class system, the organization of sexuality defines the gender system. And, as Wendy Brown suggests, "Although MacKinnon never says so explicitly, pornography presumably is to male dominance as, for Marx, liberalism is to capitalism—something institutionally securing, discursively naturalizing, ideologically obscuring, and historically perpetrating the power of the dominant" (82). If, according to Althusser's formulation, the function of ideology is to reproduce the relations of production, for MacKinnon, pornography functions to reproduce the relations of sexuality, that is, gender hierarchy. In other words, it naturalizes the subordination of women by constructing femininity in terms of sexual accessibility.

Unlike social construction theory, the Marxist theory of ideology, at least in its classic formulation, enables MacKinnon to define pornography as directly reflecting the material interests of men as the "ruling class" and sustaining the existing social order:

> Speaking socially, the beliefs of the powerful become proof, in part because the world actually arranges itself to affirm what the powerful want to see.... Beneath this, though, the world is not entirely the way the powerful say it is or want to believe it is. If it appears to be it is because power constructs the appearance of reality... (MacKinnon, *Feminism Unmodified* 164)

However, MacKinnon veers away from the classic Marxist notion of ideology as a false or distorted representation of real material conditions when she claims that pornographic "ideology" in fact turns itself into reality: "Women live in the world pornography creates" (*Theory of the State* 204).[27] Thus, she in effect wavers between a materialist and a social construction analysis. Consider, for example, the following quotation:

"Under conditions of sexual dominance pornography hides and distorts the truth while at the same time enforcing itself, imprinting itself on the world, making itself real" (*Feminism Unmodified* 130).

Does pornography then construct reality or only its appearance? MacKinnon wavers between the two options because she wants to stress both the power of pornography, the reality and totality of its harm on the one hand, and its distorted representation of women's sexuality and being on the other hand, that women, contrary to the way they are portrayed in pornography, do not enjoy being "taken and violated." Similarly, she wants to claim both that pornography *expropriates* women's sexuality (under the sexuality-work analogy), that is, women's proper sexuality, and that it *constructs* women's sexuality, that is, what is known as women's sexuality.[28] Despite the tension between these two claims, MacKinnon cannot settle for either one alone, because the social construction paradigm does not allow her to claim harm on the basis of the alienation of an authentic self, whereas the classic Marxist theory of ideology lacks an elaborate and nuanced account of how ideology forms subjectivity. It should be noted, however, that both a strict constructivist perspective and a strict materialist perspective conflict with her implicit humanist notion of the female subject.

Behavioral Conditioning. While for social construction theory the power to construct reality is an attribute of all discourse, MacKinnon ascribes to pornography a unique efficacy, that of sexual conditioning. This argument, implicit in her earlier work and explicitly developed in *Only Words*, claims that pornography conditions male erection and ejaculation to female subordination. As in the claim of production-related harm that adduces the reality of the represented acts, here she adduces the reality of the consumers' measurable physical arousal and pleasure as evidence of the conditioning process taking place: "The women are in two dimensions, but the men have sex with them in their own three-dimensional bodies, not in their mind alone. Men come doing this." The consequences of this pattern of reinforcement that pairs orgasm to images of "women being exposed, humiliated, violated . . . tortured and killed" are allegedly that "sooner or later, in one way or another, the consumers want to live out the pornography in three dimensions" (*Only Words* 12, 13).

To corroborate this description, MacKinnon cites a convicted rapist and murderer, whom she graces with the title "an honest perpetrator," who attests to undergoing such a process of conditioning. However, as Mandy Merck points out, the major support of her argument is the erection's potent status as proof for the whole alleged causal chain ending in aggression, which the erection purportedly "supports" (*Only Words* 11; Merck, "MacKinnon's Dog"). While regarding the consumers' interaction with the representations as a form of sex is probably correct both phenomenologically (true to the consumers' experience) and analytically, in an age when the proliferation of modes of mediated sex is a significant cultural phenomenon MacKinnon's argument deduces one sexual behavior—rape and abuse—from another—arousal and masturbation. And though she may have a case in claiming that pornography conditions the latter, the causal link to the former remains unsubstantiated.

Further, applying the conditioning model to pornography presupposes the existence of some kind of prior autonomous sexual response to sexual imagery. This natural, unconditioned response, for example, male arousal to the image of a naked woman, could then be paired to more specific contents, such as subordination and violence. Without such an underlying sexual reflex there can be no conditioning, just as in Pavlov's famous experiment the pairing of salivation to the sound of the bell relied on the involuntary reflex of salivation to the taste of food. Yet MacKinnon makes no analytic effort to distinguish the unconditioned response—a "natural" sexual reflex—from the conditioned one—our learned, "pornographic" sexuality—and her persistent use of the language of social construction is at odds with such a distinction. A further objection to the conditioning model consists in the claim that it misconstrues the nature of sexual arousal. As Elizabeth Cowie points out, there is a prevalent assumption that pornography induces arousal as a reflex response to its visual content, while in fact the sexual image that arouses us is "already a highly coded entity" ("Pornography and Fantasy" 135). Therefore, arousal is the product of a complex signifying process and has more to do with connotation and implied narrative than with simple visual stimuli.

Linguistic Performativity. The conditioning argument serves to substantiate MacKinnon's definition of pornography as performative "speech" rather than a merely expressive one. At stake here is her attempt to remove pornography from the realm of legally protected expression by claiming that it should more properly be regarded as an act, like certain other verbal behaviors legally considered to be acts, such as libel, blackmail, sexual harassment, discriminatory statements, or saying "kill" to a trained attack dog. To undermine the distinction between speech and act, MacKinnon mobilizes, beside the known legal exceptions, a model derived from linguistics: J. L. Austin's speech act theory. According to Austin, there exists a special category of utterances—performatives—that do not describe a state of affairs but rather perform an action or, in saying something, do something (J. L. Austin, *How to Do Things with Words*).[29] MacKinnon claims such status for pornography, thus adopting its legal categorization as "speech" but defining it exactly as that kind of speech that subordinates the property valued and protected by the First Amendment—expression of ideas—to a mode of effectivity that is not conscious persuasion but a much more direct and involuntary transitivity, like unconscious conditioning and habituation.

Whereas the conditioning model treats the pornographic representation as a visual stimulus, speech act theory, as Mandy Merck points out, requires reading it as an utterance, and that utterance for MacKinnon is "'get her,' pointing at all women" ("MacKinnon's Dog" 8; *Only Words* 15). This transcription of what pornography, all pornography, is saying involves of course considerable translation. Further, paraphrasing pornography's message as a command assigns its mode of action in Austinian terms to the category of perlocution rather than that of illocution, the speech act proper (Merck, "MacKinnon's Dog"; Butler, *Excitable Speech*). A perlocutionary act is defined by its consequences, which are separable from the act of enunciation itself, while an illocutionary act produces its effect in the very act of saying something. A ship is christened by the very pronouncement of the right formula in the right circumstances, while an utterance like "get her" depends for its effect on the compliance of its addressee. However, while transcribing the pornographic utterance as a command, MacKinnon in no way sees its efficacy as contingent. On the contrary, she attributes to pornography the capacity to turn itself into reality, to construct "the social reality of what a woman is" (*Only Words* 17). As an act of speech that possesses the power to change the state of things through enunciation itself, the efficaciousness of the pornographic utterance should be conceived not on the model of perlocution but on that of illocution. Thus, as Judith Butler points out, the pornographic utterance is figured as akin to the divine "let there be light," the only imperative that holds such sovereign illocutionary power: "The visual field [of pornography] operates as a subject with the power to bring into being what it names, to wield an efficacious power analogous to the divine performative" (*Excitable Speech* 66). The question remains, of course, what is the ground for attributing such sovereign power to pornography.

The Flaws of the Antiporn Position

This section will not offer a comprehensive critique of MacKinnon's position on pornography but will attempt, based on the many existing critiques, to identify its major weaknesses, some of which have been hinted at in the previous section.

First, as has often been noted by her critics, MacKinnon offers an ahistorical and monolithic conception of pornography,[30] regarding it as inextricably to male power, irrespective of its specific material and cultural context. By positing the subordination of women as the defining core of this representational regime, MacKinnon erases its historicity as a phenomenon whose emergence in eighteenth-century Europe was linked to a whole array of social, economic, and technological developments, whose definitional boundaries have been continually contested, and which from its inception has been subjected to politically motivated legal regulation (Hunt; Kendrick). In thus sheering pornography of history, she banishes from sight any of its shaping forces and affinities that cannot be reduced to misogyny and occludes the continuity of her own project with the history of regulation of pornography. Moreover, as Gayle Rubin points out, it is this ahistorical notion of pornography that allows antiporn feminists to regard it as a prime cause of women's oppression, an argument that fails to take account of the modernity of pornography ("Misguided" 270).[31]

MacKinnon's definition of pornography is based on its late twentieth-century incarnation as a phenomenon of unprecedented cultural salience and a multibillion-dollar industry. More specifically, it is based on the mainstream of this industry, that is, commercial heterosexual pornography, with its distinctive conditions of production and specific generic conventions. Yet this definition is taken to describe pornography per se, thus eliding not only its historical mutability but also the variety of its contemporary manifestations, hence, its potential for further change. Marginal representations are defined either as not pornographic or, more often, as identical in their meaning and function to mainstream ones.

The pornography produced on the margins of the industry—gay male pornography, lesbian pornography, and straight pornography produced by women for female consumption—is largely ignored by MacKinnon, and when it is discussed, as in the following quote, it is treated as a variant of mainstream porn, manifesting and upholding the same ideology of gender hierarchy:

> Pornography's multiple variations on and departures from the male dominant/female submissive sexual/gender theme are not exceptions to these gender regularities. They affirm them. The capacity of gender reversals (dominatrixes) and inversions (homosexuality) to stimulate sexual excitement is derived precisely from their mimicry or parody or negation or reversal of the standard arrangement. This affirms rather than undermines or qualifies the standard sexual arrangement . . . (*Theory of the State* 144)

Thus, even when single-gendered, pornography is still *about* female subordination, since sex is perceived to be hierarchical and hierarchy is perceived to be gendered. In a telling passage MacKinnon says: "It may also be that sexuality is so gender marked that it carries dominance and submission with it, whatever the gender of the participants" (*Theory of the State* 142). Dominance and submission are entirely conflated with male and female, this logic making it impossible to undermine gender hierarchy, since every inversion or subversion of it inevitably refers back to it, thus being deemed to uphold it. When men are penetrated or dominated, they are "used in the place of women,"[32] and when women take the role of sadist, they are merely imitating male dominance, thus affirming it as the ruling paradigm.

We can see, then, that the problem lies in two planes. First, MacKinnon's version of social construction theory assumes a fixed relation between (pornographic) discourse and (male) power, or in other words, that every pornographic representation, regardless of its social context, target audience, and conditions of production, inevitably carries the same meaning and fulfills the same political function of upholding male dominance. Yet as Foucault has persuasively argued, the relation between discourse and power is always fluid, and the same discourse can function both as an instrument of power and as a point of resistance.[33] Second, since the preceding quotes suggest that this fixity characterizes not only sexual representation but sexual practice as well, it appears that MacKinnon's conception of pornography as univocal and static goes hand in hand with a totalizing and static conception of male domination: "Our status as a group relative to men has almost never, if ever, been much changed from what it is" (*Feminism Unmodified* 167). The picture she paints is an ahistorical picture of timeless, changeless, oppression, yet paradoxically, this picture is at odds with her insistence on the centrality of pornography as an apparatus of male domination, if we bear in mind the distinct modernity of pornography. It is hard to imagine how such an immutable structure of domination could be affected by the abolition of such a recent phenomenon like pornography.

Another cluster of problems revolves around MacKinnon's theorization of sexuality. MacKinnon's critique of pornography is derived from the central role assigned to sexuality in her theory of gender. As noted earlier, MacKinnon defines gender as the social organization of sexuality under male dominance, in correspondence to the Marxist model that defines class as the social organization of labor under the domination of capital. Gender oppression consists in men's appropriation of female sexuality, all other manifestations of it being derivative, and pornography is both an instance of this appropriation and a major process constructing/organizing sexuality, hence, gender.

This theoretical account is problematic in several respects. As Wendy Brown points out, Marx "rooted his argument about labor as power in labor's generativity—its capacity to produce a surplus" (81n4). Sexuality, on the other hand, has no similar generativity that might account for its exploitation, unless one regards reproduction as that generativity, which MacKinnon does not. Neither does MacKinnon regard sexual pleasure itself to be the equivalent of surplus, since men's sexual exploitation of women does not necessarily entail that women are deprived of sexual pleasure; MacKinnon's claim is that women do get sexual pleasure but such that is learned, that is, not proper to them, and incompatible with their humanity. Therefore, as Brown suggests, in the absence of any kind of motivating profit, the raison d'être for the appropriation of women's sexuality "would seem to recur, darkly, to the intrinsic pleasures of male sexual dominance" (93).

These pleasures are for MacKinnon both learned and determinative. Thus, she alternately holds pornography accountable for constructing men's desires and men's view of women and quotes it as evidence of what it is that men want sexually.[34] Yet the prime originator in her theory of gender appears, in the final account, to be innate male sexuality: "Masculinity precedes male as femininity precedes female, and male sexual desire defines both" (*Theory of the State* 131). Male sexuality is posited (if somewhat tentatively) as the determining factor of the entire system of gender hierarchy: "[P]erhaps the sexes are unequal so that men can be sexually aroused" (145). Thus, MacKinnon seems to entertain simultaneously a social constructionist view of sexuality in general and an implicitly essentialist view of male sexuality.[35] Yet, even if we neglect the theoretical incoherence of this position, an essentialist view of male sexuality would undermine her very project, which is ultimately that of reforming heterosexuality. If the problem lies in essential male sexuality, what hope can there be of changing heterosexual sexuality and the relations between the sexes in general?[36]

To go back to the role of sexuality in MacKinnon's theory of gender, this poses two further problems pointed out by Brown. First, by positing sexuality as the single mechanism of gender oppression, MacKinnon ignores the "construction and regulation of gender by a panoply of discourses, activities, and distinctions other than sexuality," for example, the feminization of reproductive work, and the gendered division of labor, among others (Brown 86).[37] Second, sexuality itself is reduced by MacKinnon to a single social relation rather than "a complex nonschema of discourses and economies, which are constitutive not only of the semiotics of gender but of race and class formations" (Brown 83). In fact, as Brown observes, MacKinnon's equation of gender with sexuality is symptomatic of the contemporary tendency "to read gender as almost wholly constituted by the (heterosexual) organization of desire" (86), a tendency that Brown attributes to the destabilization of those other sites of gender construction mentioned earlier. In addition, the central place of sexuality in MacKinnon's theory of gender takes part in the constantly growing discursive deployment of sexuality characterized by Foucault, a feature it shares with the discourse of pornography itself, thus leading Brown to the assertion that MacKinnon's theory "mirrors" pornography rather than decodes it (87).

As noted, MacKinnon's critique of pornography in fact depends on a critique of heterosexuality itself. MacKinnon's writings evince a conception of heterosexual intercourse, derived from Andrea Dworkin's work,[38] as an inherently violent and violating act, a concrete manifestation and enactment of male dominance and female submission. The penis is figured as a weapon, and penile penetration is conceived as a violation of bodily integrity and subjective autonomy, as an act of possession and use. Intercourse so conceived is inherently opposed to freedom and equality, with the result that any substantive distinction between intercourse and rape is eroded: "[T]he major distinction between intercourse (normal) and rape (abnormal) is that the normal happens so often that one cannot get anyone to see anything wrong with it" (*Theory of the State* 146). Thus, MacKinnon is led to the paradox of wondering "whether a good fuck is any compensation for getting fucked" (*Feminism Unmodified* 61).

This question begs the corresponding question, posed by Drucilla Cornell, "Why is it the end of the world 'to be fucked'?" (152). As Cornell, Lynne Segal, and others point out, in her conception of intercourse, MacKinnon in fact buys into the symbolic meanings of sex constructed by pornography as well as by other dominant discourses of sex and gender. She subscribes to the identification of the phallus, as the symbol of male power, with the penis, and of 'being fucked' with loss of subjectivity. Instead of contesting the symbolic meanings attached to penetration in a male-dominant culture, she adopts the meanings and rejects the practice. Thus, as Cornell points out, she in effect endorses "a view of selfhood and, more particularly, of the body, defined from the side of the masculine," a view that identifies selfhood with inviolable bodily sovereignty (154). MacKinnon's subscription to the male point of view is apparent in her recurrent use of the four-letter word in all its declensions. This usage conveys, beside a degree of feminist bravado, a conviction that in saying it she says it all. When she describes women's having sex as their "getting fucked" she adopts the point of view embedded in the term without problematizing it and posits it as a neutral description, the way things really are.

This equation of the male viewpoint with objective reality brings us to a related problem: the totalizing quality of MacKinnon's theory of oppression and its implications for the possibility of female resistance. As Wendy Brown observes, MacKinnon appropriates Marxism's "science of domination" but produces an account of gender oppression that lacks the historical and dialectical dimension of Marxism. Sexism is posited as "utterly static—without a history or a dynamic of transformation to open a different future," and women as the oppressed class are seen to have "no cultural meaning or existence other than [their] derivation [from the dominant class]" and "no inner resources for the development of consciousness or agency." Their subjectivity is reduced to their subject position (93). This equation of women's subjectivity with their subject position under patriarchy is problematic both theoretically and politically. As Drucilla Cornell notes, MacKinnon's reduction of feminine "reality" to "the sexualized object we are for *them*" relies on the notion that male power endows the male gaze with the capacity to construct reality completely. Yet this capacity is dubious: "What 'is' cannot be reduced to the way one particular group 'sees' reality" (130, 131). Further, if women's consciousness is constituted entirely, then a female point of view, hence, a feminist critique, should be impossible. Yet MacKinnon's critique of pornography is explicitly based on just such an allegedly foreclosed point of view, a contradiction she does not address.

Obviously, women are assumed to have some epistemological access to reality, yet this access is judged on the basis of content; true knowledge for MacKinnon is women's knowledge of their victimization, while women's accounts of sexual pleasure and sexual empowerment are dismissed as false consciousness. Such an attitude, as Cornell observes, is decidedly nonfeminist in that it effectively takes part in the silencing of women. Moreover, when women's sexuality and consciousness are regarded as wholly constituted, no room is left for agency. If women's sexuality is not properly their own, since it is constructed according to the interests of male sexuality, female sexual agency is a meaningless concept. Thus, the whole realm of sex becomes strictly oppressive for women, and feminist resistance can be conceived only in terms of defending against male sexuality.

To go back to the harms of pornography, discussed in the previous section, two main objections to MacKinnon's account arise. First, her account of harm in the production process is based on an extremely naive reading of pornographic representations; represented violence is read as real violence, represented pain is read as actual pain.[39] (However, this strategy of interpretation is inconsistent, since she takes representations of women's pleasure to be a sham, thus exactly reversing the traditional reading of pornography, which takes the pleasure to be real and the suffering faked.) In this, MacKinnon in fact buys into the documentary myth of the hardcore genre, which is one of its major seductions. She is also oblivious to the degree of interpretation incorporated in her own purportedly neutral description of what is seen in pornography, her use of terms like "exposed," "taken," "used," "possessed," and "violated" reflecting a point of view that posits women as entirely passive and acted upon.[40] A more skeptical approach would deem it impossible to deduce the realities of the making of the representation from the representation itself.[41] The accounts provided by pornography models themselves offer a far more reliable source of information. Yet if one credits accounts of coercion and abuse, one must also credit accounts of free choice or even empowerment.[42]

Second, MacKinnon's account of harm in the reception process assumes that by conditioning male sexual arousal and pleasure to female subordination, pornography induces imitation in real life or, at the very least, shapes men's attitudes toward women, thus eventually constructing reality itself. This account may be contested by introducing an understanding of pornography in terms of fantasy. While MacKinnon claims that in pornography art and life imitate each other to the point of being indistinguishable, a different relation between the two may be posited, one in which pornography serves as a compensatory fantasy either soothing perennial male anxieties, such as fears of impotence and female rejection, or staging "an allegory of masculine willfulness and feminine submission" in response to a historical crisis in male dominance, in a futile attempt "to shore up or stabilize" it.[43]

According to such an argument, pornography is understood as fantasy both as the product of a collective male unconscious and in terms of its function in the psychic life of its consumers.[44] In a broader sense, all genres of fiction, as Elizabeth Cowie suggests, may be regarded as "public forms of fantasy" (149). Even aside from its probable compensatory dimension, applying the psychoanalytic understanding of fantasy to pornography means that it cannot be reduced to mere wishful thinking since "there is no straightforward connection between the dynamics of desire in fantasy and the satisfactions sought in material reality" (Segal, "Sweet Sorrows" 70). In fact, while MacKinnon adduces the sexual pleasure involved in the consumption of pornography as evidence for its status as "real sex," this element only reinforces its reading as fantasy since, as Lesley Stern points out, the activity of fantasizing is gratifying in its own right, regardless of any attempt to act out the fantasy (56). Moreover, as Elizabeth Cowie stresses, even sexual gratification is, in a sense, an extraneous element, since rather than being "a simple means to physical sexual gratification," pornography represents "the desire to desire," and its pleasure lies in arousal itself ("Pornography and Fantasy" 137).

Further, according to the theory of fantasy offered by Laplanche and Pontalis, the content of the fantasy gives no clue as to the subject's identifications, since fantasy "is not the object of desire but its setting" ("Fantasy and the Origins of Sexuality" 26). In other words, fantasy does not represent the attainment of a wished-for object but rather provides the mise-en-scène of desire. The subject's desire is invested in the scenario as a whole, and her/his identifications may shift between the different positions of desire (active or passive) in it and, hence, not necessarily adhere to gender lines.

The Anti-Antiporn Position

The Critique of Antiporn Strategy

As noted earlier, since the antiporn camp has been the agenda setter in the debate, anti-antiporn texts are chiefly engaged in a critique of its arguments, and most of the critiques developed in the previous section have been outlined in anti-antiporn writings with varying degrees of elaboration. Alongside critiques of its theoretical analysis, one prevalent objection to antiporn feminism, particularly in the early stages of the debate, concerns its political strategy. Antiporn feminists are faulted for forming political alliances with fundamentalist and ultraconservative circles, with people and organizations that have taken decidedly antifeminist positions on issues like the right to abortion, the Equal Rights Amendment, and civil rights issues in general and whose interest in banning pornography is based on religious conviction, sexual conservatism, and bigotry.[45]

They are also faulted for their reliance on state power in their attempted antipornography legislation. Critiques of this strategy call attention to the fact that when censorship is employed by the state, it is usually aimed first and foremost against sexual minorities and not against misogynist mainstream pornography.[46] They point out that as long as law enforcement is in the hands of a male-dominated government, legal system, and police, there is little chance that "feminist" antiporn legislation will be interpreted and enforced according to feminist sensibilities. As Lisa Duggan asserts, "a 'feminist issue' or 'feminist law' does not exist in the abstract: it is the alignment of political and cultural forces that gives meaning to issues and laws" ("Censorship" 68). And Ellen Willis concludes, "In a male supremacist society, the only obscenity law that will not be used against women is no law at all" (466). Since the antiporn campaign took place in the Reagan and Bush era, in a political climate marked by the strengthening of the New Right, the erosion of feminist gains, and increased homophobia and sexual repression, many anti-antiporn feminists warned that antiporn feminism is playing into the hands of reactionary forces, and that restrictions on sexual representation may endanger access to information on contraception, safe sex, and women's sexuality.

The Arguments for Pornography

The critiques of the antiporn analysis and strategy rely on a "positive" argument—an argument about the potential value of sexual representations for women and feminism—which, though often not elaborated, is at least implicit in most anti-antiporn texts. Although most critics of the antiporn position do not directly address the question of what women stand to gain from pornography, they do outline a theory of sexuality that is very different from MacKinnon's and that suggests a different relation of women to the field of sexual representation.

Many writers point out that the antiporn position is based on highly traditional, stereotypical notions of masculinity and femininity, the "characterization of male sexuality as compulsive and violent and female sexuality as muted and ethereal" (Echols 442). It is also observed that this view of sexuality replicates the one held by nineteenth-century feminists in the social purity movement, with their notions of male vice and female virtue and their view of male sexuality as predatory and women's mission as that of defending against and curbing it. Proponents of the anti-antiporn position stress the need to pull away from such a polarized view of male and female sexuality, and they point out that a major aspect of women's oppression has been the restriction of their sexual behavior and the construction of female sexuality as passive, responsive, and lethargic. The picture of male predators and female victims painted by antiporn feminists is thus seen as unwittingly reproducing and upholding precisely the oppressive patriarchal construction of female sexuality.

Anti-antiporners reject the view of sexuality as a domain offering women nothing but danger and victimization, hence, the opposition of women's liberation to sexual liberation.[47] Sexuality is seen not as the origin and core of women's oppression but merely as one of the sites within which it is constituted, and the salient feature of women's relation to sex becomes not exploitation through forced participation but rather exclusion from the realm of sexuality and restriction of sexual expression. The most radical articulation of this point of view is provided by Gayle Rubin:

> Part of the modern ideology of sex is that lust is the province of men, purity that of women. Women have been to some extent excluded from the modern sexual system. It is no accident that pornography and the perversions have been considered part of the male domain. In the sex industry, women have been excluded from most production and consumption, and allowed to participate primarily as workers. In order to participate in the "perversions," women have had to overcome serious limitations on their social mobility, their economic resources, and their sexual freedoms. ("Thinking Sex" 307–308)

Women are thus viewed as a sexually underprivileged group that must struggle to gain full erotic rights, and pornography, along with the perversions, is perceived as a site of male privilege that women ought to appropriate rather than try to eliminate.

Rubin's argument is anchored, like many other anti-antiporn texts,[48] in the libertarian discourse that posits sexual pleasure as one of the fundamental human goods, sexual liberation as an individual and societal goal and sees Western culture as sexually repressed or "sex-negative" and sexual expression as politically progressive. In regard to pornography, the libertarian premise may lead to two opposing valuations. Pornography can be regarded either as a symptom of a repressive society, which would wither away in utopia, as Ellen Willis suggests, or as an antidote to repression, promoting sexual self-knowledge and growth, as Pat Califia suggests. At any rate, the sexism of most porn is regarded by anti-antiporners not as inherent to the genre but as a reflection of a sexist culture and an inevitable characteristic of a genre that is "the product of a male imagination and aimed at a male market" (Willis 462). The implication is that once women remedy the bias that makes pornography a male territory, pornography made by and for women would be different. And Gayle Rubin explicitly suggests that porn would become more attuned to women's fantasies and more infused with feminist awareness when more women and more feminists become involved in the production of sexually explicit material ("Misguided" 272).

It is worth noting that the appropriation of the libertarian discourse by women requires a conceptual distinction (precisely the one refused by MacKinnon) between sexuality and gender, and such a distinction is indeed called for by Rubin. Rubin offers a theory of sexual oppression as separate from and irreducible to gender oppression and promotes an understanding of sexuality as inflected by gender, not subsumed under it, thus declaring feminism inadequate as a theory of sexuality ("Thinking Sex" 309).

While sex radicals like Rubin and Califia seem to posit women's relation to pornography as a question of equal access, there is also another strand of anti-antiporn thinking that focuses on questions of subjectivity. This strand of thinking, taking its cue both from the social construction theory of sexuality and from feminist film theory, refuses "complicity with the victim syndrome which reduces pleasure to male pleasure and equates this with male power" (Stern 53) yet rejects also the unproblematized libertarian notion of pleasure. It regards pleasure and subjectivity as constructed through discursive or textual practices and is interested in the capacity of sexual representations to offer new constructions of female sexuality.

As Michel Foucault has demonstrated, the discursive regime of sexuality dominating modern Western society constitutes "sex" as the core of the subject. This pivotal role assigned to sex in the paradigm of modern subjectivity poses an ineluctable challenge to women to recast themselves in these terms, that is, as desiring subjects and sexual agents rather than sexual objects.[49] While MacKinnon revolts against the reduction of women to sexual objects, anti-antiporn feminists believe that this reduction can be effectively countered only by means of opposing constructions.

Feminist film theory nourishes anti-antiporn thinking through its focus on the question of female spectatorial pleasure and desire. Laura Mulvey's influential essay "Visual Pleasure and Narrative Cinema" opened up two decades of feminist theoretical engagement with a nexus of questions concerning the relations between pleasure, spectatorship, and sexual difference in the cinema. In this essay, Mulvey analyzes the structure of visual pleasure in classical Hollywood cinema as founded on the polarity of man as bearer of the gaze and woman as its passive object. According to her analysis, the cinematic apparatus constructs a gaze by means of the fusion of three looks: that of the camera, that of the male protagonist, and that of the spectator. The way these looks are structured produces the spectator position as necessarily masculine and constructs woman as spectacle. While the strength of Mulvey's model was in exposing the oppressiveness of popular cinema, the extensive discussion sparked by her text tried to find loopholes in the monolithic structure she described in order to make space for the female spectator and allow a theorization of female resistance. It therefore moved away from the analysis of the polarized structure of the gaze to the exploration of the types of pleasure and identification open to women as spectators.

This move is exactly analogous to the one performed by anti-antiporn feminists in relation to MacKinnon's analysis. As Lesley Stern suggests, feminist film theory may "correct" the antiporn vision both by "problematizing the visible" and shifting the focus from "what we see" to "how we see," and by shifting the focus from male pleasure to female pleasure, "either 'uncovering' this in what is established as pornography, or generating its presence in feminist visual erotica" (53). Stern calls for "constructing and exploring diverse sexualities *for* feminism" (60), and this call is echoed in Linda Williams's appreciative observation, based on her study of pornographic films, of "the remarkable decentering effects [for dominant sexuality] of proliferating sexual representations," by which she refers to gay, lesbian, bisexual, and sadomasochistic pornographies ("Second Thoughts" 56). Further, while the discussion of female spectatorship that has developed within feminist film theory is linked to the specificities of the visual medium in general and the cinematic apparatus in particular, its questions, its motivations, and the directions it opens are generalizable beyond the visual realm, since the problem of theorizing the female spectator is obviously synecdochal to the larger one of theorizing the female subject.

To sum up then, the strand of anti-antiporn thinking influenced by social construction theory and feminist film theory recognizes the defining role of sexuality in the paradigm of modern subjectivity and seeks to rearticulate the position of women vis-à-vis this paradigm, which constitutes them at the same time that it excludes them. In other words, it seeks to reconceive women as sexual subjects. In view of the growing prominence of pornography in the array of social discourses constructing sexuality, and in view of its singular equation with the field of sexuality,[50] the anti-antiporn position regards it as a resource that women can and should appropriate for the construction of female sexual subjectivity or subjectivities. Such an appropriation entails both the mounting of alternative sexual representations by women and an inquiry and affirmation of the pleasures and identifications available to women as consumers of both mainstream and marginal pornography.

Summing Up the Debate

To recapitulate, we can see that the feminist pornography debate, rather than displaying a thesis-antithesis structure, is founded on a number of asymmetries, a number of essential differences in focus between the two camps. Foremost among these is the antiporn camp's focus on harm versus the opposing camp's focus on subjectivity. Antiporn feminists stress women's victimization in and through pornography and in the realm of sexuality in general, while anti-antiporners posit women not as helpless sexual victims but as sexual subjects in the making; rather than focus on pornography's current harms to women, anti-antiporners explore its promise. This first difference corresponds to a second one, which might be viewed either as its cause or as its logical outcome: the antiporn focus on mainstream (i.e., male-produced, commercial, heterosexual) pornography versus the anti-antiporn focus on marginal representations. Another essential difference is the one between the two camps' approach to representation: the antiporn position understands representation on the model of action and tends to elide any distinction between the two; the anti-antiporn position understands representation on the model of fantasy, sometimes failing to distinguish between private unconscious fantasies and ready-made public ones.[51]

A key difference in the debate concerns the theorization of the relation between discourse and power. This issue is worth exploring at some length, since it is responsible for the optimism of the anti-antiporn position concerning the prospects of feminist appropriations of pornography and the pessimism of the antiporn position in regarding pornography as irredeemable for women. On this point one can place Judith Butler as MacKinnon's opponent. In her book *Excitable Speech*, Butler sets forth a theory of linguistic performativity that can be seen as elaborating a theoretical intuition that underscores many anti-antiporn texts. Following upon Jacques Derrida's critique of J. L. Austin's speech act theory, Butler offers an understanding of performativity "not as the act by which a subject brings into being what she/he names, but, rather, as that reiterative power of discourse to produce the phenomena that it regulates and constrains" (*Bodies That Matter* 2).[52] She regards the power of discourse to bring into effect what it names as originating not in the subject producing the utterance but in the utterance's citation or reiteration of preexisting norms, norms that acquire their regulatory force through the very process of reiteration. This view rejects efforts such as MacKinnon's to make individual subjects legally accountable for the injury effected by their discourse—whether racist speech or pornographic representations—since the injurious power of the utterance is derived not from the speaker but from a community and history of speakers that are being invoked every time the injurious term or the objectifying depiction is "cited" (*Excitable Speech*).

However, this fundamental citationality of all discourse is responsible not only for its power to injure but also for its susceptibility to recontextualization. To quote Derrida, whose formulation lays the ground for Butler's argument,

> Every sign, linguistic or non-linguistic, spoken or written . . . can be *cited*, put between quotation marks; in so doing it can break with every given context, engendering an infinity of new contexts in a manner which is absolutely illimitable. This does not imply that the mark is valid outside of a context, but on the contrary that there are only contexts *without any center or absolute anchoring*. (qtd. in *Bodies That Matter* 185–186, second emphasis mine)

According to Derrida, the essential *iterability* of the sign means that it can be infinitely repeated, endlessly grafted to new contexts and thus—since signification is always context-dependent—is never selfsame but signifies differently according to context. This fundamental attribute of discourse is for Butler the key to resistance. The politics she advocates is one that "exploit[s] speech itself for its insurrectionary effects" (*Excitable*

Speech 162) and opposes injurious speech acts through appropriative recontextualization, as exemplified by the appropriation of racial slurs in rap music or of the term "queer" by gays. This suggestion is in line with Butler's argument for the power of lesbian and gay styles to undermine the heterosexual gender norms of which they form unauthorized "imitations" (*Gender Trouble* 137–138), and the same line of argument would seem to call for feminist reappropriations of pornography as a strategic countermeasure to the objectifying constructions of women in pornography.

MacKinnon, on the other hand, cannot envisage any such reappropriation. According to her,

> the situation in which women presently find ourselves with respect to pornography is one in which more *pornography* is inconsistent with rectifying or even counterbalancing its damage through speech, because so long as the pornography exists in the way it does there will not be more speech by women. (*Feminism Unmodified* 193)

For MacKinnon, the harm of pornographic speech cannot be remedied through more speech, not to mention more pornographic speech. Far from engendering female speech, the only effect pornography can possibly have on women is that of silencing. Female pornographic speech is to her an oxymoron. If we look for the reason for MacKinnon's dismissal of the very possibility of expropriation of pornographic discourse by women, we can see that counter to Derrida's assertion, adopted by Butler, that "there are only contexts without any center or absolute anchoring," MacKinnon believes pornographic discourse to be anchored by male power, which fixes its meaning and its performative effects. Alternately, one may say that MacKinnon views male domination as an exhaustive and immutable context, which prevents any recontextualization of pornography.

Butler (responding to Pierre Bourdieu's account of the performative) objects to the argument that "language itself can only act to the extent that it is 'backed' by social power" and claims that to support it "one needs to supply a theory of how it is that social power 'backs' language" (*Excitable Speech* 158). MacKinnon, as we have seen, provides at most a rudimentary and incoherent account of such "backing," through her recourse to the theoretical models of ideology, social construction, and conditioning. On the other hand, unless she is suggesting a strictly autonomous agency of language, Butler too cannot be exempted from offering a theory of the relations between social power and language. Butler faults Derrida for regarding the performative's break with existing context as a structural feature of every utterance, a view that renders him unable to explain "how it is that certain utterances break from prior contexts with more ease than others" (150). Yet while she criticizes him for neglecting the social analysis of performativity, she too fails to provide such an analysis, since she is incapable of specifying under what conditions "the improper use of the performative can succeed in producing the effect of authority" (158) and when it would only result in an infelicity, under what conditions "the rehearsal of the conventional formulae in non-conventional ways" (147) would result in performative force and when it would not be able to lay hold of the power invested in these formulae, or what conditions make possible the recontextualization of a derogatory term.

Consequently, if MacKinnon sees discourse as tethered to its context by social power and fails to take account of instances of recontextualization, Butler stresses the recontextualizability of discourse and, despite her admission that "contexts inhere in certain speech acts in ways that are very difficult to shake" (*Excitable Speech* 161), fails to take account of the social forces that bind certain discourses to their context, preventing their reappropriation. In this sense, their theories are symmetrically opposed—MacKinnon provides an account of discursive oppression that makes no allowance for resistance, while Butler provides an account of discursive resistance that fails to analyze the workings of social power to constrain discursive redeployment. Both, however, are guilty of ahistoricism: MacKinnon's theory leaves no room for processes of recontextualization, thus failing to account for historical dynamism, and Butler's theory describes the linguistic mechanism whereby such processes take place *when they do* but fails to account for the conditions that enable or disenable them.

To locate the source of the differences in focus between the two camps, one needs to go, however, beyond the theoretical realm, to the plain of identification. The key to the debate seems to lie in the emphasis placed on harm and victimization by the one camp and on female sexual subjectivity by the other. I believe that Teresa de Lauretis comes close to the heart of the matter when she speculates that

> it is the hold of a socially constructed and subjective internalized identification with the victim's or "feminine" position that ... prevents "Dworkin" from fantasizing herself in the other place and taking up the aggressor's or "masculine" position. ... It is that imaginary identification with the victim's position that both limits the interpretive possibilities for "Dworkin" as viewer of the pornographic text and makes her feel constricted in a fantasy scenario that her subjecthood will not accept as hers. ("On the Subject of Fantasy" 81–82)[53]

De Lauretis suggests, correctly in my opinion, that antiporn feminists are interpellated by the pornographic text to the victim position, an interpellation they refuse but that nevertheless determines their response to pornography and forecloses any other identification. As de Lauretis aptly puts it, "'Dworkin' resists seeing herself in the mass-produced pornographic fantasy, in which yet she does see herself" (82). In Althusserian terms, antiporn feminists are the "bad subjects," those who hear the hail of ideology, recognize that it is addressed to them, but do not turn around. Specifying the kind of interpellation that is at work for anti-antiporn feminists is somewhat more complicated. They do not seem to be interpellated by the pornographic text to the "feminine" position. Their stance seems rather to represent a reaction to being barred from interpellation to the "masculine" position, the position of desiring subject and sexual aggressor. To revert to the terms of the Althusserian allegory once more, they hear the hail that pornography directs to the male consumer whom it constructs as the subject of its fantasy and recognize that it is not addressed to them. Antiporn feminists refuse to occupy the place assigned them by the pornographic text, while anti-antiporn feminists can find no place for themselves in it. The former refuse to recognize themselves in the image the pornographic text offers them, while the latter would like the text to address them when it doesn't.

As de Lauretis argues, counter to some reductive applications of Laplanche and Pontalis's theory of fantasy, the subject cannot "pick and choose any or all of the subject positions inscribed in a film" (or any other representation) ("On the Subject of Fantasy" 75). Its range of identifications is bounded by its historical situatedness, its positioning along the dimensions of gender, race, sexuality, among other categories, as well as its individual history. To ask why certain women are interpellated by pornography in one way while others are interpellated in another would entail an inquiry into the complex web of social and intrapsychic factors that shape identification, an inquiry that risks getting mired in psychological speculation. However, while identifications can be neither legislated nor judged, understanding the debate as motivated by opposing identifications does not invalidate the critical examination of the positions to which these identifications give rise either in terms of their theoretical coherence or in terms of their political efficacy.

Porn Wars: The Next Generation

While contemporary antiporn feminism consists of several voices, in extracting the essentials of this position I will refer mostly to two works: *Pornified*, by journalist Pamela Paul, and *Pornland*, by media scholar Gail Dines, whom I find the most articulate and persuasive spokesperson of this camp.

The first thing that distinguishes present-day antiporn feminism from its predecessor is the fact that it locates its intervention in the specificity of the present cultural moment, emphasizing the unparalleled nature of this moment in terms of the unprecedented visibility and accessibility of pornography and what is described as its seamless integration into pop culture (Paul 4). Paul and Dines describe a culture saturated with pornography, one in which the lines between pornography and popular culture have completely blurred and in which pornography is shaping young people's sexuality to an unprecedented degree. Dines describes this "seismic change" as "a massive social experiment" of alarmingly unforeseeable consequences, whose architects are a mercenary group of (mostly) men, the pornographers (Dines ix–xi). The narrative posits a complete rupture with what we have previously known as and about pornography (both Paul and Dines argue that "most women and some men have an idea of pornography that is 20 years out of date" [Dines xviii]). As Smith and Attwood astutely note, we have here a "complex narrative of nostalgia [for the days of softcore *Playboy*-type pornography] and futurology . . . where pornography is acknowledged as an already existing feature of the landscape, but one that has developed outside the knowledge of 'ordinary' adults and needs urgent redress" (Smith and Attwood 43). It is thus possible to maintain the ubiquity and hypervisibility of pornography and at the same time present it as an unknown and alarming reality that needs to be exposed.[54] Our porn-saturated culture is represented as a dystopia come true, in which the pornographers in a kind of stealth attack have managed to "hijack" our sexuality (Dines xxxi).

There are several comments to be made about this account. First, while it is undoubtedly true that the internet has dramatically facilitated access, including children's access to an unlimited quantity and range of pornographic representations, the break with the past is tendentiously exaggerated in the service of alarmism. First-wave antiporn feminism has already responded to a multimillion-dollar industry producing thousands of new titles annually, and while the internet increased the facility of distribution and the privacy of consumption, the video revolution was arguably a no less momentous sea change. Whereas first-wave antiporn directed its attack specifically against pornography, present-day antiporn critique is targeted equally at the popular culture, which it sees as transformed by pornography. The underlying narrative is one in which a profit-driven porn industry employs its huge resources to gain acceptability and infiltrate mainstream culture, and consequently, with images that not so long ago qualified as softcore porn now a regular part of pop culture, hardcore porn is becoming ever more extreme in an attempt to satisfy its desensitized consumers. Here, too, the phenomena these critics describe under the rubric of the "pornification" of culture (e.g., sexually explicit music videos, porn stars gaining celebrity status, pole dancing as a form of exercise, highly sexualized styles of dress for women and girls, etc.) are indicative indeed of an ongoing cultural process of sexualization whereby sex is becoming more visible in Western cultures (Attwood xiii). But while antiporn feminists see the porn industry as the prime mover behind this development, there are more fundamental social processes driving it, notably the changing boundaries between the public and the private, and the process (whose origins were described by Foucault and its contemporary manifestations by Anthony Giddens) of sex becoming central to the creation and expression of the individual's self (xv). The narrative that locates the blame for the sexualization of culture in "the pornographers" is a reductive explanation that ignores the multiple social factors shaping this process. Interestingly, Dworkin and MacKinnon avoid such reductive explanatory accounts that locate accountability in a specifiable group. For them, pornography is an instrument of patriarchal ideology that functions to sustain male domination, but it is this type of account, of course, that earns them with Pamela Paul the unflattering (not to say dismissive) label of "feminist hardliners" (Paul 258). Paul abstracts their position on sexuality as "all women are victims and all sex is rape" and charges them with alienating through this extreme position "what may otherwise be a natural broad-based following among women," drowning all other feminist critiques of pornography (258–259).[55]

This disassociation from first-generation antiporners is interesting, especially since, as we shall soon see, current antiporn feminism has more in common with it than it sometimes cares to acknowledge. However, one fundamental difference consists in their theories of sexuality. As opposed to MacKinnon and Dworkin's deep suspicion of all (heterosexual) sex, Paul and Dines propose a notion of a natural and healthy sexuality, which they oppose to "porn sex." Thus, in the preface to her book, Dines refuses the antiporn/pro-sex dichotomy and asks:

> But what if you are a feminist who is pro-sex in the real sense of the word, pro that wonderful, fun, and deliciously creative force that bathes the body in delight and pleasure, and what you are actually against is porn sex? A kind of sex that is debased, dehumanized, formulaic, and generic . . . (x)

According to the outlook they propose, then, sex is basically healthy and benign but warped by pornography. Indeed, as Smith and Attwood remark, "Recent antiporn feminist work does not focus particularly on the problematic aspects of gender in porn. . . . Instead it seems more concerned with the idea of 'healthy sexuality' . . ." (50). And what is considered healthy sexuality and set against "porn sex" is always a sexuality that is relational and involves intimacy, connection, and tenderness, as well as creativity. In both Paul's and Dines's books, one of the chief harms of pornography consumption by men is its detrimental effects on (heterosexual) relationships, indicating a view that not only privileges relationships but is judgmental of sex outside the context of relationship or romance. As Smith and Attwood rightly note, the characterizations of healthy sex indicate a very narrow conception of good sexuality, one that has no room for casual sex, kinky sex, or rough sex and that lacks a conception of benign sexual variation, to use Gayle Rubin's term, either in regard to sexual practices or in regard to people's motivations for having sex.[56]

What the notion of a natural, healthy sexuality affords is to construe men as victims of pornography just as much as women. Indeed, Dines's book devotes two chapters to men, explaining how male socialization "grooms" men into porn consumption and describing men's relation to pornography in terms of sexual dependency. It is easy to note the predominance of the addiction paradigm in current antiporn writings, a paradigm that draws both on medical and self-help discourses.[57] The benefit of this paradigm is that it avoids the gender conflict paradigm of radical feminism (as well as taps into the popular self-help ideology), thereby opening the way to include men in the antiporn movement "as they too are being dehumanized and diminished by the images they consume" (Dines 164). The contemporary antiporn movement interpellates men, then, not as oppressors called to relinquish their privileges but rather as abused victims. But since with men as victims too some "bad guys" must be identified, these are found in the form of the pornographers described as "a savvy group of capitalists" (Dines 83). Overall, Dines's critique of pornography seems to be rooted in a general distrust toward commercial popular culture reminiscent of late Marxist critiques of the culture industry.[58] She likens the pornography industry to the fast food industry (Paul likens it to the tobacco industry), in itself not an inappropriate analogy but one that bespeaks a deep suspicion of everything that is mass-produced and, as Smith and Attwood remark, a distrust of mediation of any kind, whether in the form of industry, commerce, or representation (Smith and Attwood 51). Her construction of the notion of an "authentic sexuality"—"one that develops organically out of life experiences, one's peer group, personality traits, family and community affiliations"—curiously assumes the possibility of a sexuality untainted by cultural representations and seems to bespeak a longing for a society in which mass media does not exist (Dines xi).

The belief in a natural, healthy sexuality that pornography warps and the construction of men as victims of pornography result in a switch from juridical strategies of intervention to educational ones. In the conclusion of her book, titled "Fighting Back," Dines calls for a movement that will resist porn culture, one that will include men and that she proposes to build through grassroots education about the true nature and effects of porn. Interestingly, the major consciousness-raising tool she proposes, and one that she herself helped develop, is a slide show, the same tool that was used thirty years earlier by WAP.[59] Contrary to first-wave antiporn, though, Dines stresses that an antiporn movement "can't only be about what's wrong in the world" but "needs to offer a mobilizing vision" of an alternative sexuality "based on equality, dignity, and respect" (164). The emphasis on holding out an alternative positive vision of heterosexual sexuality might be one of the lessons drawn from the earlier campaign that lacked such a vision and was therefore particularly vulnerable to accusations of being anti-sex. Though, as mentioned, the vision held out is a rather narrow and sanitized one. In a similar vein, Paul proposes that one of the chief solutions to the problem of pornography is proper sex education (257). In other words, both of them make the reasonable proposition that the way to neutralize pornography's pernicious effect is to provide effective counternarratives about sexuality.

Paul is also less shy about exploring various ideas for regulation (including the idea of criminalizing the giving and receiving of payment to perform sexual acts), especially in the form of restrictions on the distribution of pornography. She maintains, however, that the greatest potential for change lies in quelling the demand by means of measures similar to those that are used in relation to cigarette smoking and through the conjoined efforts of the government, the media, public institutions, and private citizens (Paul 261–265).

Another aspect in which current antiporn feminism differs from its predecessor is the way in which it formulates its claims about the efficacy of pornography. Instead of the behavioral conditioning model or linguistic performativity model MacKinnon employed, what we get from present-day antiporn feminists are far more cautious statements that ground the claims about the effects of pornography on both the individual and cultural level in the by now widespread recognition of the effects of media in general. Consider, for example, this statement by Dines: "Human beings develop their identity and sense of reality out of the stories the culture tells, and while pornography is not the only producer of stories about sex, relationships, and sexuality, it is possibly the most powerful" (82). This assertion gains credence by the fact that by now, as opposed to twenty or thirty years ago, porn has indeed become a major purveyor of sexual information and sexual narratives not only for adults but for preadolescents as well. By invoking, for example, the effect of fashion advertising on the steep rise in the consumption of cosmetic surgery, she reminds us of the power of images to construct reality for their viewers and "the cumulative effect of the subtextual themes found in the system of images" (81).[60] If women are compelled to shape their bodies according the model of beauty they are bombarded with by mass media, even when they know the images are manipulated, then similarly, she contends, it would be fantastical to think that men can masturbate to porn images and walk away from them untouched by their misogyny, even when they know that these are performances of sex that do not reflect mundane sexuality. Both Paul and Dines, in their books, make a strong case for the way porn shapes men's standards of female attractiveness, ideas about female sexuality, and expectations about sex. Dines also supports her claim concerning the pernicious effects of misogynous pornography through an analogy to the way that racist images function. As she explains, the efficacy of sexist or racist images arises from a social context saturated by racist or sexist ideology: "These images never stand alone but are implicated in the broader system of messages that legitimize the ongoing oppression of a group, and their power is often derived ... from strengthening and normalizing the ideology that condones oppression" (Dines 87).

The racial analogy is not unique to Dines but has been utilized repeatedly by the first generation of antiporn activists. MacKinnon, for instance, employs it several times in her attempts to undermine the legal distinction between speech and act. Thus, she brings the example of a sign saying "Whites Only" as an act of racial discrimination (recognized by the law as such) effected precisely through its expressive content; and of cross burning as an act of racial terrorism and incitement to violence (though not recognized by the US Supreme Court as such) whose harm is brought about through the message it conveys (*Only Words* 9, 23). To get closer to the subject of pornography, she draws an analogy between photographs of lynching and snuff films and finally between these two and bondage pictures of Asian models in *Penthouse* magazine (23–25). The first two are comparable as documentations of (presumably) real-life murders that are also expressions of a supremacist ideology, whose consumers derive pleasure from watching them; the third extends the analogy to the realm of stylized violence (BDSM imagery), whose erotics draws on racist and orientalist ideology. Typically to MacKinnon, this three-part analogy works to erode the distinction between documentation and representation, real-life violence and stylized violence, and the slippage is achieved by exploiting the figure of the lynching, whose traumatic toxicity attaches to anything brought into contact with it.

Generally, the racial analogy in antiporn discourse argues, as Kobena Mercer summarizes, that "just as black people are degraded by racist speech and hurt by racial violence, so women are harmed and victimized by sexist and misogynist representations which portray, and thus promote, the hatred and fear of women that erupt in all acts of male violence" (Mercer 461). The function of the racial analogy has been both to bolster the assertion of a causal relation between pornography and violence against women by likening it to the causal relation between racist hate speech and racial violence, and, as Mercer suggests, "to elicit a moral response of horror and outrage that lends further credence to the antiporn argument" (462). While Dines in the passage quoted earlier explicitly eschews the claim of a simple causal relation and offers a more complex systemic model of influence, she does invoke the outrage aroused by images of racist violence in an attempt to effect a defamiliarization and reframing of mainstream porn so as to underscore its sexism and misogyny:

> Imagine what would happen if suddenly we saw a slew of dramas and sitcoms on television where, say, blacks or Jews were repeatedly referred to in a racist or anti-Semitic way, where they got their hair pulled, faces slapped, and chocked by white men pushing foreign objects into their mouths. (88)

Criticism directed against the use that the antiporn camp made of the racial analogy pointed out that while it reduces race to rhetoric, it fails to offer an analysis of racial representation in pornography (Mercer 462).[61] The latter omission has been rectified by Dines, who devotes one of the chapters of her book to the ways in which race functions in pornography, showing how pornography exploits and reinforces racial stereotypes and "sexualizes the racism in ways that make the actual racism invisible" (Dines 140).

A feature that contemporary antiporn feminism has in common with its predecessor is the focus on mainstream pornography, that is, commercial heterosexual pornography for male consumption. Contemporary writings no longer ignore the existence of porn by women, but they generally dismiss it either as "more of the same thing" or as too marginal to have an effect. Thus, Dines asserts: "My experience with porn produced by women is that it uses the same codes and conventions adopted in mainstream porn, even when they try to market it as something different, and that it's not necessarily any more ethical in its production than porn produced by men" (Dines et al., "Arresting

Images" 20). And Paul makes it clear that she is skeptical of the project of feminist porn, since it is unclear its message is getting through "amid the barrage of male-oriented pornography out there" and since its alternative images are less likely to be attractive to the mainstream man (270). On the whole, she seems to suggest an incompatibility in sexual tastes and sensibilities that results in the fact that women and men are attracted to different types of sexual representations: "Most men do not find truly female-targeted erotica appealing," and "true male-oriented pornography still offends the vast majority of women" (123).

Aside from the objection that feminist porn is ineffectual in subverting the message of mainstream porn, Paul goes on to wonder "is it even desirable for women to become producers and consumers of pornography?" as "equality should come from elevating women to where men hold an advantage, not lowering them to share the costs of pornography with men" (271). This rhetoric of not having women sink to the level of men is curiously reminiscent of nineteenth-century discourse on women's moral superiority. In the conclusion to her book, Paul states: "Pornography is at its core the commercialization of women, turning men into consumers, and women into a product to be used and discarded" (274). However, any attempt to change this division of labor and redress the balance is dismissed as either immaterial or undesirable. The rise in women's pornographic production online is described as "women . . . increasingly in charge of selling themselves" (111), that is, even when they are producers of alternative images, Paul still sees women as sexual commodities rather than sexual subjects, and the rise in women's consumption of porn is explained as a product of the cultural pressure to do so in a pornified culture.

To sum up, like first-generation antiporn feminism, contemporary texts concentrate on pornography's harm. However, notably, the focus is almost exclusively on consumption-related harm, and significantly it is not only women that figure as the victims of pornography; much attention is devoted to the harm to men and to heterosexual relationships. As I have just shown, despite an acknowledgment of the existence of porn by women, the stress on mainstream porn remains, and the skepticism concerning women's ability to reshape pornography attests to an implicit belief in a fixed relationship between (pornographic) discourse and (patriarchal) power. Contrary to its predecessor, contemporary antiporn writing does not elide the difference between representation and action but offers a more nuanced analysis of the cultural efficacy of representations, though occasionally, some formulations come very close to MacKinnon's totalizing assertions, for example, "The porn business does not just construct and sell a product; it constructs a world in which the product *can* be sold" (Dines 46). Last, but not least, while present-day antiporn writings usually eschew the definitional stumbling block, when a definition for pornography is offered it is one that relies on the kinds of definitions drafted by traditional antiporn feminism, such as "sexually explicit material that sexualizes hierarchy, objectification, submission, and/or violence."[62] It is interesting that while the criteria of hierarchy, objectification, submission, and violence are all found in MacKinnon and Dworkin's definition of pornography in the ordinance, the contemporary definition curiously lacks an allusion to women, that is, this is a definition that plays down the dimension of sexual politics (though this dimension is evident in the slide show from which the definition is derived).

Meanwhile, on the other side of the feminist divide, there is new scholarship that studies porn by women and affirms its value. The two texts I will take as representative of this trend are *After Pornified*, by Anne Sabo (2011), and *The Feminist Porn Book* (Taormino et al. 2013). Sabo's book is a survey of what she calls "re-visioned porn" by women, a survey that starts with Candida Royalle's films and goes on to review contemporary porn by women both in Europe and the United States. Sabo defines re-visioned porn as characterized by "a sincere commitment to radically change porn, featuring female and male sexuality with respect and realism" and operating as "a vehicle for women to explore their own sexuality and define it for themselves" (6). In her list of criteria that distinguish Royalle's porn, as well as other porn by women, from mainstream porn, beside its high cinematic production value, she includes a gender democratic gaze; the use of subversive role play; an alternative symbolic to portray sexual agency, desire, and pleasure; and the portrayal of a more gender-egalitarian society. The definition of feminist porn offered by the editors of *The Feminist Porn Book* resonates with Sabo's definition of re-visioned porn and expands it by alluding also to labor conditions and representational politics not restricted to gender. Feminist porn, they state,

> aims to build community, to expand liberal views on gender and sexuality, and to educate and empower performers and audiences. It favors fair, ethical working conditions for sex workers

and the inclusion of underrepresented identities and practices. Feminist porn vigorously challenges the hegemonic depictions of gender, sex roles, and the pleasure and power of mainstream porn. (15)

The Feminist Porn Book is a collection that combines writings by feminist porn scholars and feminist porn producers, organized around the notion of a feminist porn movement: "a forty-year-long movement of thinkers, viewers, and makers, grounded in their desire to use pornography to explore new sexualities in representation" (13). As noted earlier, the editors of the collection understand the category of "feminist porn" as encoding a political vision that animates both porn production and scholarship.

Both Sabo's book and *The Feminist Porn Book* are in dialog with contemporary antiporn feminism. In *After Pornified*, the dialog is manifest first of all in the book's very title, the word "after" signaling that what *Pornified* tells us about pornography is not the whole story. Sabo criticizes Dines for her generalizations and for providing a picture of mainstream porn that is slanted toward the extreme but is otherwise sympathetic of the concerns she raises. However, precisely in light of these concerns, she regards alternative pornography by women to be an antidote to mainstream porn's harmful effects. As she plainly puts it: "The great thing about porn affecting us is that it can actually have a good effect on us" (Sabo 198). Hence, she suggests, "re-visioned porn by women is ... becoming a real counterweight to the negative sexualization of women (and men!) perpetuated by the entertainment industry and all other porn" (8). Sabo invokes Dines's call for a counter-ideology that would disrupt the messages of (mainstream) porn, quoting her assertion that such counter-ideology "would have to be as powerful and as pleasurable as porn," and she correctly points out that alternative pornography by women meets precisely these criteria, that is, it provides a different vision of heterosexual sex that is both egalitarian and pleasurable.[63]

The Feminist Porn Book stakes a more adversarial position vis-à-vis antiporn feminism, particularly in Clarissa Smith and Feona Attwood's chapter. Their critique situates the resurgence of the antiporn movement within the trope of "sex panics" and underscores the underlying narrative of the family under threat and the constructions of "natural" sexuality and "proper" relationships at work in antiporn discourse

(45–47). But while contemporary antiporn feminism indeed holds out a rather sanitized ideal of natural and healthy sexuality, contemporary pro-sex feminism, on the other hand, appears to ignore or underestimate the increased misogyny of mainstream porn. Antiporn scholars stress the growing prevalence and popularity of what used to be considered extreme pornography. Practices like double penetration, multiple men ejaculating on a woman's face (bukkake), gagging, and ATM have become almost staples of mainstream porn.[64] As Meagan Tyler points out, even the pornography industry itself has acknowledged the trend toward more extreme pornography, and Ana Bridges demonstrates based on content analysis studies a marked increase in the prevalence of mild forms of aggression, such as spanking, slapping, and hair pulling, directed toward women (Tyler; Bridges).

These tendencies are hardly addressed in contemporary anti-antiporn writings, which dismiss the concerns raised by antiporn feminists as a mixture of alarmism and sexual conservatism.[65] While such attributes are indeed present in antiporn discourse, they do not warrant writing off its claims concerning the aggravated misogyny of mainstream porn. Take for example Smith and Attwood's assertion that, "for Dines, anal sex, ejaculation on a woman's body or face, and more than one man having sex with one woman are degrading" (50). Such an inference may well be correct, and yet while it is true that none of these practices in and of itself necessarily signifies degradation, nevertheless, many videos in which several men have sex with a single woman are characterized by a homosocial dynamic in which male bonding takes place at the expense of the woman, who figures as a passive object lacking agency and is often mocked and insulted. Similarly, when ejaculation on a woman's face occurs within the context of a sexual interaction also characterized by nonreciprocal oral sex, verbal abuse, and mechanistic thrusting with no attention to the stimulation of the woman, it signifies differently than within the context of a passionate mutual exchange where the partners enjoy each other's bodily fluids. As I noted in my discussion of MacKinnon and Dworkin, the notions of subordination, objectification, and degradation are highly slippery and subjective, and applying them to representations of sex is bound to yield considerable controversy. In this respect, current antiporn feminism is plagued by the same definitional and interpretive problems as its predecessor.[66] Nevertheless, it does not follow that these notions are irrelevant for reading pornographic texts, only that labeling certain acts, expressions, or modes of representation degrading or objectifying should be grounded in careful and context-sensitive readings.

However, mainstream porn figures only marginally in The Feminist Porn Book and After Pornified, both of which focus on pornography by women as their main topic. Consequently, there is hardly any overlap between the objects of discussion of the two camps. As in the previous round of the debate, for each, the signifier "pornography" denotes a different object. Even a more specialized term such as "gonzo" is ascribed wholly different significations. Dines defines it as a genre "which depicts hard-core, body-punishing sex in which women are demeaned and debased," while Sabo uses the term in its technical porn-industry sense as denoting the use of a first-person camera and employs it to describe, for instance, Anna Span's style of shooting (Dines xi; Sabo 92).[67] While it is true that it is predominantly in the subgenre of gonzo that hardcore porn has become more extreme, the fact that Dines supplants its formal attributes with what is currently its most notorious content is a move typical of antiporn feminism that more generally defines pornography according to its most unappealing manifestations. As in the previous round of the debate, each camp depicts an entirely different picture of the field of contemporary porn: in one, pornography is a ruthless, strictly profit-driven industry characterized by escalating misogyny that has hijacked contemporary culture and perverted our sexuality; in the other, pornography is a heterogeneous and multivocal field of representation—in which women are increasingly active participants—and fraught with possibility for redefining sexuality and empowering women. While pornography has continued to evolve, the basic differend between the positions remains.

The following chapters are dedicated to an evaluation of the "positive" claim of anti-antiporn feminism, the claim that pornography can be appropriated to construct women as sexual subjects. Reading select contemporary pornographic texts written or produced by women for female consumption, I look at the ways in which they tackle the problem of female sexual subjectivity to see what promise they may hold for feminist thought. As noted, I employ the notion of "phantasmatic strategies" to refer to the various solutions such texts work out to the problem of envisioning women as sexual subjects, clustering them into four broad categories: cross-identification with gay male sexuality, recoding penetration, resignifying the phallus, and a performative understanding of gender.

TWO

The Phantasmatic Gay Man

Cross-Identification in Women's Pornography

In pornographic fiction by women and lesbian porn in particular, gay male sexuality comes up not infrequently either as a site of fantasy or as an implicit or acknowledged model. I understand this phenomenon in terms of cross-identification, an identification that crosses boundaries of gender and sexuality. There are different varieties of cross-identification at work in pornographic works by women. Moreover, such identification may take place on different narrative planes; there is identification by characters, authorial identification, and identification as intertextuality or cross-cultural influence. Chapter 6 will discuss the nexus of cross-gender desire and identification in the pornographic topos of cross-gender queer sex. In the present chapter, I discuss two discrete phenomena: male homoerotic fantasy in pornography written by heterosexual women and the modeling of lesbian sexual fantasy and pornography on gay male sexual fantasy and pornography. Admittedly, these are phenomena of a completely different order, but they share a phantasmatic investment in male homoeroticism, either directly or as a mediating figure or intertext. My aim in this chapter is both to document the existence and scope of cross-gender identification in women's pornography and to explore what is at stake when women—straight and gay—identify phantasmatically with gay men and with homoeroticism. I will attempt to show that this type of identification works as a phantasmatic strategy that enables women to recode their sexuality and thus gain symbolic access to sexual subjectivity. In fact, cross-identification might be regarded as a master strategy, in the sense that its workings to a large degree underlie and enable those phantasmatic strategies that are the focus of the next chapters.

The last section of the chapter will examine theorizations of identification in general, and cross-identification in particular, but I will begin by invoking the notion of identification in a rather loose and general sense, as a placeholder for a certain type of phantasmatic investment. Admittedly, my use of the term "identification" to designate the cluster of phenomena I'll be referring to already contains an interpretive claim regarding their meaning and function. Laplanche and Pontalis in *The Language of Psychoanalysis* define identification as the "psychological process whereby the subject assimilates an aspect, property or attribute of the other and is transformed, wholly or partially, after the model the other provides" ("Identification" 205). Hence, in grouping the phantasmatic investments I discuss under the heading "identification," I am making a claim concerning both the idealization that underlies them and their transformative function.

Identification with Male Homoeroticism in Anne Rice's *Beauty* Trilogy

I turn first to a discussion of cross-gender authorial identification in Anne Rice's trilogy, *The Erotic Adventures of Sleeping Beauty*. The three volumes of the *Beauty* trilogy—*The Claiming of Sleeping Beauty*, *Beauty's Punishment*, and *Beauty's Release*—appeared in the United States in 1983, 1984, and 1985, respectively, under the pseudonym A. N. Roquelaure and a few years later were acknowledged by the novelist Anne Rice as her work.[1] The fictional world of the trilogy is a perverted fairy tale world. Beauty, its main protagonist, is identified as the heroine of the tale of Sleeping Beauty, the first volume providing the tale with an alternative ending, in which the prince does not wake Beauty with a kiss but strips her, rapes her, and carries her off to his kingdom to be his sex slave. This alternative resolution of the tale provides the point of departure for a sadomasochistic erotic saga, which involves not only Beauty and the prince but many other characters, too, both slaves and masters. The three books elaborate an expansive and intricate system of erotic domination, coextensive with the entire fictional world. At the center of this system is the court of the queen, the prince's mother, furnished with hundreds of pleasure slaves, all princes and princesses from neighboring kingdoms. But erotic domination is practiced not only at the court but also in the adjacent village, where rebellious slaves are sent to serve; and although the neighboring countries do not maintain analogous institutions, they are obliged to take part in this one by supplying young representatives of their royal families for a period of several years' servitude. The system of erotic domination extends also further away, to the oriental sultanate to which a number of the slaves are kidnapped and where most of the third book takes place.[2]

While the system of erotic domination projected by the text is a total one, the master/slave division is fundamentally arbitrary. This arbitrariness is underscored both by the temporariness and reversibility of the slave status—after several years' servitude the slaves return to their home countries where they resume their former social role—and by the noble birth of the slaves. Far from corresponding to the social hierarchy, the master/slave division reverses it, with members of the highest social rank reduced to sexual playthings (their subhuman status signaled by their constant nakedness) and subordinated both to their peers and to their inferiors. The master/slave division is thus deessentialized and not seen to reflect any inherent attribute of the subject either as an individual or as a member of a group. While the *Beauty* books recognize that some individuals are naturally more disposed toward one role rather than the other, they seem to suggest that every person is capable of both, a claim borne out by several instances of role switching.

The text not only denaturalizes sexual roles (master/slave) by representing them as arbitrary and learned, it also provides a detailed description of the socialization into the slave role, a socialization that involves the molding of individual desire itself and the fashioning of a slave subjectivity. The slaves undergo a process that can best be described as behavioral conditioning, linking sexual arousal with physical pain and humiliation. This process takes place in the course of their daily "education," but there exists also a special institution, the Training Hall, dedicated to this particular purpose. Sexual responsiveness is cultivated and valued in the slaves, and not for any practical purpose.[3] Their arousal is important not because it enhances their use value but because it signifies their slave subjectivity, that is, that their desire is in complicity with their treatment.

In her book *Sexual Politics*, Kate Millet suggests that patriarchal regimes divide the sexes along three parameters: status, role, and temperament, with women's role and temperament reflecting and sustaining their inferior status (26). In the Beauty trilogy we find the sexual roles of master and slave disjoined from social status (as well as from the gender division), and far from attempting to naturalize temperamental differences as patriarchal societies do, the narrative focuses on the various apparatuses for the cultivation of role-appropriate temperament. Read as a commentary on the dominant sex/gender system,[4] the Beauty books subvert the ideology that regards sexual temperament as natural—and role and status as its derivations—and unveil the mechanisms that mold sexual temperament according to role.

One of the seemingly most progressive aspects of the *Beauty* trilogy is its assimilation of same-sex sexuality. The text abounds with male-male desire and sexual practice and does not at any point problematize same-sex sexuality in general. There is no question of the legitimacy of same-sex desire, and nowhere are same-sex and cross-sex desire seen as conflicting or mutually exclusive. However, female-female desire is far less prevalent than either male-female or male-male desire, and there is no instance in the text of a woman possessing a female pleasure slave on a long-term noncommercial basis. The one major instance of female-female desire, Beauty's affair with Inanna, the sultan's wife, in the third volume, stands out in the text in its egalitarianism and total lack of power play. The only other direct erotic interaction between women occurs between Beauty and Mistress Lockley, the village innkeeper. Yet, significantly, when Mistress Lockley takes Beauty to her bed, it is together with another male slave; even this is not an exclusive female-female interaction. And although Mistress Lockley owns Beauty, she does not have exclusive sexual possession of her; since she employs her slaves as a commodity in a commercial exchange, she doesn't enjoy unlimited access to them.

While the first volume of the trilogy centers on heterosexual desire, the next two volumes focus increasingly on male-male desire. *Beauty's Punishment* features Tristan as a second protagonist alongside Beauty, and his erotic interactions are mostly with his master, Nicholas, and with other male slaves. In *Beauty's Release* Laurent replaces Tristan as Beauty's co-protagonist, and until the final chapter, when he comes to claim her as his bride after both of them have been freed and restored to their original rank, most of his erotic interactions too are with men, both masters and fellow slaves. Not only does homoeroticism occupy an increasingly central place as the trilogy evolves, but interestingly, the two men's stories are narrated in the first person, whereas Beauty's story is given in the third person, mostly in free indirect discourse.

As Wayne Booth asserts, the mere distinction between first- and third-person narration "will tell us nothing of importance unless we become more precise and describe how the particular qualities of the narrators relate to specific effects" (150). Since Booth, the proliferating narratological literature on point of view has come up with no definite answers regarding the respective function and significance of first-person versus third-person narration. These seem to be very much context dependent. Thus, first-person narration may heighten identification with the narrator but may also function as a distancing device, and similarly, free indirect discourse may serve "both as a mode of ironic distancing from characters and as a mode of empathetic identification with characters" (McHale 275). In our case, however, I believe it safe to assume that the shift to first-person narration in Tristan and Laurent's stories signals a heightened degree of identification with their characters. In pornographic fiction, the "dual voice" that is the defining feature of free indirect discourse, often takes the form of a subtle alternation between the protagonist's point of view and an external point of view that objectifies her/him. Such an alternation is highly effective erotically since it allows us both to "view" the character from the outside as an erotic object and to share her consciousness of her own objectification and her sense of arousal. This is the type of narration that we find in the chapters telling Beauty's story, whereas with Tristan and Laurent, the first-person narrative limits us to a more narrow identification with their own experience. We do "see" them as erotic objects but only through their own eyes; they relay to us the objectifying gaze aimed at them through their consciousness and internalization of it. Moreover, their characters are consequently represented as more reflexive and introspective than Beauty.

The sense that, in the *Beauty* trilogy, first-person narration signals greater intimacy and identification with the characters finds corroboration in the *Roquelaure Reader*, "the official guide to the Sleeping Beauty Novels," written in cooperation with Anne Rice. After quoting Rice, who says that Prince Alexi was her favorite character in *The Claiming of Sleeping Beauty* (he inaugurates the pattern of male first-person narration by telling his story to Beauty), Katherine Ramsland asserts that in the second novel, Rice is clearly more interested in her new character, Tristan, than in Beauty. She goes on to remark, "*More comfortable in the male perspective, and more excited by it*, Rice reached for greater intimacy by telling Tristan's story *as if it was hers*" (44, my emphasis). A little later, Ramsland explains that the character of Laurent saved the book for Rice when "she had grown tired of Beauty, and Tristan's story had reached a sense of closure." But she also provides additional motivation for the author's investment in Laurent's character, saying that "more than any other character, he is the image of the man Rice wanted to be" (46).

Rice's authorial identification with male characters appears to be a recurrent feature of her writing; in fact, after a series of male protagonists *The Claiming* is apparently "the first of Rice's published novels to describe a predominantly female experience" (Ramsland 40), yet we have seen how Beauty gradually cedes her center-stage position to the male characters.[5] *The Roquelaure Reader* also notes Rice's investment in homoerotic themes from the very beginning of her writing career in college. These literary investments in male characters and homoerotic narratives are explicitly tied by the *Reader* to Rice's phantasmatic investment in gay men and gay male relationships, her fascination with various aspects of gay male culture and experience, and her identification and close relationship with actual gay men. Rice is quoted saying: "I knew when I was young, about twenty-four, that I wished I was a gay man. . . . That was a common fantasy of mine. I felt that the physical response I had to men must mean I'm like a gay man" (Ramsland 14–15). Significantly, Rice ties her identification with gay men to the quality of her sexual response to men:

> I often see men in the bluntly sexual way that gay men do. . . . In my youth, I frightened other women when I spoke bluntly about men's bodies and how I liked them. I was told repeatedly that "women don't feel like that." I was given the impression by other women that I was abnormal. I wanted to see naked men. I wanted to feel their penises. I wanted to be a gay man. I want to run with gay men. Be one of them. (Ramsland 16)

Clearly, then, Rice's identification with gay men functions for her as a means of reconciling her sexual attraction to men with sexual "aims" and modes of sexual expression that are incompatible with normative femininity. Rice expressly equates her gay male identification with a desire for sexual agency, a need to express sexual feelings and obtain recognition of them, and a desire for sexual freedom and perhaps also sexual community. She also relates her preference for writing from a male point of view to the social repression of female sexuality: "'For years,' she explains, 'I felt so enraged about repressive forces that it was easier to write from the viewpoint of a male'" (Ramsland 40).

If we go back to the *Beauty* trilogy, we can see that the work indeed finds it problematic to portray female sexual agency. As noted, the work's main erotic force does not hinge on the power differential between women and men: the slaves at the queen's court are both female and male, and so are their masters. However, if we examine the gender-power correlation more closely, we find that it is neither negligible nor all that different from the traditional one. The kingdom is indeed run by a woman, but that is only due to the late king's death; the women of the court possess male pleasure slaves, but among the laity, women seem to take only a secondary, accessory role in regard to the slaves: when Prince Alexi is sent to the kitchen as punishment, those are primarily the men who torment and abuse him, and when a woman does partake of these amusements, she does so through the mediation of a man. Gender and class interact, then, but basically, the social structure depicted is a patriarchal one, in which women's access to power, and to sexual power in particular, is limited.

One laywoman who does possess slaves and interacts with them directly is Mistress Lockley, the village innkeeper. Yet, though she has complete authority over her slaves, the nature of her relation to them is ambiguous since she keeps them not only for her own pleasure and as a subsidiary labor force but, perhaps chiefly, for commercial purposes, as erotic entertainment for her guests, mostly men. As noted, since she employs her slaves as a commodity in a commercial exchange, she does not have unlimited access to them and therefore does not enjoy the authority and ownership of a true proprietor. In this type of relation between gender and economy, we find the imprint of dominant ideology: since women are deemed unable to "possess" others sexually and capable only of being possessed, their own sexuality and that of others has no use value for them, only exchange value. Therefore, if they wish to rise above the status of commodity, they may do so only by becoming sexual traders; sexual proprietors they cannot be.

Similarly to the issue of female power, the issue of female desire is also revealed to be problematic on closer inspection. Even when women in the text practice erotic domination, as the court ladies do, the scenes that they conduct differ significantly from those conducted by men. When the queen and Lady Juliana engage Beauty in a session of spanking, whipping, and fetching games, these practices, though accompanied by manifestations of desire on both sides, strangely lack sexual consummation, which always follows in similar scenes where men are the dominants: although it is considered part of the torture to leave the slaves unsatisfied, the masters do not place any value on their own abstinence. A similar pattern emerges also with male slaves: the queen is more prone to have Prince Alexi fellate other slaves than to use him for her own pleasure, and Lady Elvira is usually satisfied simply to watch Laurent chase and mount female slaves in the garden. Both women are described as "cold."

It seems, then, that the text finds it hard to portray a combination of female sadism and female desire; in its underlying female psychology, the two more plausible types are the voluptuous masochist and the cold sadist. An exception to this rule we find, once more, in Mistress Lockley, who does take Beauty and another male slave to her bed and allows them to gratify her. Yet, this exception is related to her class affiliation: as a laywoman she falls under the type of the "natural" countrywoman whose voluptuousness is part of her lower nature.[6] Moreover, the scene still differs from the analogous male-dominated ones in two respects: it does not incorporate or immediately follow discipline or abuse (in the plot sequence, three chapters separate "Mistress Lockley's Discipline" from "Mistress Lockley's Affections"), and the sexual interaction itself is surprisingly egalitarian and almost devoid of any manifestations of power. All in all, it is hard to avoid the sense that, according to the work's implicit assumptions, while female sadism is sexy, female sexuality is not quite reconcilable with sexual dominance and sexual aggression.

What emerges, then, is a link between Rice's authorial identification with male characters and male same-sex eroticism and her inability to envision female sexual agency. Interestingly, Rice accounts for her identification with gay men in terms of her (active) desire to look at men's naked bodies and touch them, yet the male characters in the *Beauty* trilogy, whose story is given in the first person and whom Rice testifies to identifying with, are men who are stripped, put on display, and handled. These male characters function in the text mostly in a receptive and submissive capacity, as objects of penetration and domination for other men. So that while these male characters provide vehicles for the expression of "active" desires that are proscribed for women, they, even more importantly, provide vehicles for the expression of "passive," submissive, and masochistic desires, *without marking these as feminine*. Rice's authorial identification with these submissive male characters enables her to identify with a masochistic position without doing so *qua* woman; that is, it enables her to circumvent the essentialist equation of femaleness and masochism.[7] This conclusion is supported by Katherine Ramsland's depiction of the way Rice treats the character of Alexi (the first male slave featured in the trilogy, and the first one to give his story in the first person):

> Alexi was the epitome, for Rice, of the male masochist. To defy the stereotype of female passivity and illustrate how strongly masochistic desires can affect men, Rice went into lengthy detail about his experiences. Throughout his ordeal, Alexi exhibits the anxiety, weakness, fear, and subjugation normally associated with women. He cries over things done to him but also finds them arousing and craves more. (41)

True, Ramsland formulates Rice's authorial motivations in didactic rather than identificatory terms, but she does underscore the fact that the submissive male protagonists of the *Beauty* trilogy display sexual and emotional attributes that are traditionally attributed to women. And the fact that Rice chose to render their experience—rather than Beauty's—in the first person calls for an explanation.

Kaja Silverman in "Masochism and Male Subjectivity" raises a similar question concerning the significance of the cross-gendered identification in the female masochistic fantasy analyzed by Freud in his essay "A Child Is Being Beaten." The manifest content of this fantasy is as follows: "Some boys are being beaten, [I am probably looking on]," and Freud reconstructs in analysis two prior phases, the second of which remains unconscious: 1. "My father is beating the child [whom I hate]," and 2. "I am being beaten by my father" (Silverman 47). While Freud focuses on the transgressive Oedipal desire of the analytically (re)constructed second phase, Silverman calls attention to the manifest content of the fantasy. The final phase, she says,

> attests to three transgressive desires, not one of which Freud remarks upon . . . : to the desire that it be boys rather than

girls who be loved/disciplined in this way; to the desire to be a boy while being so treated by the father; and finally, to the desire to occupy a male subject position in some more general sense, but one under the sign of femininity rather than that of masculinity. (48)

She claims that Freud "deflects attention away from the burning question of what it might mean, apart from simple disguise, for a female subject to represent herself in phantasy as a group of passive boys" (49).

Silverman does not offer a straightforward answer to this question, but she does indicate that the beating fantasy involves an identification with male homosexuality, an identification that transgresses and challenges the very binary logic of gender. For if

> [the position of] (passive) male homosexuality... has itself been constituted through identification with the mother... what emerges is a situation in which each sex has access to femininity through its imaginary alignment with the other, and in which *femininity is* thus both *radically denatured*, and posited as the privileged term. (50, my emphasis)

If a woman has access to femininity by means of a phantasmatic identification with "feminine" males, whose own divergence from normative masculinity is conceived in terms of their phantasmatic identification with the mother, then not only is the causal relation between femaleness and femininity broken, but "feminine"—that is, passive or masochistic—desires in a woman acquire a sense of transgressiveness that they lack when seen as biologically determined. When these "feminine" desires are mediated through a male subject position and reinscribed as transgressive, they allow for a sense of agency that is predicated on the paradigm of choice implicit in male homosexual subjectivity and seemingly absent from female heterosexual subjectivity. In other words, the gap between anatomy or biological function and sexual aim allows the male homosexual subject to symbolically maintain sexual agency even when forfeiting phallic power; and by means of phantasmatic identification with this subject position the heterosexual woman can gain access to a sexual subjectivity from which she is barred by a lack of phallic power seen as inherent rather than perverse.[8] Perhaps this is what Silverman implies when she says: "[I]t is clearly not the same thing, socially or psychically, for the girl to be loved/beaten by the father as it is for the boy," and that "the girl might be said to seek access to that difference through her identification with the boy . . ." (50).

The question of the significance or function of a woman author's (and of a woman consumer's) phantasmatic investment in male-male eroticism is raised also by "slash" fiction, a genre of fan fiction that takes famous fictional same-sex media couples, mostly male ones, and imagines romantic and erotic relations between them.[9] Constance Penley, who writes about the K/S fandom, describes the slash genre as "a unique hybrid genre of romance, pornography, and utopian science fiction" (480) and reports that the fandom that produces and consumes these fictional works is almost 100 percent female and mostly heterosexual.[10] One of the questions that preoccupy Penley is, What are the fans' motivations "for writing their erotic fantasies across the bodies of two men" (483)? Although there are many aspects of K/S fiction that are unique, so that some of the answers Penley offers to this question have to do with the specificities of the *Star Trek* universe and the particular characters of Kirk and Spock, others do seem generalizable and relevant to the *Beauty* trilogy as well.

Perhaps Penley's major answer to the question "Why two men?" has to do with the "radical equality" possible between two male characters that is both incompatible with the traditional heterosexual romance formula (as well as with the traditional heterosexual pornographic formula) and unimaginable in a patriarchal world:

> When [Kirk and Spock] do get together, they do so as a couple in which love and work can be shared. Their passionate lifetime union is only an extension of the friendship and loyalty they have always felt for each other while working as Captain and first officer on the bridge of the *Enterprise*. (Penley 490)

In the *Star Trek* fictional universe, as (to a somewhat lesser extent) in contemporary society, women do not enjoy equal opportunities; heterosexual unions are therefore predicated on inequality. To imagine an equal romantic or sexual relationship is to imagine a same-sex one,[11] and since women's limited access to opportunity makes their characters less interesting and less amenable to identification, it is easier to imagine two men together. Citing Lamb and Veith, Penley asserts that we still live in a patriarchal culture, and it is thus not possible to imagine two women passionately in love with one another who go out and save the galaxy once a week (Penley 490). Virginia Woolf's Chloe and Olivia are still a utopia.[12] As Anne Kustritz argues, the radical equality of the male characters enables also a transformation of the way that sexual intercourse is constructed: depicted in heterosexual fiction as a conquest resulting in the devaluation of the woman, in slash fiction sex is portrayed as "an expression of trust rather than an act of domination" (Kustritz 377). While in slash fiction the choice of a same-sex male couple serves to bypass the heterosexual erotics of dominance and submission, in the *Beauty* trilogy the focus on homoeroticism serves to decouple the erotics of dominance and submission from gender hierarchy, thereby also denaturalizing it.

Another aspect that Penley comments on is the fact that most stories do not depict Kirk and Spock as homosexual, that is, as having homosexual identities. This is an aspect that K/S fiction shares with the *Beauty* trilogy since, as I have shown, none of the male slaves in *Beauty* is assumed either to have a stable or exclusive preference for men or to be conscious of such a preference as a distinctive trait or an identity factor. Penley suggests that this peculiar feature is attributable to the phantasmatic freedom it allows:

> I think it allows a much greater range of identification and desire for the women: in the fantasy one can *be* Kirk or Spock (a possible phallic identification) and also still *have* (as sexual objects) either or both of them since, as heterosexuals, they are not *un*available to women. (488, emphasis in the original)

In other words, the space between same-sex desire and homosexual identity allows women to hold these men as objects of both identification and desire. To take Penley's point a little further, what male-male sexuality as a fantasy scenario offers heterosexual women is the chance to both love a man and "be" a man, that is, it obliterates the compulsory split between identification and desire.[13] To put it differently, it provides an assurance that desiring *a man* does not exclude identifying with masculinity or desiring *as a man*. The flip side of this freedom to identify with masculinity is, as Penley notes, the fans' rejection of the female body "as a terrain of fantasy or utopian thinking" (i.e., the female body is rejected not only as an object of desire but also as the object of phantasmatic identification), though she hastens to clarify that "the female body they are rejecting is the body of the woman as it has been constituted in this culture" (498).[14]

On the other hand, women's phantasmatic investment in male-male sexuality can be viewed not only from the perspective of the range of female desires and identifications it opens up but also as an attempt to "'retool' masculinity," as Penley puts it (498). In K/S fiction, Kirk and Spock represent ideal male types and interact with each other in ways that women would like men to interact with them. And if Penley mentions sensitivity and nurturing as attributes of the desirable "retooled male," one may also add penetrability and—in the *Beauty* trilogy—even submissiveness.[15]

To go back to the *Beauty* trilogy, both Silverman's reading of the beating fantasy discussed by Freud and Penley's reading of K/S fiction support my claim that Rice's cross-gender authorial identification with male-male desire, and particularly with "passive" and masochistic homosexual desire, provides a phantasmatic apparatus for resignifying desires traditionally coded feminine and enables the alignment of male object choice and masculine identification. As I have argued, when "feminine" desires are mediated through a male subject position and thereby severed from biological determinism and reinscribed as transgressive, they become compatible with sexual subjectivity. Moreover, identifying with men whose masculinity is humiliated by the celebrated masculinity of other men enables Rice to pay tribute to phallic power and exploit its erotic potential while at the same time subverting it and turning it against itself.[16]

However, the subversive value of this strategy is not unqualified, since it relies on an underlying symbolic scheme that posits the phallus as the indispensable agent of sexual domination. Hence, the "feminization" of the male characters does not entail any significant sexual empowerment of the female characters, since while men may be penetrated, women cannot be envisioned as penetrating: the novel abounds with leather, wooden, and stone phalli, but they are never usurped by a woman to penetrate another woman or man *in the context of a sexual act*. Imagining a woman possessing the phallus poses an insurmountable difficulty for the *Beauty* trilogy. Here, as we shall see in the following chapters, contemporary lesbian and queer pornography have more to offer.[17] As we have seen, despite the impression of a pluralistic and progressive sexual politics, *Beauty* fails to envision a radical change in female power or in the construction of female desire.

Influence, Appropriation, and the
Gay Male Intertext in Lesbian Sex Culture

When it comes to lesbian cross-identification with gay men, not only do we find gay male pornography authored by lesbians, but we can also note the extensive influence of gay male porn on lesbian porn. Both these phenomena are anchored in the context of the formative and wide-ranging influence that the far more developed gay male sex culture holds over the lesbian sex culture that has emerged in North America and Europe since the late seventies.[18] Lesbian cross-identification with gay male sexuality covers the entire spectrum from consumption of gay male porn, erotic investment in gay male fantasies, role play on the theme of male-male sex, and writing gay male erotica—on the individual level—to the collective borrowing and adaptation of gay male erotic identities and styles, sexual attitudes, sexual etiquette, ideals, and fantasies. While for heterosexual women, their phantasmatic identification with homoeroticism appears to remain bound to the actual figure of male-male sex, for lesbians, gay male sexuality functions not only as a figure of individual fantasy but as a "cultural intertext," subject to collective transformation and performative reinscription. In the following chapters, I will look closely at specific themes and ideological constructs that lesbian porn derives from gay male porn. In the present chapter, however, I would like both to document the various forms of lesbian cross-identification with gay men in the sphere of sexuality and to analyze the cultural conditions and the emotional and political investments that underpin it.[19]

In 1989, the lesbian sex magazine *On Our Backs* published an article on lesbians who enjoy gay male porn. In it four women respond to an identical set of questions concerning their preferences in gay porn and its appeal for them. Their responses reveal several types of motives for consuming gay male porn. First, there is the preference by default, due to the scarcity of lesbian porn—and especially of lesbian s/m porn—compared to the large variety and higher quality of its male counterpart. With heterosexual or gay male porn from which to choose, the respondents opt for the latter, a choice motivated both by a preference for same-sex eroticism ("I am usually more comfortable with same-sex material even if the sex is male") and by an aversion to the sexism that permeates heterosexual porn ("although gay male porn lacks women with whom to identify, it is generally less overtly sexist") ("When Girls

Look at Boys" 43, 30). But the respondents also report a positive preference for gay porn owing to a number of factors. One of the respondents remarks that as a butch who feels alienated to some degree from her femaleness and uncomfortable with femininity, she finds it easier to identify with images of two men. She thus reminds us of the common discrepancy between assigned gender and gender identification, and the fact that spectatorial or readerly identification is more likely to hinge on the latter. Further, once gender identity is not reduced to the binary categories of heterogender (man/woman), the affinity between lesbian and gay male masculinity becomes more apparent.[20] Both lesbian culture and gay male culture have produced alternative masculinities.[21] Such queer masculinities may have a lot in common, especially since lesbian culture has not always been hospitable to butches and butches who do not identify as women may be uncomfortable with the category "lesbian," an identification with gay male masculinity—both in the sexual realm and beyond it—is natural for butches who look for models of nondominant masculinity.

Another interviewee locates the attraction of gay male porn not in what gay male and lesbian sexuality have in common but rather in those features that distinguish the former from the latter. She alludes to "the simple, physical, raw sex" of gay male porn as opposed to the romanticism of lesbian porn ("When Girls" 43) and also to what she terms the "selfishness" of gay male sexuality, "each taking their own pleasure from the other, not for the benefit of anyone but themselves, and apologizing to no one" ("When Girls" 31, 42). At stake here are the different protocols and the different ethos of lesbian and gay male sex, which derive from the different constructions of male and female sexuality in general: for men sexual pleasure is constructed as something to be *taken*, for women sexual pleasure is constructed as something to be *gotten*; in gay male sex each participant is responsible for his own pleasure, in lesbian sex each participant is expected to take care of the other's pleasure. And while giving another woman pleasure is the lesbian claim to phallic endowment,[22] the male phallus, whether gay or straight, is largely defined by the ability to take pleasure in the other or even subject the other to one's own pleasure. The attraction to the selfishness of gay male sex signifies, then, a longing for a different definition of sexual subjectivity, a more male type of phallus.

Writing several years later, in a cultural climate in which the joint identity category "queer" has gained currency, Carol Queen and

Lawrence Schimel reiterate many of these motives for lesbian consumption of gay porn:

> Female viewers or readers who are dykes or bisexuals may also appreciate the specifically homoerotic, male-on-male dynamic of porn made for gay men. Here, a woman porn consumer finds no pesky heterosexual assumptions or sex-role stereotypes (at least none that relate directly to her); even the emphasis on a relationship that often marks lesbian erotica is usually absent. What she gets, instead, is hot homo-sex—and a chance to voyeuristically appreciate male sexuality *without calling her own orientation into question.* (14, emphasis added)

The latter point is an important one in light of the threat—not only to a stable sense of identity but also to community membership—posed by cross-sex attraction, a threat made more acute by the political dimension of lesbian identity, that is, its opposition to male power.

As mentioned, lesbians are not merely consumers of gay male porn; along with consuming and adapting ready-made fantasies, some also take an active part in the elaboration of gay male pornographic discourse, especially in the genre of prose fiction. Most of this work is published in gay men's pornographic magazines and books—usually though not always under male pen names—but Pat Califia has also included gay male stories in her collections of lesbian porn.[23] A forum specifically designated for such work was provided by *Switch Hitters*, an anthology devoted to gay male erotica by lesbians and lesbian erotica by gay men, which appeared in 1996. As the editors, Carol Queen and Lawrence Schimel, note, instances of the former are far more common than those of the latter, due among other things to the much larger and better-paying market for gay male porn (14).[24] Of course, as indicated by the discussion so far and as I will go on to show more extensively, lesbians' interest in gay male porn is not strictly commercial, and the fact that lesbians are more phantasmatically involved with gay male sexuality than vice versa has much to do with the different state of development of gay male versus lesbian sex culture.[25]

To begin to explore the issues involved, I would like to look at a story that explicitly thematizes lesbian identification with gay men and gay male sexuality, "The Journal," by Roberta Stone, which appeared in the collection *Herotica 2*.[26] The story's protagonist-narrator is a lesbian on holiday in the mixed gay resort of Provincetown. The temporarily single narrator, whose relationship pattern seems to be one of serial monogamy, shares a house with her longtime friend Vicki, who is also uninvolved at the moment. One Sunday morning, opting to stay home instead of going out to cruise the crowd of lesbians leaving church, she begins to write a sexual fantasy about a gay man in Provincetown, Peter, who meets a handsome butch stranger (at that same church service) and later that night goes home with him. The scenes of the fantasy are crosscut with parallel scenes from the narrator's day, and while Peter goes home with the unknown leatherman and has rough sex with him, the narrator and Vicki suddenly realize their mutual attraction and go home to have tender vanilla sex. The plot structure, which fosters a point-by-point comparison between the (equally stereotypical) lesbian and gay male narratives, provides an ironic commentary about the differences between the two sexual cultures: lesbians find cruising an exasperating task, gay-men cruise effortlessly; gay men have casual sex, lesbians mate "in the family"; gay men have wild sophisticated sex, use toys, and role-play, lesbians have intimate and meaningful sex; and where gay men just have good sex, lesbians immediately "get married" following a hot sexual encounter (to Vicki's question "Are we still friends?" the narrator replies, "I think we're more than that now") (Stone 42).

"The Journal" illustrates, then, the function of gay male sexuality as a fantasy terrain for lesbians as well as highlights the ambivalent status of this fantasy. On the one hand, the less adventurous, more sedentary lesbian sexuality seems to fall short on all counts compared to gay male sexuality. The fantasy, after all, is an envious one; the thought that drives the narrator to elaborate her fantasy is: "I wish I had the energy to cruise. I can just picture what I'd be doing if I were a gay man" (30). Later on, when she explains to Vicki what she's writing, she justifies the gender switch saying: "After all, it couldn't be as boring as the last five months of my life" (presumably, the period of time that she has been out of a relationship) (31). The implication is that lesbian sex life is centered on relationships, so that when the narrator tries to imagine having sex outside the bounds of a relationship, she creates a gay male fantasy alter ego to cast in a scenario of casual sex. Gay men signify—for lesbians but also for straight culture—the realm of casual sex, public sex, toys, and role-playing, from which lesbians feel barred by the norms of lesbian culture and individual disposition; when imaginary access to this realm is sought, gay men and gay male culture provide the medium.

On the other hand, when the two women in the story are about to have sex and Vicki asks to read what the narrator has written, the latter responds: "It's just trash. Just a fantasy. Real life doesn't happen that way" (38). Fantasy is subordinated to reality, and with it implicitly, wild gay male sex is subordinated to tender lesbian sex. The envious cross-gendered fantasy is denigrated compared to real sex between women, and lesbian sexuality ends up being reaffirmed as hot and deeply satisfying despite its greater conventionality. The story ends with the lesbian narrative, giving it the weight of closure, and proper hierarchy is restored.

Yet, the neat subordination of gay male fantasy to lesbian reality remains troubled by a few elements. First, the narrator writes the fictional narrative in her journal, a fact that grants it a certain autobiographical status. It is, after all, *her* fantasy, *her* phantasmatic identification, and as such represents something about her; it is *her* story, for what one writes in one's journal is one's own story.[27] Further, since the story bears the title "The Journal," the whole text—both the first-person sequences *and* the fantasy sequences—assumes the status of a journal entry. Second, and relatedly, the cross-cutting technique not only juxtaposes the two narratives, but also—since the fantasy scenario is always one step ahead of the real-life narrative—the former can be seen to nourish the latter, as sexual fantasy nourishes sexual practice. Understood this way, the vanilla encounter between the two women friends is not simply the inferior (more conventional) or superior (more authentic) counterpart of the s/m encounter between the two male strangers, it is also phantasmatically sustained by it and therefore may be seen to incorporate it.

While "The Journal" explicitly thematizes the issue of lesbians' phantasmatic identification with gay men, it nevertheless maintains a clear distinction between lesbian and gay male sexuality. As we have seen, the two appear to inhabit opposite poles and are defined over against each other. True, the story allocates to gay male sexuality a phantasmatic space inside lesbian subjectivity, yet it treats lesbian sexuality—at least in its manifest forms—as a completely autonomous system. However, much contemporary lesbian erotic fiction erases these clear boundaries and borrows extensively from gay male erotic fiction and gay male sexual culture.

The envious comparison allegorically staged by the story is found on another register in lesbian political and theoretical writing that advocates borrowing from gay male sex culture and/or acknowledges lesbians' debt to it. In a piece published in 1991 and bearing the title "Lesbian Sex/Gay Sex: What's the Difference?" Julia Creet points out "the importance of gay male sexual representations to lesbian explorations of sexuality and identity" (32). She notes the rapprochement between lesbians and gay men spurred by the AIDS crisis, specifically the shared discussion of sexuality and the heightened exposure to each other's sexual imagery promoted by AIDS activism and the safe-sex discourse it gave rise to. She sees "lesbians' increased use of style" and, in the realm of sexual imagery, the recent prominence of the dildo, as signs of gay male influence and does not only record this influence but also enthusiastically endorses it:

> Our brothers have created institutions out of fantasies, while we lesbians are still arguing over whether to engage in fantasy in the first place. They have not been shy about their extensive repertoire; we need only the inclination to look. (30–31)

What lesbian culture lacks is "images to represent and words to articulate what it is that we desire and do" (31). And since gay male culture is sexually articulate, as much as lesbian culture is sexually inarticulate (an observation Creet quotes from Marilyn Frye), it makes sense to take advantage of the close ties between the cultures to acquire some of the "sexual literacy" gay men possess.

Creet also quotes Pat Califia, who acknowledges her sexual debt to gay men and gay male culture:

> Gay male friends and lovers have taught me things that I would have never learned in the lesbian community. I can't exaggerate my admiration for the well-developed technology, etiquette, attitudes and institutions that gay men have developed to express their sexuality. (Califia, "Gay Men, Lesbians" 187)

The choice of Califia is not a chance one. Califia is both a founding figure for lesbian porn and one of the pioneers and public spokespeople of lesbian sex culture, and she has also (as the former writer of a sex-advice column for men in the *Advocate*) been known for her intimate affiliation with gay male culture. In fact, through her fictional and journalistic writing alike, Califia has been one of the chief agents of mediation and translation between gay male and lesbian sexuality. More than a decade after the piece quoted by Creet was published, Califia again notes the significant influence that gay male culture had on her:

> Gay men have got institutions and traditions that allow them to be sexually adventurous in ways that women usually are not. When I was trying to create a life for myself as a sexually adventurous woman, I wanted to see what I could find in those traditions that could be useful for me and other women. . . . I loved the fact that men would walk into bars, grab each other's nipples, and pat each other on the crotch. They could have this ten-second conversation and then go off and fuck. I didn't know any women who could do that. (Califia, "Identity Sedition" 99–100)

As Creet, Califia, Queen and Schimel, and others note, looking up to gay men and their sexual culture has particularly characterized s/m dykes, who often found a hostile reception in the lesbian world and who looked for models and for solidarity to the gay male leather community.[28] Writing about the Catacombs, a gay male s/m and fisting club that operated in San Francisco from the mid-seventies to the mid-eighties, Gayle Rubin provides insight into the actual workings of gay male influence on lesbian s/m culture as well as reveals the foundational role of this influence in the very emergence of lesbian s/m. Rubin describes how the founders of the lesbian s/m community were initiated into the world of leather under the auspices of a gay male sexual institution. She records the process whereby in the late seventies a few lesbians gained access to the Catacombs, first joining the men's parties and then starting a tradition of women's parties in the same space. In this way, the nascent San Francisco lesbian s/m community, which later became "instrumental in the emergence of organized lesbian S/M nationally," acquired its "party and play technology" through its first members' access to an institution of the gay male leather community ("Catacombs" 130). Where Rubin offers an ethnographic account of that cross-cultural contact, Califia, in the piece quoted previously, provides an insider's first-person account of the experience of being in that all-male space and the formative influence it had on her identifications and political commitments:

[My] politics are based on personal experiences with crossing all kinds of boundaries and combining categories of people and erotic experiences in what were, in the beginning, new and unusual ways.... The way I felt the first time I saw two men have sex with each other was a defining moment for me ... ("Identity Sedition" 93)

Califia notes that her identification with gay leathermen, and with gay men in general, is reinforced by the ravages of AIDS, that is, it is fueled by loss and the need to both commemorate and embody the mourned objects: "In part, I continue to write gay male porn because I refuse to give in to grief.... My sexuality and my pornography are a living memorial" ("Identity Sedition" 94).[29]

Though the leather-dyke community provides the paradigmatic example of gay male influence on the lesbian sex culture, the latter phenomenon is of a far wider scope and itself forms one aspect of the larger rapprochement between lesbians and gay men since the 1980s. The roots of this rapprochement, whose foremost token is the genderless identity category "queer" that has emerged in the late eighties, are usually traced back to two major causes. The first is the AIDS crisis and the lesbian mobilization in response to it, which brought gay men and lesbians closer. The second is the move in the lesbian world away from the lesbian feminism of the seventies, with its sexual restrictiveness and its definition of lesbianism in terms of woman identification, and the turning to gay male culture for its positive valuation of sexuality and affirmation of sexual variation. While the rise of the women's movement in the seventies emphasized the gender divide, fostered the alliance between lesbians and straight women, and cultivated women-only cultural spaces, the eighties and nineties saw the renewal and reaffirmation of the ties between lesbians and gay men that had characterized gay life earlier in the twentieth century, both in working-class bar culture and in upper-class and bohemian circles. The reemergence of joint institutions and cultural spaces enhanced the cultural contact between lesbians and gay men, which to a certain extent has never ceased to exist, and concomitantly the increased contiguity fostered cross-gender identification and a growing sense of shared identity. However, as Esther Newton and other lesbian critics point out, the "apparent convergence" between lesbians and gay men "has resulted from lesbians moving closer to gay men and gay male culture than the reverse" and implies primarily lesbians' adoption of aspects of gay male culture such as "camp theatricality and modes of sexual behavior and imagery" (Newton, "'Dickless Tracy'" 67, 89).

The symptoms of gay male influence on lesbian culture are many and varied. They include lesbians' reembracing of style, which brought about the lesbian chic of the eighties, and the adoption of drag with the emergence of drag king performances and competitions. In the sexual realm, one notes the prominence the dildo has acquired in lesbian sexual representations, not just as an instrument of penetration but as the center of erotic ritual that is sucked, packed, and whose phallic reference is fully exploited.[30] Another symptom is the way in which fisting, a traditionally gay male sexual practice, has increasingly displaced finger-fucking in contemporary lesbian sexual discourse (Merck, "Lesbian Hand" 168); and the erotic style of daddy-boy (or its derivative, daddy-girl) that has gained currency in lesbian sexual representation and practice in the nineties is quite literally drawn from gay male culture. Lesbian safe-sex discourse is also a direct transposition of its gay male counterpart, and it is arguable that in light of the low risk of HIV infection through female-female sex, the functions of lesbian safe-sex discourse have more to do with phantasmatic identification with gay men and the dissemination of gay male sexual attitudes and styles than with health education.[31]

Some lesbian feminist critics like Sheila Jeffreys regard the very emergence of lesbian pornography and lesbian s/m as deplorable products of gay male influence. Jeffreys labels this influence a "slavish imitation" of gay male cultural forms, "however inappropriate to lesbian experience" (142), and explains it as a simple reflection of male hegemony in the gay community and as a manifestation of the general backlash against feminism that has affected the lesbian community as well. According to her, both gay male sexuality and gay male cultural forms uphold male supremacy; hence, their adoption by lesbians is intrinsically paradoxical and represents a failure of feminism. Jeffreys diagnoses all those manifestations of gay male influence noted earlier as symptoms of lesbian self-effacement, a moving away from authentic lesbian values, and the resubordination of lesbianism to homosexuality.[32] Beside its reliance on an essentialist notion of lesbianism, and the reductiveness of an analysis that equates lesbianism with loyalty to women and male homosexuality with an attachment to masculinity and male supremacy, the problem with Jeffreys's critique is that it views the lesbian adoption of gay male forms as a completely passive process and fails to ask what needs motivate the borrowing or, conversely, what it is that lesbians stand to gain from it.[33]

My contention is that, as I will demonstrate in the following chapters, the extensive borrowing from gay male sexual culture is motivated by the felt need to articulate female sexual subjectivity; so that what seems to Jeffreys and others as a move away from feminist identifications and commitments is in fact informed by a feminist project. If we accept Marilyn Frye's observation that lesbian culture is sexually inarticulate but understand her as alluding to more than a lack of sexual vocabulary, we can go on to ask what it is in lesbian sexuality that seeks articulation and why it is that the gay male idiom is found so useful for articulating it. As in the case of straight women's investment in male homoeroticism, it seems safe to assume that lesbian identification with gay male sexuality serves to legitimate and resignify passive, receptive, and masochistic desires. Such desires, traditionally coded feminine and branded by the lesbian feminist orthodoxy as symptoms of patriarchal false consciousness, are transcoded in gay male culture, as will be shown in the following chapter; and if for gay men these desires may still bear some traces of femininity, for lesbians their routing through gay masculinity redeems them from their feminine coding and their relation to gender oppression. Similarly, identification with gay male sexuality also gives scope to aggressive, penetrative, or sadistic desires in women, desires that lesbian feminism denounced as masculine and patriarchal. Routing such desires through an identification with male homoeroticism does not of course counter their labeling as masculine, but it does decouple them from hetero-patriarchal oppression in the sense that they are not directed toward women.[34]

In addition, the "phallicizing" of lesbian sexuality through the influence of gay male culture preempts its inscription as pre-Oedipal, immature, and pertaining to the axis of identification rather than that of desire (Case, "The Student"). The dildo and penetration function as markers of post-Oedipal sexuality, that is, *real* sexuality. And finally, what the gay male model affords, as opposed to the heterosexual model that informs traditional butch-femme relations, is ownership of the phallus that does not entail that one's partner lacks it. As Esther Newton points out, the mannish lesbian of the beginning of the twentieth century inscribed herself as a sexual subject by adopting the inversion paradigm, but her feminine partner's desire remained inarticulable ("Manish Lesbian"). By adopting gay male sexuality as a model, the lesbian can inscribe herself as phallic and desiring without positing an irreducible difference between her partner and her.

Thinking Cross-Identification

The two major queer theoretical interventions on the subject of identification are Judith Butler's notion of gender as melancholic identification and Eve Kosofsky Sedgwick's matrix of gay identities and identifications.

In her essay "Melancholy Gender/Refused Identification," Butler applies Freud's notion of melancholia as the ego's identification with a lost object to the realm of gender identification. According to this logic, normative gender identification is read as the trace of foreclosed and unmourned homosexual attachment: the prohibition on homosexuality both preempts the possibility of homosexual attachment and, by disavowing its loss, makes it into one that cannot be grieved; and since Freud specifies that ungrieved loss results in melancholic incorporation of the lost object, the ungrievable loss of homosexual possibilities results in normative gender identification. Thus, the girl becomes the woman she "never loved" and "never lost" and the boy the man he "never loved" and "never lost."

According to Freud, the resolution of the Oedipus complex forms an exception to the rule that abandoned objects are incorporated into the ego through identification, because in it object cathexis is replaced by identification not with the loved parent but with the parent of the opposite sex ("The Ego and the Id" 32). Butler's counterclaim is that the Oedipus complex already presupposes a prohibition on homosexuality and that the direct substitution of identification for desire does take place, only prior to Oedipality. Butler's adoption of Freud's notion of this kind of tradeoff between desire and identification—a tradeoff based on the fundamentally heterosexual logic that defines them as mutually exclusive[35]—is a strategic move, an exercise in what she terms "hyperbolic theory," aimed to demonstrate that this heterosexual logic itself inevitably leads to the assertion of the constitutive role of homosexuality.

However, when applied to cross-gender identification in gay men and lesbians, the tradeoff model must explain it as the result of abandoned heterosexual cathexis—a clearly unsatisfactory explanation—first because there is, of course, no cultural prohibition on heterosexuality that would necessitate giving up heterosexual attachments and transforming them into identification, and second, because homosexual identity does not mandate cross-gender identification in the same way that heterosexual identity mandates same-sex identification, that is, normative gender identity.[36] It is perhaps feasible to claim that while normative gender identification is founded on the loss of homosexual object choice—when such homosexual attachments are not renounced, cross-gender identifications are made possible—but such a claim would require positing the existence of identification not founded on loss.[37] As for our subject of discussion in this chapter, the tradeoff model can account neither for straight women's identification with gay men nor for lesbians' identification with them. After all, the former have not relinquished their cross-sex desire, and the latter's choice of gay men rather than straight ones remains unexplained. It seems better, then, not to take the melancholic model of identification (i.e., identification as compensating for lost object cathexis) as a prototype of identification in general. For if identification often involves desire, the view of the two as transforming into each other still prevents acknowledging their more complex interrelations and particularly the possibility of their coexistence.

Further, in his discussion of identification in *Group Psychology and the Analysis of the Ego*, Freud himself lists the regressive substitute for an abandoned libidinal object choice as only one of three modes of identification. Another mode is the identification that is formed with a person "who is not an object of the sexual instinct" on the basis of a shared "common quality" (107–108). The example Freud gives of such identification is that of a girl who reacts with a fit of hysterics to a letter from her lover, and her friends who envy her illicit love affair "catch" the fit. Freud explains that the mechanism behind the symptom "is that of identification based upon the possibility or desire of putting oneself in the same situation." The shared "common quality," according to him, is "openness to a similar emotion." But it is worth stressing, that identification in this case (as in the first and simplest mode of identification, e.g., a boy's pre-Oedipal identification with his father) is founded on a *desired* attribute of the other and not based on an existing shared quality. Of the three modes of identification in Freud's typology, it is this mode that seems to me the most relevant to the cross-gender identifications explored in this chapter. The friends' identification with the girl's desire—their desire to desire as she does—is reminiscent of women's literary identifications with gay men's sexuality, identification founded on the desire to conceive themselves as desiring subjects after the gay male model.

A more contemporary psychoanalytic discussion of identification, which can shed light on women's identifications with gay men, is offered by Jessica Benjamin in her book *The Bonds of Love*. Discussing what in Freud's typology is the first mode of identification, identification as "the original form of emotional tie with an object," which she terms "identificatory love," Benjamin (following Freud) points out its developmental importance for the little boy whose identification with the father helps him solve the conflict of the rapprochement phase between the need for autonomy and fear of loss. The solution entails recognizing oneself in the father as a subject of desire. Unlike Freud, Benjamin both underscores the homoerotic character of this "ideal love" of the boy for his father and notes that girls too seek to identify with their fathers and thereby gain recognition of their own desire. Fathers' usual unavailability for such identification, their failure to confer recognition on their daughters, is the cause for what psychoanalysis designates "penis envy," which is actually "the longing for just such a homoerotic bond as boys may achieve, just such an identificatory love." According to Benjamin, it is this longing that finds expression in the female beating fantasy described in "A Child Is Being Beaten": "[I]t is the woman's wish *to be like* the powerful father, and to be recognized by him as *like*, that the fantasy simultaneously punishes and gratifies" (Benjamin 111). Similarly, then, it makes sense that women's quest to conceive themselves as sexual subjects should find expression in phantasmatic identification with male homoeroticism. For if "the problem of woman's desire" stems from the unavailability of the father for the girl's identificatory love, recognition as a desiring subject remains bound for women to the paradigm of male homoerotic relationship.

Probably the queer theorist to pay most attention to cross-identification is Eve Kosofsky Sedgwick.[38] Sedgwick suggests two definitional axes for mapping gay identities and identifications: universalizing and minoritizing sexual definition (homosexuality perceived as a universal human attribute or as a minority identity) and separatist or integrative gender definition (homosexuality defined as gender liminality or, on the contrary, as affirming one's gender membership and strengthening the bonds to one's gender). As she asserts, "One thing that does emerge with clarity from this complex and contradictory map of sexual and gender definition is that the possible grounds to be found there for alliance and cross-identification among various groups will also be plural" (*Epistemology* 89). If we try to employ Sedgwick's grid to map the two types of cross-identification discussed in this chapter, we find that Anne Rice's gay male authorial identification is based on a universalizing sexual definition. As we saw, homo/hetero sexual identity categories are entirely absent from the *Beauty* world, and sexual acts are not seen to express or testify to an inner identity core. Lesbian identification with gay men, on the other hand, is grounded in a minoritizing sexual definition, that is, a sense of belonging to the same minority group[39] (or to similarly situated minority groups).

When it comes to gender definition, things are more complicated. Accounting for gay men's identification with straight women and lesbians, Sedgwick places both under the topos of gender inversion: "[G]ay men have looked to identify with straight women (on the grounds that they are also 'feminine' or also desire men), or with lesbians (on the grounds that they occupy a similarly liminal position" (*Epistemology* 89). Yet in our case, gender liminality appears to play a far less definitive role. In the *Beauty* trilogy, the author's identification with the male protagonists is based on a similarity of both object (men) and aim (passive, receptive, and masochistic); yet (a) neither these aims nor the characters themselves are defined in the text as feminine, and (b) these sexual aims are not exclusive and come combined with "active" ones. Moreover, as Rice herself testifies, it is these characters' masculinity, no less than their "feminine" traits, which fuels her identification.

In lesbian identification with gay men, as the evidence quoted previously shows, identification is often grounded in a sense of shared masculinity, but in that case the trope of gender liminality is applied to lesbianism alone while male homosexuality is understood under the topos of gender separatism. Interestingly, then, in women's identification with gay men, gender liminality is no longer the presiding trope, a fact that attests both to the decline of the inversion model of homosexuality and the masculinization of gay male culture, and to the fact that what motivates this identification is a desire to move away from sexually restrictive definitions of femininity rather than a fixed feminine identity. In other words, when both straight women and lesbians identify with gay men, they do so not because they recognize gay men's femininity but precisely because gay men escape definitions of femininity, which they would like to escape as well.[40]

It is essential, therefore, to complicate Sedgwick's mapping with the understanding that identification is not based simply on existing similarities; it also involves the assimilation of a desired aspect of the other. Consequently, the otherness of the object is no less important than its sameness for the formation of identification. This otherness is requisite for the dynamic aspect of identification stressed by the psychoanalytic literature, that is, the transformation of the subject by the identifications s/he forms. To reiterate the definition by Laplanche and Pontalis cited at the beginning of this chapter, identification is the "psychological process whereby the subject assimilates an aspect, property or attribute of the other and is transformed, wholly or partially, after the model the other provides" ("Identification" 205). Thus, resemblance is as much the product of identification as it is its foundation. For instance, the attainment of appropriate gender identity through identification with the parent of the same sex is one of the chief functions of the Oedipus complex. Identification in this case seemingly relies on prior resemblance—sameness of sex—but more crucially it establishes resemblance, shaping the child's gender identity according to the model provided by the same-sex parent.

Furthermore, to take full cognizance of the fact that all identification is identification with the other, that as Diana Fuss puts it, "Identification is the detour through the other that defines a self" (2), is to radically problematize the difference between identification and cross-identification. By definition, all identification is identification across, if only across intersubjective boundaries. Therefore, the difference between identification and cross-identification is revealed to depend on the contingent and politically stabilized distinction between attributes that define identity—such as gender and sexual object choice—and attributes that do not. And for that very reason, identifications that cut across recognized identity boundaries threaten to expose the contingence of these boundaries as well as to destabilize identity itself. As Diana Fuss points out, identification both founds identity and undermines it:

> At the very same time that identification sets into motion the complicated dynamic of recognition and misrecognition that brings a sense of identity into being, it also immediately calls that identity into question. . . . Identification is a process that

keeps identity at a distance, that prevents identity from ever approximating the status of an ontological given, even as it makes possible the *illusion* of identity as immediate, secure, and totalizable. (2)

If character is no more than sedimented identifications, as Freud asserts in "The Ego and the Id," identifications that exceed the bounds of normative identity, for example, identifications across gender and sexuality, have the power not only to disrupt identity but also to inaugurate new identity formations, as instanced by the identity category "queer," a category describing an unprecedented configuration of identifications between gay men, lesbians, bisexuals, transgendered people, and other sexual and gender nonconformers.[41]

My discussion of cross-gender identification in pornography by women has inquired after the motivations behind these identifications, motivations that I locate not in a loss to be made up for but rather in a desired reconfiguration of identity. My perspective then stresses the dynamic dimension of identification, identification as the assimilation of a desired aspect or attribute of the other. Further, I propose an understanding of identification—and specifically of collective identification or identification as it functions in public forms of fantasy—as a strategic political tool, that is, a springboard for transforming notions of female sexuality and articulating female sexual subjectivity.

THREE

Refiguring Penetration

Dworkin: The Woman Possessed

One of the major conceptual stumbling blocks for thinking of women as sexual subjects is the prevailing view of sexual penetration as inherently inimical to subjectivity. Probably the most elaborate and poignant adumbration of this view is provided by Andrea Dworkin in her book *Intercourse*. Dworkin's book is concerned with the cultural meanings of heterosexual intercourse "in a man-made world," that is, under conditions of male domination. These meanings she extracts from a broad range of cultural texts—fiction, religious and legal literature, and sexological texts—as well as through a more general cultural analysis. From all these sources she derives an equation of intercourse with possession, domination, ownership, invasion, and violation, entailing for the woman loss of identity, integrity, and privacy.

Dworkin transcribes the social signification of intercourse thus:

> Intercourse is commonly written about and comprehended as a form of possession or an act of possession in which, during which, because of which, a man inhabits a woman, physically covering her and overwhelming her and at the same time penetrating her; and this physical relation to her—over her and inside her—is his possession of her. He has her, or, when he is done, he has had her. By thrusting into her, he takes her over. His thrusting into her is taken to be her capitulation to him

as a conqueror; it is a physical surrender of herself to him; he occupies and rules her, expresses his elemental dominance over her, by his possession of her in the fuck. (*Intercourse* 63)

Dworkin is ostensibly recording cultural meanings—intercourse as it is "commonly written about and comprehended"—but she is also making claims about the experiential reality of both participants in the act: "Alone together, a man fucks a woman; he possesses her; the act is an act of possession in and of itself; the man and the woman experience it as such" (79). Furthermore: "Being owned and being fucked are or have been virtually synonymous experiences in the lives of women. He owns you; he fucks you. The fucking conveys the quality of the ownership: he owns you inside out" (66). Or:

> Women feel the fuck—when it works, when it overwhelms—as possession; and feel possession as deeply erotic.... And therefore, being possessed is phenomenologically real for women; and sex itself is an experience of diminishing self-possession, an erosion of self. (67)

This equation of male-defined cultural meanings and women's subjective experience of sexuality is explained by the fact that in a male-dominated society, these meanings both echo women's total social experience of being dominated and inform and saturate actual sexual practice. They are transmitted via this practice, thereby shaping women's sexuality, forging intimate links between the experience of sexual pleasure and the sense of being possessed:

> Because a woman's capacity to feel sexual pleasure is developed within the narrow confines of male sexual dominance, internally there is no separate being.... There is only the flesh-and-blood reality of being a sensate being whose body experiences sexual intensity, sexual pleasure and sexual identity in being possessed: in being owned and fucked. (67)

Dworkin draws attention to the political dimension of intercourse, its "exemplary" function as an expression, assertion, and rationalization of male dominance, its role in communicating to women their inferior status. She highlights its status as a social imperative and the highly codified and regulated nature of this allegedly private act, thus revealing society's role both in prescribing the practice and in backing its meanings. Yet while, on the one hand, she seems to attribute the cultural meanings of intercourse to the social reality of male power, that is, to see these interpretations of the act as contingent on the context of gender hierarchy, on the other hand, she voices the suspicion that the act itself is incompatible with women's freedom and equality, and further, might even be "a basis of or a key to women's continuing social and sexual inequality" (128). Efforts to reform the circumstances that surround intercourse, she warns, efforts aiming to allow intercourse to be experienced in a world of gender equality, still fail to "address the question of whether intercourse itself can be an expression of sexual equality" (126–127). This suspicion that intercourse is unamenable to reform because inherently hierarchical and opposed to women's humanity runs counter to Dworkin's initial line of argument that exposes the arbitrariness of equating intercourse with the man's possession of the woman:

> Remarkably it is not the man who is considered possessed in intercourse, even though he (his penis) is buried inside another human being.... He is not possessed even though he is terrified of never getting his cock back because she has it engulfed inside her, and it is small compared with the vagina around it pulling it in and pushing it out.... He is not possessed even though he rolls over dead and useless afterward, shrunk into oblivion: this does not make him hers by virtue of the nature of the act ... (65)[1]

In this passage, Dworkin underscores the tendentiousness of the normative reading of intercourse and seems to suggest that bodily acts are amenable to divergent and competing interpretations, the winning interpretation being the one that is backed by social power. However, in a later chapter, she does select one feature of this corporeal interaction—the penetration of the woman's body and *not* the anxiety-evoking engulfment of the penis—as paramount for defining the meaning and significance of the interaction, and she sees it as bearing an inherent meaning integral to the bodily experience itself.

The disruption of bodily boundaries is described by Dworkin as essentially invasive and abusive, incompatible with the standard of humanity and citizenship:

> There is the outline of the body, distinct, separate, its integrity an illusion, a tragic deception because unseen there is a slit between the legs, and he has to push into it. *There is never a real privacy of the body that can coexist with intercourse; with being entered* . . .
>
> A human being has a body that is inviolate; and when it is violated, it is abused. A woman has a body that is penetrated in intercourse: permeable, its corporeal solidity a lie . . .
>
> She, a human being, is supposed to have a privacy that is absolute; except that she, a woman, has a hole between her legs that men can, must, do enter. This hole, her hole is synonymous with entry. (122, my emphasis)

Dworkin is right of course to object to the definition of women as made to be entered, their anatomy prescribing their "use" (while the rectum, the bodily orifice common to both sexes, is not regarded as "synonymous with entry"); she is also right in criticizing the double standard of humanity, according to which what is considered a fundamental violation of bodily integrity for human beings in general is regarded as not only the "normal use" of women but also the affirmation of their human potential.

However, Dworkin's exposure of this double standard goes hand in hand with an endorsement of the dominant masculinist view of subjectivity, a view that equates bodily integrity with impermeability and that relies on an image of the human body as a closed autonomous unit, with every disruption of its hermetic contours spelling danger and disaster (hence, the tragedy of the treacherous, invisible female slit). If one's sense of integrity, autonomy, agency, and self-determination all depend on an experience of bodily inviolability, understood as impermeable boundaries, then genital penetration inevitably has destructive consequences for women's subjectivity:

> In the experience of intercourse she loses the capacity for integrity because her body—the basis of privacy and freedom in the material world for all human beings—is entered and

occupied; the boundaries of her physical body are—neutrally speaking—violated. (137)

It also has inevitable implications for women's political status, leading Dworkin to ask: "Can an occupied people—physically occupied inside, internally invaded—be free" (124).[2]

There are questions to be asked here about "invasion," "occupation," and "violation" qualifying as "neutral" descriptions, not merely because of their pejorative connotations but also in terms of their descriptive adequacy: In what sense is a woman *occupied* by the penis or its bearer? In what sense are her corporeal boundaries violated? Does the temporary presence of the penis in the vagina qualify as occupation? Is it an invasion because any bodily penetration is construed as invasive or because this particular type of entry is regarded as a hostile one? Does Dworkin consider penile penetration to be a violation of bodily boundaries in the same way as breaking the skin? While Dworkin rejects the functional determinism that deduces from the existence of the vagina the imperative of penile penetration, she commits the diametrically opposite error, claiming that bodily integrity forecloses penetration. Thus, she substitutes for the construction of the female body as hole, a construction no less imaginary and normative of the properly human body as a hermetically closed unit.

In fact, two questions arise from Dworkin's equation of intercourse with possession: 1. Is she not unwittingly subscribing to the heroics of phallic mystique by affirming that penile penetration in and of itself *is* indeed possession, violation, and so forth, that it does achieve all that dominant ideology attributes to it?[3] Dworkin's description of the catastrophic consequences of intercourse for women is an example of her subscription to phallic mystique, albeit in its darker version:

> The physical rigors of sexual possession—of being possessed—overwhelm the body's vitality ... [the woman's] insides are worn away over time, and she, possessed, becomes weak, depleted, usurped in all her physical and mental energies and capacities. ...This sexual possession is a sensual state of being that borders on antibeing until it ends in death. (*Intercourse* 67)

This description, inflected by the discussion of Bashevis Singer's tale of spiritual-possession-ending-in-death that follows it, suggests perhaps the effects of prolonged violent rape, but Dworkin offers it as a representation of the phenomenological reality of being sexually possessed, that is, what actually happens to women when they are "fucked."

2. Does her view of penetration as loss of self not rely on a masculinist model of the subject? This latter question is raised by Drucilla Cornell in response to the writings of Catharine MacKinnon, Dworkin's partner in the battle against pornography, who acknowledges Dworkin's influence on her thinking on sexuality. Responding to MacKinnon's recasting of the gender division as "those who fuck" and "those who get fucked" and her question "whether a good fuck is any compensation for getting fucked," Cornell poses the opposite question: "But why is it the end of the world 'to be fucked'?" ("Feminism Always Modified" 153, 152). Her answer is that the catastrophic view of being fucked is a specifically male one, stemming from the fear of having the attributes of a woman in a system of gender opposition and hierarchy. In such a system, the subject is defined, "from the side of the masculine," as seeking freedom rather than intimacy and the body is figured as impermeable and imperiled. It is this masculine notion of subjectivity, claims Cornell, that MacKinnon, following Dworkin, adopts:

> Under MacKinnon's view of the individual or the subject, the body inevitably figures as the barrier in which the self hides and guards itself as the illusionary weapon—the phallus—in which "it" asserts itself against others. But why figure the body in this way? Why not figure the body as a threshold or as a position of receptivity? As receptivity the body gives access. To welcome accessibility is to affirm *openness* to the other. To shut oneself off, on the other hand, is *loss* of sensual pleasure... The endless erection of a barrier against "being fucked" is seen for what it is, a defense mechanism that creates a fort for the self at the expense of jouissance ... it is only if one accepts a masculine view of the self, of the body and of carnality, that "being fucked" *appears* so terrifying. (Cornell 154, emphasis in the original)

Cornell, then, suggests that the problem is not with "getting fucked" but "with the system of gender representations that define the masculine, and the self, correspondingly, as the one who does not 'get fucked'" (152–153). MacKinnon and Dworkin select the wrong target for attack when they reject the practice itself rather than its cultural significations, thus embracing a masculine model of subjectivity instead of radically questioning it. By a masculine model of subjectivity (or of selfhood, as she puts it), I take Cornell to mean one that reflects male anxieties of differentiation, not one that arises naturally from male embodiment. And though Cornell, following Irigaray and Cixous, goes on to stress feminine difference and the need to articulate feminine desire and pleasure "beyond 'the old dream of symmetry'" (Cornell 155), I would like to read her as suggesting not merely an alternative model of *female* subjectivity, one that derives feminine values from female anatomy, receptivity from the vagina; I would like to read her as offering the metaphor of the-body-as-threshold-rather-than-barrier as the ground for an alternative model of *human* subjectivity, female *and* male. Otherwise, this alternate model would remain locked in a binary, that is to say, heteronormative paradigm of sexual difference, with female and male embodiment each giving rise to incommensurable forms of subjectivity.

As Cornell's critique makes clear, the dread and derogation of penetration indicate not only a particular notion of the body but also a particular ethics, a general view of the self's relations with others. The privileging of one libidinal position over another is also the affirmation of an ethical position. Hence, to contest the cultural significations of intercourse is also to contest dominant ethics. Cornell's rejection of a masculine model of subjectivity that stresses freedom and impermeability in favor of one that stresses openness and receptivity recalls Jessica Benjamin's critique of the "false differentiation" constitutive of male identity and, hence, of the norm of individuality in general. Following Nancy Chodorow, Benjamin claims that owing to socialization and child-rearing patterns, the male experience of differentiation in our society stresses "difference over sharing, separation over connection, boundaries over communion, self-sufficiency over dependency," thus preventing the mutual recognition that is the condition for true differentiation (76). Benjamin's account of the male child's experience of differentiation explains why it is that, as Cornell notes, the masculine model of subjectivity upholds freedom over intimacy and accessibility. And while Cornell and Benjamin both criticize the dominant masculine model of subjectivity and suggest a different definition of subjectivity underwritten by a different ethics, Benjamin's account, lodged in object-relations theory, has the advantage of understanding male and female developmental narratives as grounded in contingent cultural conditions, thus avoiding the essentialism of grounding subjectivity in anatomy.

To recapitulate, Dworkin and MacKinnon's view of intercourse is masculinist both in its aggrandizement of penile power and in its notion of penetration as opposed to subjectivity. It attributes to the penis, hence, its owner, the power to possess and occupy and equates being penetrated with a disastrous loss of self. Dworkin admits to the difficulty of separating "the act of intercourse from the social reality of male power"—social, economic, political, and physical—that constructs both the meaning and the current practice of intercourse (*Intercourse* 127). She impugns intercourse as a phenomenological whole without attempting to separate the bodily practice from the political context in which it takes place or from the cultural meanings that inform and shape it[4] and also without subjecting the corporeal practice itself to a more meticulous scrutiny. Consequently, she fails to make some not so negligible distinctions regarding what it is exactly that she indicts in the practice known as heterosexual intercourse.

Dworkin refers occasionally to the hierarchical topography of the missionary position but rejects the sexual position of the woman on top as a fake alternative that does not affect the basic power relations of the act; she mentions Shere Hite's suggestion of intercourse without thrusting (presumably to minimize the invasive and aggressive dimension of the act) but dismisses that too as one of the utopian programs for reforming intercourse that women elaborate. Her text indicates quite clearly that she regards penetration itself to be the chief evil, but she does not specify whether the problem lies in the vulnerability that attaches to the very experience of having a bodily orifice penetrated by another person, or whether it has to do more specifically with the fact that the pleasure of the male partner is taken to be the chief motivation for the act, thus turning the penetrated woman into a mere vehicle, a subservient means to the obtainment of penile pleasure. In the context of heterosexual intercourse, orthodoxly defined as the insertion of the penis into the vagina ending in ejaculation, this distinction is indeed immaterial, since penetration is synonymous to the penis, every other form of penetration seen as either heralding or imitating it. But once we go beyond the heterosexual context or even beyond the orthodox definition of heterosexual sex, the distinction between penetration as selfishly motivated or altruistically motivated, penetration as taking or as giving, does acquire significance and opens the way, as we shall see later on in this chapter, for rewriting the cultural significations of penetration, which Dworkin regards to be so immanent and immutable. By restricting herself to a consideration of heterosexual sex as it is orthodoxly prescribed and read, and excluding other practices and understandings, she *ipso facto* subscribes to and reinforces a heteronormative and monolithic construction of "sexual intercourse" as an incontestable amalgam of practices and meanings.

Bataille: The Self Dissolved

Dworkin's description of intercourse as violating the integrity of the woman's body and selfhood echoes Georges Bataille's notion of eroticism as akin to violence and death. Bataille defines eroticism as the quintessentially human quest to bring some measure of continuity into an existence founded on discontinuity, the discontinuity that defines the individual and the living creature in general as a bounded, separate being. While a complete dissolution of boundaries comes about only in death, sex is a partial, temporary dissolution, a state of momentary continuity with another creature. Bataille characterizes this continuity not as a harmonious merging but as inherently violent and violating, because it involves loss of self-possession and dissolution of the boundaries that define our very individuality. "What does physical eroticism signify," he asks, "if not a violation of the very being of its practitioners?—a violation bordering on death, bordering on murder?" (17). This formulation already indicates that while the themes of violation, broken boundaries, and loss of integrity are common to Dworkin and Bataille,[5] the two differ significantly in that Dworkin views the loss of self as characterizing the female partner alone while Bataille sees it as mutual. Moreover, while for Dworkin the violence is transitive—enacted by the man on the woman—for Bataille the violence is intransitive and impersonal, engulfing the man and the woman alike:

> The passive, female side is essentially the one that is dissolved as a separate entity. But for the male partner the dissolution of the passive partner means one thing only: it is paving the way for a fusion where both are mingled, attaining at length the same degree of dissolution. (Bataille 17)

For Bataille, the dissolution of individuality brought about by the sexual act has to do not only with penetration, not only with the disruption of the physical contours of the body. It is there already in the state of sexual arousal with the loss of self-possession it entails: reason, utility—the guiding principles of normal discontinuous existence—are suspended, and the sexual drive takes command. It is there too in the nakedness that precedes and heralds the sexual act, a nakedness that is symbolic of dispossession because it means the stripping away of all the signifiers of social identity and implies defenselessness and vulnerability. The sexual act itself is described in terms of the body in a state of turmoil usurping the agency of rational will:

> [The erotic convulsion] gives free rein to extravagant organs whose blind activity goes on beyond the considered will of the lovers. Their considered will is followed by the animal activity of these swollen organs. They are animated by a violence outside the control of reason.... The urges of the flesh pass all bounds in the absence of controlling will. Flesh is the extravagance within us set up against the law of decency. (92)

If the self is identified with the "controlling will," then the sexual act dissolves it. The engorged sexual organs themselves are figured as "extravagant," out of bounds, typifying the excessive character of the erotic.

Bataille does assign penetration a central role in the erotic dissolution of the self, but his understanding of it is informed by his understanding of religious sacrifice:

> The lover strips the beloved of her identity no less than the blood-stained priest his human or animal victim. The woman in the hands of her assailant is despoiled of her being. With her modesty she loses the firm barrier that once separated her from others and made her impenetrable. She is brusquely laid open to the violence of the sexual urges set loose in the organs of reproduction; she is laid open to the impersonal violence that overwhelms her from without. (90)

The act of sacrifice is a deliberate transgression of the taboo on murder. This act of violence "deprives the creature of its limited particularity and bestows on it the limitless, infinite nature of sacred things" (90). The spectacular death of the sacrificial object at the hands of the priest serves to reveal to the onlookers the continuity of all existence with which the formerly discontinuous being is now one. As the priest and the bystanders take part vicariously in the transition to continuity undergone by the victim, so the male partner shares in the dissolution of the woman's boundaries: "The female partner in eroticism was seen as the victim, the male as the sacrificer, both during the consummation losing themselves in the continuity established by the first destructive act" (18). Note in the earlier quotation the equivocal nature of the violence; the violence is as much the violence of the male perpetrator as the impersonal violence "set loose in the organs of reproduction" (his, hers, or both?). As the priest is only an agent of higher powers, so the male is but an agent of an impersonal force; he functions as the vehicle of erotic violence, but he too falls prey to it.

For Bataille, violation and self-loss are defining features of eroticism. One might say, then, that penetration for him is the concrete manifestation of the boundary dissolution that is the essence of the erotic. Furthermore, Bataille expands the scope of the category "eroticism" beyond the realm of the body; he distinguishes three kinds of eroticism: physical, emotional, and religious and in all three spheres defines the erotic as the quest for continuity, a continuity that necessarily transgresses the boundaries of selfhood. In view of this broader meaning of the erotic, sexual penetration turns out to be merely one aspect of it, one instance of a general principle, rooted not in contingent social conditions and power relations but in human nature itself. Or, to state it differently, it is not heterosexual penetration that is the ultimate locus of violence; the violence is in being wrenched out of one's individuality, and that is the fundamental principle of eroticism in all its forms. On the other hand, one must not underestimate the force of Bataille's sacrifice analogy. If the man is the sacrificer and the woman the victim, penetration is unequivocally inscribed as an act of destruction, if only of a "slight degree" (18).

Bersani: The Heroics of Self-Shattering

Another thinker who theorizes sex as self-shattering is Leo Bersani in his essay "Is the Rectum a Grave?" Though Bersani makes passing reference to Bataille's work, his thinking on the subject, developed more extensively in his book *The Freudian Body*, relies not on Bataille but on Freud's *Three Essays on Sexuality*. Recapitulating his argument in *The Freudian Body*, he traces in Freud's *Three Essays* a line of thinking that holds that

> sexual pleasure occurs whenever a certain threshold of intensity is reached, when the organization of the self is momentarily disturbed by sensations or affective processes somehow "beyond" those connected with psychic organization.... Freud keeps returning to a line of speculation in which the opposition between pleasure and pain becomes irrelevant, in which the sexual emerges as the *jouissance* of exploded limits, as the ecstatic suffering into which the human organism momentarily plunges when it is "pressed beyond a certain threshold of endurance." (Bersani, "Rectum" 217)

While the notion that sexuality involves a shattering of psychic organization recalls Bataille's definition of eroticism as dissolution of the self's boundaries, Bersani's "shattering" has nothing to do with a metaphysical quest for continuity. Rather, it is a notion of a quasi-biological order, referring to an overload of stimuli that exceed the capacity of the psychic apparatus to bind them. If sexuality breaks the opposition between pleasure and unpleasure—finding pleasure in succumbing to intense stimuli instead of defending against them and seeking to heighten tension rather than to discharge it—then sexuality is a "tautology for masochism." All sexuality is inherently masochistic. Bersani goes on to speculate that this masochistic quality of sexuality has an evolutionary adaptive function, since it "allows the infant to survive, indeed to find pleasure in, the painful and characteristically human period during which infants are shattered with stimuli for which they have not yet developed defensive or integrative ego structures" (217).

In "Is the Rectum a Grave?" Bersani expounds this theory of sexuality in the context of a discussion of homophobia and the discourse of homosexual promiscuity in the AIDS era. He accounts for homophobic discourses and sentiments by adumbrating the fantasy of male anal receptivity that he believes underlies them: the "seductive and intolerable image of a grown man, legs high in the air, unable to refuse the suicidal ecstasy of being a woman" (212). To demonstrate the cultural equation of anal receptivity with self-destruction, Bersani cites John Boswell and Michel Foucault, who both record a taboo on "passive" anal sex for men across cultures and historical periods, a taboo that dates back to classical antiquity. Following Foucault's analysis of the Greek sexual ethos, Bersani notes that this taboo stems from a notion that "to be penetrated is to abdicate power," a notion that he finds again in MacKinnon and Dworkin's work, though presented from a different moral perspective (212). If the ancient Athenians were concerned about the male citizen sacrificing his bodily autonomy and therefore his political authority by submitting to another man and becoming a vehicle for his pleasure, Dworkin, as we have seen, is concerned about the implications of heterosexual intercourse for women's sense of privacy and integrity and their political status. The resemblance between the ancient Greeks' view of sex and Dworkin and MacKinnon's is, after all, not that surprising, since as noted earlier, the latter's notion that penetration is irreconcilable with subjectivity indicates their adoption of the dominant ideology's phallic mystique and a masculine model of subjectivity.

The conception of (penetrative) sex as hierarchical and destructive provides a point of convergence for an analysis of homophobia and an analysis of sexism. Bersani sees this conception as lying at the root of the hatred of gay men, who abdicate male power by submitting to penetration, while Dworkin and MacKinnon derive from it the low status of women, who are seen as lusting for self-annihilation. Paradoxically, though an obvious strategy for both a feminist project and an antihomophobic one would be to oppose this hierarchical view of sex and affirm an alternative egalitarian one, both Dworkin and MacKinnon and Bersani—and herein lies their affinity—reject this option. For Dworkin, the hierarchical view is a valid description of sex as it is practiced and experienced in a male-dominated world, while Bersani suggests that the value of sex lies precisely in its destructive aspect. Bersani commends Dworkin and MacKinnon for their courageous indictment of sex, their "refusal to prettify it," but as soon as he notes his affinity to them he parts with them on the normative level: though they indict sex *as we currently know it*, their ultimate project is to reform it, whereas he celebrates "the inestimable value of sex as—at least in certain of its *ineradicable* aspects—anticommunal, antiegaliterian, antinurturing, antiloving" (215, emphasis added). In fact, even when he agrees with Dworkin and MacKinnon, Bersani divests their critique of pornography and heterosexual sex of its political dimension, reading it merely as an expression of moral revulsion directed at immanent and immutable features of sex itself.

It is via this route that we get to self-shattering as the ultimate, ineradicable truth of sex. Dworkin and MacKinnon are right, according to Bersani, about the violent nature of sex, but they are wrong about the sources and direction of this violence. The violence, he suggests, is inherent to the sexual rather than contingent on social divisions of power and self-directed rather than other-directed. However, before this ultimate truth can be recognized, there are still "anatomical considerations" to be taken into account, for Bersani faces a difficulty similar to Bataille's: The truth of sex as self-shattering/self-dissolution is common to both sexes, but men and women are still positioned differently in relation to penetration, and penetration is equated with subordination or violation. Or, in Bersani's more circuitous formulation: "Human bodies are constructed in such a way that it is, or at least has been, almost impossible not to associate mastery and subordination with the experience of our most intense pleasures" (216). Bataille resolves this difficulty by means of the sacrifice model and the man/sacrificer's vicarious participation in the woman/victim's dissolution. Bersani, on his part, resorts to the notion of "the fantasmatic potential of the human body—the fantasies engendered by its sexual anatomy and the specific moves it makes in taking sexual pleasure" (216),[6] a notion that, he asserts, evades the charge of essentialism because it makes no descriptive claim about the essence of sexuality. In other words, he claims that men and women's different sexual equipment and differing roles in heterosexual copulation give rise (spontaneously and ineluctably) to fantasies of mastery and subordination, fantasies that in turn shape social structures of mastery and subordination (and not vice versa). Thus, he upholds the dominant cultural meanings of penetration but seeks to prevent anatomy from becoming destiny by interposing the notion of fantasy, intimately linked to bodily experience on the one hand but amenable to cultural intervention and ideological exploitation on the other.

However, beyond the fantasies of mastery and subordination lies the more fundamental truth of sex as self-shattering, and Bersani suggests that "sex as self-hyperbole is perhaps a repression of sex as self-abolition" (218). Further, sexuality can be experienced in terms of mastery and subordination only within a relational context; viewed from a solipsistic perspective, sex can only be experienced as a disintegration of the self, the very opposite of mastery. Bersani goes so far as to say that it is "*the degeneration of the sexual into a relationship that condemns sexuality to becoming a struggle for power*" (218, emphasis in the original); where there is no relationship there are no power differentials and consequently no hierarchy and no domination.[7] For Bersani, the disintegration of the self (especially the male self) in sex is ethically and politically valuable. Since "the self which the sexual shatters provides the basis on which sexuality is associated with power," the self-shattering jouissance could be thought of "as our primary hygienic practice of nonviolence" (218, 222).

These considerations lead Bersani to celebrate the value of male anal receptivity. According to his famous provocative formulation, "The rectum is the grave in which the masculine ideal (an ideal shared—differently—by men and women) of proud subjectivity is buried" (222). In other words, through their sexual practice, and particularly through submitting to penetration, gay men undermine their identification with phallocentrism and battle their internalized homophobia. Since men, owing to the "fantasmatic potential" of their genitalia, are especially prone to experience sexual pleasure as "self swelling" or a "phallicizing of the ego" (218), gay men's choice to experience sexual pleasure as powerlessness is a radical and subversive one. Thus, male homosexuality, as metonymic to anal receptivity, acquires an exemplary status as emblematic of sex itself, and gay men are figured as heroic pioneers: "Male homosexuality advertises the risk of the sexual itself as the risk of self dismissal, of *losing sight* of the self, and in so doing it proposes and dangerously represents *jouissance* as a mode of ascesis" (222, emphasis in the original).

"Is the Rectum a Grave?" has been the target of several feminist critiques, but even before questioning its sexual politics, it is important to point out a significant slippage in its argument. On the one hand, Bersani presents the disintegration of the self as the mark of the sexual in general: sexual pleasure is the experience of being shattered by an overload of stimuli. On the other hand, in his celebration of anal receptivity he equates the experience of shattering and disintegration more specifically with being penetrated. If self-shattering characterizes the sexual in general, then from a solipsistic point of view, anal pleasure should be no different from other forms of sexual pleasure. The privileging of anal receptivity as particularly "shattering" signals that in operation here is the very relational perspective that Bersani seeks to overthrow; this perspective represents penetration as an act that polarizes persons, an act that expresses and reinforces power and powerlessness. Thus, while Bersani begins by pronouncing sexuality itself a tautology for masochism, he eventually relapses into the more traditional equation of masochism with the "feminine" position of sexual receptivity.

Moreover, this feminine position gains heroic status only when associated with men. In its "natural" association with women, it is devoid of heroism or transgression. As Mandy Merck points out, Bersani's celebration of anal receptivity as the position of utmost political subversion and existential risk ends up reprivileging masculinity and reinforces the traditional alignment of femininity with domesticity and tameness and masculinity with wildness and with the sexual itself:

> In his comparisons of heterosexual women and homosexual men, Bersani seems at times to be describing two different 'femininities.' A cursory reading of his rendition of rectal sex reveals a heroic rhetoric of 'demolition,' 'danger' and 'sacrifice' ... which is nowhere attributed to vaginal penetration. Might it be Bersani's view that male 'femininity' is butcher than its female equivalent, precisely because the subject's masculinity is at stake? ("Savage Nights" 221)

Similarly, Carole-Anne Tyler in her critique of Bersani derives from his argument the implicit conclusion that "gay men are the better women, represented as better equipped to undo identity" (40).[8] No doubt, it is descriptively correct to claim that for men being penetrated is far more transgressive than for women, for whom on the contrary, penetration is mandatory; however, Bersani claims to be talking about more than just social transgression. And when he presents "the risk of self-dismissal" as available only to men, he reinscribes self-dismissal as natural for women and, therefore, no risk and no achievement.

Tyler resists the slippage in Bersani's essay between sex as death of the subject and penetration as annihilation when she says: "If he is right to insist that women, like men, can experience a phallicizing of the ego ... then he should be willing to concede that promiscuous anal sex is no more a guarantee of the self-shattering death of the subject than is vaginal sex." And she astutely goes on to point out the self-contradictory nature of the heroic discourse of self-dismissal: "In fact, in this essay promiscuous anal sex has exactly a phallicizing function, swelling the ego of the theoretical impersonator (as "feminine masochist") at the expense of women" (40).

Bersani seems to align himself with the feminist project of contesting phallocentrism, but his definition of phallocentrism is an idiosyncratic one:

> Phallocentrism is exactly that: not primarily the denial of power to women (although it has obviously also led to that, everywhere and at all times), but above all the denial of the *value* of powerlessness in both men and women. I don't mean the value of gentleness, or nonaggressiveness, or even of passivity, but rather a more radical disintegration and humiliation of the self. ("Rectum" 217)

According to such a definition, women's problem in a phallocentric society is not being powerless but being devalued as such, as though the assignment of social value to powerlessness could compensate for subordination and lack of control over one's life. Embracing and celebrating powerlessness is hardly a plausible feminist agenda, at least not for women.[9] Bersani seems oblivious to the fact that the valuation of powerlessness can only have meaning as a corrective to an obsession with power, and only those who have power can abdicate it, assuming, that is, that sexual receptivity is indeed an abdication of power. Since, as Mandy Merck points out, "nothing in the anal receptivity of the penetrated male precludes possession [of the penis] in actuality, let alone his identification with its potency" ("Savage Nights" 228).

Pornographic Reinscriptions

The previous section has documented the wide currency of the equation of sexual receptivity with powerlessness, dispossession, violation, victimization, and a range of similar meanings, all of which are antithetical to the notions of subjectivity and agency. As we have seen, this equation prevails not only in popular culture, nor merely in the high-theoretical products of the "straight mind," but also in influential strands of feminist and gay male thought. In what follows we will look at how pornographic writing by women, both straight and lesbian, represents penetration, what strategies of resignification it employs in dealing with its dominant cultural meanings, and what alternative significations it constructs to make penetration compatible with sexual subjectivity.

Rewriting Heterosexual Penetration

First, it should be noted that in contemporary pornographic fiction by women, penile penetration is generally demoted from its privileged status. If we take as an example *Herotica 2*, the second volume in a series of popular collections of women's erotic fiction, we will find that out of sixteen stories that feature heterosexual sex (the collection as a whole includes twenty-six stories, eight of which are about lesbian sex and two about masturbation), only nine represent penile penetration, vaginal or anal, either actual or fantasized; in the other stories men pleasure women orally and manually. In two of the stories the male protagonists are even incapable of penile penetration, one suffering from impotence due to a medical condition and the other paralyzed from the waist down, yet their satisfactory sexual performance is stressed. In another story, the woman protagonist, who initiates the sex, goes down on her boyfriend while fantasizing that *she* is anally fucking *him* with an imaginary cock.[10] It is worth noting that in the discourse of penetration, oral sex represents a special case, since it disrupts the neat alignment of the inserter/insertee division with the active/passive binary. In oral sex it is the receptive partner (the one who takes in his/her partner's penis) who is usually the more active one.[11] Female-authored heterosexual porn stories, like the one mentioned, often stress the active aspect of giving head, the sense of agency and control of another's pleasure, thus removing it from the frame of penetration and resignifying it as a form of active fucking. The active penetration fantasy in the story can be understood, then, as lending a culturally legible expression to the protagonist's sense of sexual aggression, which she finds difficult to articulate from a feminine position.

Assuming that this statistic reflects not only a (conscious or unconscious) editorial decision, we can note a tendency in contemporary erotic writing by women to counter the prevailing cultural assumption according to which heterosexual sex equals penile penetration, or at least penile penetration is its defining core (all "the rest" counting as foreplay, unnecessary frills, concessions to female demands, or simply perversion), and female sexual gratification is incomplete without it. A first strategy for dealing with the pejorative significations of penetration is then to downplay its importance, that is, reveal penile penetration as inessential to women's sexual gratification and not defining of heterosexual sex. Secondly, stories that do represent penile penetration often contest its dominant meanings and delineate alternative ones.

Such is the story "Claudia's Cheeks," by Catherine Tavel, in which it is the woman protagonist who asks her male partner to penetrate her anally and who directs and controls the sex. As the story tells us, this bout of anal sex functions to rectify a previous traumatic experience of painful and nonconsensual anal sex with a brutal, inconsiderate lover. Whereas in the early encounter between the inexperienced eighteen-year-old Claudia and her older lover Claudia is passive, helpless, coerced, and derives no pleasure from the act, in the later encounter she is in command and enjoys a powerful orgasm while her partner's climax is not mentioned. The differences in power relations correspond to and are conveyed by differences in physical position: unlike the first encounter when she was in her partner's grip, her motion restricted while he thrust into her, in the second encounter it is Claudia who moves on her partner's penis while he remains motionless. And the text states that "for the first time in her life, she felt that *she* was doing the fucking and not getting fucked. And Claudia liked it. She liked it a lot" ("Claudia's Cheeks" 181). Hence, while Dworkin dismisses both the woman-on-top position and the option of intercourse without thrusting as ways of altering the significance of penetrative sex, the story suggests that the factors of posture and movement do make a difference in terms of the experienced meaning of the act.

After describing Claudia's climax, the closing lines of the story state: "And do you know what it felt like? It felt like power. You see, Claudia had finally learned how to get on top using her bottom" (181). The depiction of being penetrated in terms of activity and power is even more striking because it is anal penetration at stake. Since anal penetration does not involve direct genital stimulation for the female partner, it is often represented in pornographic literature (and in culture in general) as abusive, sadistic, and humiliating,[12] that is, as carrying to extreme the pejorative meanings that attach to penetration in general.[13] Hence, representing anal penetration as not only enjoyable but also an empowering experience is a gesture that contests the penetration = violation equation by reclaiming the most infamous and abjected type of sexual penetration.

A major theme of the story is Claudia's continual objectification because of her "big, bouncy, beautiful ass," which is the part of her that attracts most attention from men to the neglect of her other qualities. Repeatedly subjected to a fragmenting, fetishizing gaze that often translates into a corresponding sexual practice in the men she sleeps with, Claudia nevertheless manages in the final sexual encounter to attain sexual agency. Unlike traditional male-authored pornography in which women are depicted as perfectly happy with their sexual objectification and subordination, "Claudia's Cheeks," then, does not offer a utopian view of heterosexual sexuality. It does depict and problematize sexual objectification, and it does represent an instance of sexual penetration as abusive and violating; yet, over against this option it delineates the possibility of experiencing penetration as empowering even within the frame of a predominantly sexist culture. Against the reified view proposed by Dworkin, which sees sexual penetration as signifying always and only possession and domination, the story suggests a more nuanced understanding of the act that takes into account a whole array of contextual factors, such as consent, the power differential between the partners, who initiates and directs the act, sexual posture, physical control (e.g., freedom of movement and thrusting), and the balance of pleasure.

Another story by Catherine Tavel, "About Penetration," which appears in *Herotica 3*, tackles the subject of penetration from a different angle. "About Penetration" is in fact a story about penetration that does not occur, and it is through this central absence that the text discusses the meanings of sexual penetration. The text tells the story of an extra-marital affair between Diane, the protagonist, and Thomas, both married. The two, who develop a deep intimacy, have phone sex and a few spells of partial sex, especially joint masturbation, but Thomas refuses to sexually penetrate Diane "with his finger, his tongue or his penis" so as not to be unfaithful to his wife ("About Penetration" 64). Diane is tormented by this refusal but accepts it. In the closing episode of the story, Thomas agrees to meet Diane in the company of his friend Kenny. After dining together the three go to Kenny's house, and at Thomas's prompting Diane and Kenny have sex as he watches. The text makes it clear that Kenny is acting as a proxy for Thomas, and that Diane and Thomas experience the interaction as a mediated sexual encounter between the two of them.

Thomas's refusal to penetrate Diane is presented as an attempt to avoid full commitment and loss of control. The rationale behind it is that no penetration equals no adultery. Yet Diane, who experiences his refusal as a rejection, also suspects that Thomas is enjoying the power his refusal gives him over her and compensates himself in this way for his wife's sexual rejection of him: "It was pretty wonderful to make another woman wet, to make her squirm for you, even in her sleep, wasn't it? All that, without technically committing adultery" (66). To compensate for the absence of sexual penetration, Diane and Thomas's relations contain other forms of symbolic penetration. Diane has a pair of matching earrings made for Thomas and herself; to wear hers she pierces a hole in her ear, and the text comments: "The piercing was intensely painful yet seemed significant." When Thomas finally agrees to accept his earring and puts it through the hole in his ear, it is "almost a religious experience" for the two of them (66). Beside this ceremonial act, the major form of penetration in the story is ocular. Diane and Thomas's passion is expressed by the way they penetrate each other visually: "Whenever they were alone, or even in a crowd, their eyes would bore holes through each other" (65). The exchange of gazes in the final episode is especially charged. On the one hand, it is Diane who is particularly vulnerable in this interaction: She is doubly penetrated, both by Kenny and by Thomas's gaze, and she is both physically and mentally exposed. On the other hand, she manages to dislodge Thomas from his initial impassive stance, affirm her emotional hold over him, and involve him in the interaction by looking into his eyes. The change in the power balance comes about through Diane's first orgasm, which empowers her:

> That was the moment Diane realized her own strength. She would penetrate Thomas without even touching him. She would penetrate him with her eyes and with other things. She would take him inside that way. She would use the power generated by her orgasm to pierce him. (68)

The fact that she has managed to accomplish this is confirmed at the end of the story by Thomas, who admits that she has penetrated him with her heart, her mind, and her eyes.

The story thus reverses some of the meanings conventionally attached to sexual penetration; rather than being an expression of aggression, hostility, and subordination, sexual penetration is represented as an expression of intimacy and commitment, as implying self-exposure and risk not only for the receptive partner but for the penetrating partner as well. In refusing to penetrate Diane, Thomas refuses not only to possess her but also to be possessed himself; in refusing to "take" her, he refuses to give of himself. Contrary to the picture painted by Dworkin, Thomas wields power over Diane not by fucking her but by abstaining from doing so, and it is this abstention that she experiences as cruel and aggressive.

Further, the type of erotic possession and intense emotional connection accomplished by sexual penetration can, as Diane proves, be achieved otherwise. Similarly to Claudia in "Claudia's Cheeks," Diane feels sexually empowered in a situation that on the face of it could seem humiliating or exploitative. And she attains the strength that allows her to "penetrate" Thomas by making herself open and vulnerable. Thus, the story makes a triple statement regarding heterosexual penetration: penetration is seen as an act through which the penetrating man is possessed by the penetrated woman no less than the other way round; far from being an experience of subordination, the female partner's experience is revealed as empowering; and bodily penetration is demoted from its exclusive status as a singular means of erotic and emotional possession. The story's resignification of penetration in terms of (denied) intimacy and commitment and its valorization of sexual receptivity as openness to the other echo Cornell's notion of the body as threshold and a position of receptivity. Like Cornell, the story figures sexual receptivity as a libidinal position that implies also a valorized ethical position; and Thomas's refusal to penetrate is revealed as tantamount to an avoidance of being emotionally penetrated, a defensive stance of withdrawal from the other.

Penetration in Lesbian Sexuality

As mentioned earlier, while in heterosexual discourse penetration is practically synonymous to penile penetration, in a lesbian context this equation is broken down owing to the glaring absence of the penis from lesbian sexual exchange. This absence of necessity effects a significant rearticulation of the significations of penetration. That is because penile and nonpenile penetration represent drastically different balances of pleasure and power between sexual partners. As Ann Cvetkovich points out, "If the 'top' penetrates the bottom with a penis, then the 'top's' sexual pleasure might be assumed to be central. In contrast, if the 'top' penetrates with a finger, fist, dildo, or other nonorgasmic object, then the bottom might be considered to be the partner whose sexual pleasure is the primary goal" (134).[14] The fact that penile penetration is at least largely *assumed* to be motivated by and geared toward the genital pleasure of the penetrator gives scope to the meanings—both cultural and lived—of objectification and abuse that attach to it. When this factor of the penetrator's genital pleasure is eliminated, as is the case in lesbian sex, it is possible to see which of the standard meanings that attach to sexual penetration remain in place and which are overturned or crucially revised.[15] Of course, penetration with a finger, fist, or dildo is in no way exclusive to lesbian sex, but the *structural impossibility* of penetration with an "orgasmic object" predefines penetration in a lesbian context as altruistically rather than selfishly driven.[16]

Cvetkovich, who anticipating my preoccupation here is interested in the question of how sexual receptivity is experienced and conceived by lesbians, turns to accounts by lesbian femmes "as an important resource for lesbian representations of the experience of getting fucked" (125). Traditionally, the femme role combines both feminine gender expression and a receptive role in sex.[17] In a butch-femme erotic interaction, the butch is the "doer" while the femme is the center of erotic attention, and it is her pleasure that is the focus of the interaction. In other words, in the butch/femme division of labor, the femme is the one who "gets fucked"; yet, as Cvetkovich shows, the "rich range of figurative meanings that seem inseparable from the more specifically sexual acts signified by the 'passive' form of the verb to fuck," meanings such as "being dominated, being made weak, or being passive," are strongly contested in femme discourse (125).

The femme accounts that she cites, taken mostly from the collection *The Persistent Desire*, edited by Joan Nestle, generally challenge the notion that getting fucked is a negative experience and, more specifically, counter the equation of sexual receptivity with passivity.[18] Thus, Lyndall MacCowen does identify getting fucked with loss of control but characterizes such loss of control as a hard-won privilege rather than a liability. And many femmes "insist that the femme is active rather than passive in her sexual relation to her lover and to her own desire" and "stress the power and labor of receptivity" (Cvetkovich 131). The labor of receptivity consists of several dimensions. One of those is the work of sexual expressiveness and communication: "moaning, talking, breathing, shifting, letting her know the effect her lovemaking had on me, letting her know what I wanted" (Mykel Johnson, qtd. in Cvetkovich 131). Communicating is necessary for the femme to get exactly what she wants, but it is also (and this is less often recognized) her way to reward the butch for her attentions. Availability and openness are themselves another aspect of the labor of sexual receptivity. As Cvetkovich notes, "The assumption that a bodily orifice receiving an object or body part must either be passive or be rendered passive when penetrated does not seem credible at a strictly biological level" (130). To be sexually open to penetration requires active effort, and the femmes cited stress that the openness involved is also mental and emotional, not just physical. This openness requires overcoming inhibitions, shame, and self-hatred and an effort to let oneself be vulnerable to another.

Joan Nestle's essay "The Gift of Taking," also cited by Cvetkovich, lays particular stress on the activity involved in sexual receptivity. Nestle employs a rhetorical strategy of using the same terms, "giving" and "taking," to describe the activity of both her butch lover and herself, thus confounding the active/passive polarity. In the standard usage of the term, it is the butch who "takes" the femme, and Nestle indeed employs the term in this sense: "I want to scream out to her, 'Now, please take me now'" (119), but she also describes herself as "taking" and "taking in" her lover's hand. "Give" is also used in the two opposite senses of giving a gift and giving in: "She is ready to assume her full power and I am ready to give to her"; "I can match her demanding with my giving, her hand with my insides" (119, 120). But as the essay's title declares, the butch's taking is also a form of giving: "Through her gift of taking, I will be given back to myself" (118). Thus, although the butch and the femme inhabit polarized roles, when translated to the more abstract language of giving and taking,[19] the exchange between them is revealed as an egalitarian one, involving a dialogic dynamic in which power and pleasure are constantly relayed between the two partners. Nestle's rhetorical strategy implies a claim that the polarity of activity and receptivity, possessing and being possessed, is merely epiphenomenal, and that a closer analysis of the butch-femme interaction reveals similar actions and affects on both sides. Further, as the last quote manifests, for Nestle being "taken" is not losing oneself but being given back to oneself, especially in the sense of being reconciled with one's body. And as much as it is an abdication of power, it is also a source of power: "My submission in this room with this woman is my source of strength, of wisdom. It informs all my abilities in the other world . . ." (117). Both Nestle and the other femmes Cvetkovich cites contest the construal of sexual intercourse in terms of a win-lose economy. The premise of the butch-femme erotic interaction is that the butch's pleasure is derived from giving her partner pleasure (a premise epitomized by the stone butch's refusal to be touched at all) (Davis and Kennedy), yet, as the accounts by femmes demonstrate, the femme's pleasure is not an entirely selfish one either and includes her sense of "giving" to the butch and responding to her erotic needs. Thus, the butch's erotic position demonstrates what is true, though less easily recognized, for the femme as well, that sexual pleasure is irreducible to genital pleasure. Hence, as Cvetkovich points out, "Appeals to biology or anatomy to determine who is getting pleasure or who is on top do not hold up in any systematic way because the experience of pleasure and the possession of power are not inherent features of any particular sexual act" (135).

The texts cited by Cvetkovich are first-person accounts of femme sexuality, published as part of the move of reclaiming and revalorizing pre-Stonewall culture, and butch-femme roles in particular, in the 1980s and 1990s. They contain explicit, even graphic depictions of sex, yet in terms of their publishing context, they are not categorized as pornography or erotica, even though Nestle's "The Gift of Taking" could easily appear in a collection of erotic fiction. I will now move on to discuss lesbian erotic fiction proper and further strategies of tackling the problem of penetration. But to do so, I will first make a detour via gay male pornography since, as hinted in chapter 2, the resignification of sexual receptivity in gay male culture has contributed significantly to its reconceptualization in lesbian pornography and lesbian sexual culture.

Penetration in Gay Male Pornography

Since the 1970s gay male culture has undergone a marked process of "virilization," by which I refer to an attachment to and reclamation of symbols and styles of hypermasculinity. Gay male leather culture with its appropriation of the straight biker look and gay male gym culture with its appropriation of bodybuilding and adoption of the muscular ideal of masculine beauty are two of the most prominent examples of this.[20] As Gayle Rubin notes,

> A masculine homosexual ... was once considered an oxymoron; such persons existed but were "unthinkable" in terms of the hegemonic models of sexuality and gender. The development of the leather community is part of a long historical process in which masculinity has been claimed, asserted, or reappropriated by male homosexuals. ("Sexual Traffic" 69)

Gay porn too has from its inception laid stress on masculinity, starting with the pre-porn-era physique magazines and continuing in the drawings of Tom of Finland with his hypermacho figures of "square-jawed cops and grinning, tattooed sailors, all with pendulous penises swinging between their perfectly flared thighs" (Simpson 133). As Mark Simpson notes, Tom of Finland's masculine iconography "has been carried over into gay video porn which, with its models' exaggerated (boyishly) masculine characteristics and appendages, resembles nothing so much as a kind of animated version of Tom's drawings" (134). Simpson goes so far as to claim that gay video porn "disavows anything faggoty" and avoids any specifically gay characterization of its dramatis personae and their setting to such a degree that it might be said to depict "'straight' men having gay sex" (132).

While Simpson may be carrying his point a bit too far, he is undoubtedly right about gay porn's attachment to masculinity and its trappings. Interestingly, this ethos of masculinity has also inflected the signification of penetration, that signally feminizing practice. It is enough to browse through a catalog of gay porn videos to note not just the abundance of titles that allude to masculinity but also the prevalence of titles like "Take It Like a Man" or "More of a Man" that link sexual receptivity to virility.

Gay male film scholars and cultural critics are divided in their opinion about the status and significance of sexual receptivity in gay male porn. Richard Dyer observes that "although the pleasure of anal sex (that is, of being anally fucked) is represented, the narrative is never organized around the desire to be fucked, but around the desire to ejaculate," and he disappointedly concludes that "although at the level of public representation gay men may be thought of as deviant and disruptive of masculine norms because we assert the pleasures of being fucked and the eroticism of the anus, in our pornography this takes a back seat" (28). On the other hand, Tom Waugh, in his evaluation of gay male pornography versus its straight male equivalent, qualifies Dyer's claims, saying that while they may be true of many theatrical films (Dyer and Waugh are both writing in the early eighties, the very beginning of the video era), "passive penetration fantasies are extremely common as narrative principles in many non-commercial films and anecdotes I have encountered (as are fellatio fantasies, active or passive, which do not seem to be organized around the narrator's ejaculation)" (31–32). It is possible that the sine qua non of external ejaculation that gay porn has inherited from mainstream porn is also partly responsible for the narrative structure Dyer observes. This conjecture gains support from the fact that in literary porn, it is quite common to find passive or receptive desires operating as the narrative drive. Complicating the picture offered by Dyer, Waugh asserts that in gay male porn, the mise-en-scène "does not privilege individual roles, top or bottom, inserter or insertee, in any systematic way," and that the gay male spectator (as opposed to his straight counterpart) is "habitually invited to identify narratively with victimization and/or penetration of the Self" (33). Mark Simpson claims that gay porn privileges the figure of the top, that it is the "mythic penetrator" who never gets fucked himself, like Jeff Stryker, who attains stardom; yet this assertion is belied both by the prevalence of role switching in gay video porn and by the existence—albeit exceptional—of gay porn stars like Joey Stefano, who made his career as an almost exclusive bottom.

While Dyer criticizes gay porn for privileging the normative masculine desire to ejaculate over the disruptive desire to get fucked, what I find interesting is precisely the way in which the desire to get fucked gets recast in a lot of gay porn *as* masculine. Bottoming as masculine is a commonplace notion in s/m or leather-oriented gay porn. In this kind of porn, the sexual exchange is often conceived on the model of an initiation rite, in which it is the older or otherwise senior partner— who is also the more masculine man—who fucks the younger or junior partner, thus in a sense imparting some of his masculinity to him and "making" him (more of) a man.[21] Beside the masculinizing influences of male-male interaction in general, the penetrator's penis and his semen always function as synecdoches of his masculinity. The penetrator's semen is often conceived as the "essence" of his manhood, and its oral or anal reception by the bottom is figured as a kind of communion in which it is not merely the essence of the individual that is internalized but, more specifically, his masculinity. Similarly, since the penis is seen to stand for the top's virility, taking it in is understood as an assimilation of his power and agency or, in other words, an assimilation of the phallus. Finally, taking in the penetrator's penis is often figured as an arduous task, which tests the insertee's endurance, self-control, and discipline, so that submitting to it successfully is itself a proof of masculinity. Thus, the refrain "take it!"—so often addressed by the top to the bottom in gay porn during the sexual act—conveys the compounded sense of the literal imperative to take in the penis and the challenge to endure the rigors of penetration.

John Preston's classic s/m novel, *Mr. Benson*, exemplifies this ethos of masculinity. The narrator who at the beginning of the story is already a leather clone into s/m, nevertheless retrospectively describes himself as a "queen," that is, not a real man, prior to his life-transforming encounter with Mr. Benson. The latter he consistently describes as the epitome of masculinity, for example, "the vision of manhood I thought the most perfect I could ever imagine" (32); there is nothing about him—from his booming voice to his calloused feet to his taste in furniture—that is not utterly manly. Mr. Benson is the "real man" the narrator had always wanted, and by obeying him he proves "how much of a man [he is]" (11). The narrator describes Benson's cock as "this essence of my man's being," and early on in their first interaction he learns that he has to "earn that cock" (20, 16). That is, contrary to the view of penetration as an act of aggression, unilaterally geared to the pleasure of the penetrator and not requiring the active cooperation of the insertee, the sexual ethos projected by the narrative constructs penetration as a privilege that needs to be won through hard work on the part of the bottom; and work is, of course, masculine and masculinizing. The bottom is constructed then not as a victim or passive vehicle but as freely choosing his receptive role and, moreover, striving to earn it. When called upon to defend his preference for polarized roles, the narrator says: "I believe there are some men able enough to give as men and some men able enough to take as men" (40) (referring here to himself as one who "gives"). Both roles are manly, and as long as the top is a "real man" rather than a fake, any kind of receptive interaction with him is manly as well.

The currency of this ideological construction is confirmed by Gayle Rubin:

> Gay male leather, including gay male SM, codes both desiring/desired subjects and desired/desiring objects as masculine. In this system, a man can be overpowered, restrained, tormented, and penetrated, yet retain his masculinity, desirability, and subjectivity. ("Sexual Traffic" 69)

Rubin's formulation highlights two key points that will be given further consideration later: 1. In gay male leather culture penetration functions as only one among several forms of domination and possession. 2. For the bottom, retaining his subjectivity goes hand in hand with retaining his masculinity, in other words, the equation of subjectivity and masculinity remains intact.[22]

The masculine construction of penetration is certainly not unique to porn and not even exclusive to leather culture but found in various segments of gay culture, alongside the construction of penetration as feminizing. In the introduction to his book, *The Masculine Marine*, which comprises interviews with marines, most of them gay, Steven Zealand attempts to account for the widely held belief among gays that when marines have sex with other men, they "demonstrate a marked, consistent preference to play the 'passive' role in anal sex" (3). He reports:

> Some Marines I have known claim that marines view being penetrated not at all as female, but as a *manly* test of endurance that, successfully withstood, leaves the bottom with *more* power. According to Captain Eric, "it takes a lot more masculinity to be a bottom than to be a top." He recites a favorite DI [drill instructor] aphorism: "pain is weakness leaving the body." (10)

All the gay marines interviewed show an intense investment in masculinity and profess both to regard themselves as masculine and to be attracted to masculine men. Thus, Corporal Keith, when asked what kind of man would make him want to bottom to him, answers "very masculine" and goes on to specify that this includes a big dick. He explains: "I think it's a challenge for myself. Can I take this thing on? I've pretty well given this impression that I'm a hard core motherfucker;

I wonder if I can really take it. I guess that's my way of proving I can" (36). Here again, the big penis both signifies the masculinity of its owner, which makes him a worthy object, and concurrently functions as a test of the speaker's own masculinity, not unlike the physical and mental ordeals that Marines undergo in boot camp, and which, successfully withstood, endow them with their aura of supermasculinity.

Resignifying Penetration through Gay-Male Identification

Gay male culture's recoding of sexual receptivity has provided new imaginary schemes for conceiving sexual receptivity in women too, mostly in lesbian contexts (as we shall see in the next section) but in heterosexual or bisexual contexts as well. For instance, in Carol Queen's short story "Sweating Profusely in Mérida: A Memoir," the female narrator's sexual receptivity is resignified by virtue of her phantasmatic identification with gay male sexuality. The text tells the story of a sex vacation that the narrator and her lover, whom the story designates only as "Boyfriend," take in the Mexican town of Mérida. Boyfriend is bisexual, though his cruising efforts are directed mostly toward men, and their relationship, far from being a conventional monogamous one, revolves around sex parties and threesomes with other men. Mexico is chosen as a holiday destination owing to Boyfriend's obsession for uncircumcised men and the assumption that Mexican men "will play with men, too . . . especially if there's a woman there" (191). The highlight of this vacation is an orgy with four Mexican men at the local bathhouse, the narrator being the only woman. During this session she is vaginally and orally penetrated many times until in the end the floor is littered with condoms and she has to be supported to the shower.

While it is evident that the narrator is the epicenter of the sexual encounter, and that for at least three of the men her presence is essential in order for them to engage in male-male sex, nevertheless she makes it clear that for her the encounter is mediated through her identification as a gay man: "I was finally in a bathhouse doing what I had always wanted to do and feeling more like a faggot than like a beautiful *gringa*" (194). She notes that most of their shared sexual partners classified her as a "beautiful girlfriend" but contests the adequacy of this label remarking: "I had a feeling most men couldn't keep up with a girlfriend who was really a faggot, or a boyfriend who was really a woman, or whatever kind of fabulous anomaly I was" (194). She also observes that part of the thrill of the experience for her lies in venturing into an exclusively male territory, "a place no woman I knew had gone before" (194).

But in what way does a phantasmatic identification with gay male sexuality resignify the sexual encounter? How is having group sex as a faggot different from having sex with a group of men as a woman? The answer seems obvious enough. First of all, group sex involving a woman and multiple men is usually associated with exploitation and coercion; and when free will is assumed on the part of the female participant she is most likely to be labeled a slut, since promiscuity in women is always condemned. However, with the narrator as a "faggot," the encounter becomes one of group sex between equal status partners, eliminating the suggestion of exploitation that results from the construction of heterosexual sex as a fundamentally unequal exchange between hierarchically positioned partners.[23] Moreover, while heterosexual sexual morality evaluates promiscuity according to a double standard that censures it in women but condones or even applauds it in men, gay male sex culture is not only based on a positive valuation of casual sex, multiple partners, and anonymous sex but has also developed institutions specifically designed to facilitate such encounters, of which the bathhouse is one. Though the bathhouse in Mérida is not the standard gay bathhouse and perhaps not a gay bathhouse at all—it does not exclude women, and sexual encounters seem to take place there only on a commercial basis—for the narrator it fulfils the fantasy of being in a gay bathhouse and having sex in the mode that such an institution designates. Having sex as a faggot stands for the ability to be lustful with men without opprobrium and to evade the heterosexual construction of sex as an exchange in which the main beneficiary is the male partner. Channeled through a gay male sensibility, feeling too weak to walk to the shower after a session of multiple penetrations by several men, becomes a badge of honor that signifies a stance of bottom machismo. Cross-identification with gay male sexuality—within the compass of sex *with* gay men—will be discussed in chapters 5 and 6 in relation to another work by Carol Queen, the novel *The Leather Daddy and the Femme*. In the present story, however, it is the space of bisexuality—her partner's bisexuality—that allows for the narrator's cross-identification.

Penetration in Lesbian S/M Porn

As noted in chapter 2, lesbian s/m culture was to a large degree modeled after gay male leather culture, one of the symbolic gains being the resignification of sexual receptivity as masculine or "butch" and therefore not antithetical to subjectivity. (This masculine symbolics is not unique to lesbian s/m and can be found in configurations of butch-butch sexuality inspired by the gay male model.[24]) To see how this masculine ethos is appropriated and redeployed in lesbian s/m pornography, I will now turn to Pat Califia's story "The Calyx of Isis."

"The Calyx of Isis" has appeared in Califia's first collection of erotic fiction, *Macho Sluts*, and is one of her best-known stories. This ninety-two-pages-long text revolves around one of the stock themes of s/m: the test. Alex, a butch dominant, is in a master-slave relationship with Roxanne, a femme submissive. As a test of Roxanne's obedience and loyalty Alex arranges an elaborate s/m scene in which she delivers her into the hands of a group of other top women who subject her to various forms of torture and sexual servitude. After a night-long session in which Roxanne proves her mettle and her commitment to Alex, the bond between them is confirmed by Alex piercing her and having her wear rings that express Alex's ownership of her.

The text employs a number of strategies to resignify penetration. First of all, as in gay male s/m fiction, sexual penetration is dislodged from its privileged status as the ultimate form of possession and domination and becomes merely one practice among others. During the night, Roxanne is subjected to a whole array of tortures and physical invasions: she is physically restrained, whipped, and caned; her entire body is covered with clothespins that are then removed by a bull whip; she is finger fucked, vaginally penetrated with a dildo, anally fisted, made to perform cunnilingus on several women and to suck the dildo of one of them; and finally she has her ears, nipples, and inner and outer labia pierced. Among these extreme physical practices, vaginal penetration does not figure prominently. All of the practices that Roxanne is subjected to signify possession and domination, yet at the same time they all function as tests of her courage, endurance, and self-control, qualities traditionally coded as masculine. The practices that the story marks as most intense in terms of both their physical rigor and the psychological experience of self-abandonment or "self-shattering" (to use Bersani's term) are the anal fisting, the removal of the clothespins and the ensuing flogging that produce in Roxanne an out-of-body experience, and the final body-piercing. On the whole, the different practices of inflicting pain figure in the text as much more intense forms of possession than sexual penetration.

Unquestionably, the most significant act of sexual penetration in the story is the anal fisting episode, which also receives the longest, most elaborate description (nine pages). The fact that it is anal, not vaginal, penetration that is represented as the ultimate claiming[25] undermines the equation of penetration with femininity, since not only is the anus the orifice common to both sexes but, as Gayle Rubin points out, anal fisting is a practice that emerged among gay leathermen and was elaborated and institutionalized within the gay community ("Elegy" 103); and it is still practiced predominantly by gay men. As if to stress this point, the two women who perform it on Roxanne specialize in cruising and fisting gay men. While described as an act of complete possession and surrender, fist fucking is nevertheless depicted as a collaborative effort in which Roxanne's active cooperation is required throughout.

As we can see, then, "The Calyx of Isis" tackles the problem of penetration by means of three complementary moves: First, by shifting the focus to anal penetration and a practice marked as gay male, penetration is universalized or defeminized, that is, reinscribed as a non-gender-specific sexual practice. Second, the context of s/m, with its plurality of techniques for creating intense bodily sensations and crossing physical and mental thresholds, dislodges penetration from its privileged status as the ultimate symbol of possession and domination. And finally, sexual receptivity itself is transvalued: like other tests of endurance, submitting to extreme forms of penetration is viewed as an achievement and shown to involve the active participation of the penetrated partner. In s/m the construction of the exchange as a ritual involving an elaborate etiquette and requiring skill and expertise lends agency to the bottom as well and displaces the active/passive binary with a standard of excellence in both roles. Further, while the experience of being fisted is described as one of loss of control and loss of self, this loss of self is figured in the language of transcendence rather than dehumanization.

To sum up, we have seen that while the culturally enshrined equation of sexual penetration with domination, victimization, and the undoing of subjectivity is reiterated and upheld in influential feminist and gay male discourses like those of Dworkin and Bersani, pornographic fiction and other sexually explicit discourses by women manage to find ways around this ideological stumbling block. In heterosexual fiction, perhaps the major strategy is rejection of the definitional and libidinal centrality of penile penetration, that is, its status as the defining core or sine qua non of heterosexual sex. When penile penetration is represented, the activity, power, and sexual agency of the penetrated woman are stressed. Similarly, discourses by and about lesbian femmes assert the activity, power, and agency of the femme as the receptive partner and the effort involved in being receptive. The absence of genital pleasure for the penetrating partner, as a structural feature of lesbian sex, compels a thorough revision and realignment of the win-lose paradigm of sex, a paradigm in which penetration is the diacritical mark that discerns winner from loser, and power, pleasure, and subjectivity all accrue to the penetrator. When this model collapses, it reveals the irreducibility of sexual pleasure to genital pleasure (not to mention the irreducibility of genital pleasure to the pleasures of penetration) and the existence of power and pleasure (though not necessarily the same kind of power and pleasure) on both sides of the active/receptive or fucker/fuckee divide.

Further, the resignification of receptivity as virile or butch in gay male sexual culture has been appropriated by lesbian porn. Gay male porn has helped break the culturally determined link between being fucked and being feminine or feminized, and its ethos of masculinity has opened the way for the emergence of the figure of the butch bottom and various types of butch-butch eroticism.[26] Even when lesbian porn does not explicitly construct the bottom position as masculine, it does frequently exploit the gay male valorization of bottoming as proof of endurance, an ability to "take it." Finally, s/m through its plurality of extreme bodily practices dislodges penetration from its status as the ultimate form of possession and domination.

As a final note, I would also like to briefly point out one example of the resignification of penetration in visual porn, an example that does not rely on the gay male trope of the masculinization of receptivity. Annie Sprinkle's *The Sluts and Goddesses Video Workshop*, codirected with Maria Beatty, is a work of educational porn, one of the hybrid genres that feminist pornography has developed. In this video Sprinkle guides a group of women (and by extension the female spectators) through a gradual and structured process of sexual transformation whose aim is to develop two sexual personae: the slut and the goddess. In the tape, Sprinkle appears both in the guise of a sex educator who addresses the spectators either onscreen lecturing calmly or in voice-over coaching and encouraging and as an active participant who demonstrates the techniques she advocates along with the other "transformation facilitators." Her sex educator persona is styled as a prim but benign matron in conservative dress and hairdo, gesturing at the 1950s model of femininity.

Toward the end of the tape, Sprinkle, aided by two friends, demonstrates female ejaculation and then a five-minute-long orgasm, which she names a "mega-gasm." The two young women who penetrate her manually are styled according to a queer quasi-leather aesthetics and display some genderbending characteristics, such as a painted mustache combined with a lace bra. In spite of this parodic allusion to masculinity, the two are clearly in an auxiliary role—their function is to deliver her orgasm—and their facial expressions and panting attest to the effort they expend for that purpose. On the other hand, Sprinkle, as the beneficiary of their exertions, is clearly neither passive nor dominated. Her being penetrated becomes irrelevant compared to the sexual power she radiates. Her orgasmic lack of control becomes a show of ultimate mastery, a display of sexual virtuosity. The excessiveness of her sexual performance makes it into an awe-inspiring spectacle.

The construction of Sprinkle's sexual performance as an achievement rather than a loss of self is abetted by several factors: First, as already noted, as opposed to penile penetration, penetration with a nonorgasmic object tends to be construed as occurring for the benefit of the receptive partner, and this construal is supported by Sprinkle's spectacularly incontestable pleasure. Second, the scene is accompanied by an insert of a digital clock and a chart that provides a graphic representation of the fluctuation in "orgasmic intensity" throughout the duration of the orgasmic event. These quantitative measures contrast with the "out of control" character of the orgasmic event, offering rational (albeit tongue-in-cheek) framing devices that impose order and structure on a bodily performance that seems chaotic and unruly and exteriorize the subjective dimension of Sprinkle's experience. Finally, Sprinkle's voice-over interprets for us what we are viewing. In this voice-over she portrays orgasmic loss of control as a liberating experience that takes deliberate effort to achieve; but more importantly, through this very splitting device the video underscores her agency, reminding us that the frenzied, nonverbal woman lying on her back screaming in

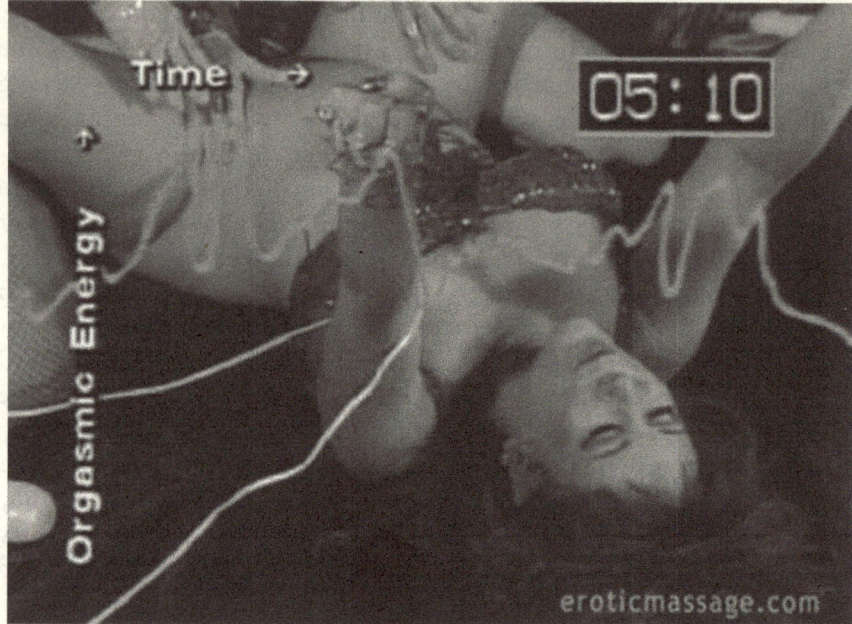

Figure 3.1. The "mega-gasm." Still from *The Sluts and Goddesses Video Workshop* (Maria Beatty/Annie Sprinkle, 1992). © Annie Sprinkle, 1992.

the throes of uncontrollable pleasure is the very one who occupies the position of narrative and expert authority. Sprinkle even "enters" the scene momentarily in her matronly incarnation, winks at the spectators, and asks whether we're having as much fun. Through these framing and splitting devices, Sprinkle controls the terms in which her sexual performance is construed and counteracts the cultural alignment of penetration with objectification and lack of agency. As Linda Williams notes in her discussion of Sprinkle, the Greeks regarded female sexual pleasure as excessive and uncontrollable, a construction that "operated to the detriment of female agency in the social sphere" ("A Provoking Agent," 189). Sprinkle, while offering a spectacular performance of the excessive pleasure of the "passive" penetrated woman, nevertheless manages to assert her sexual and discursive agency both through and around this performance.

All these representational strategies and symbolic configurations work to unravel or at least begin to pry apart the intractable cultural nexus that binds sexual penetration with femininity, passivity, possession, violation, and powerlessness. While much feminist writing has been devoted to exposing the sexism inherent in the prevailing notions of heterosexual sex, and especially the hierarchical and violent conception of penetration, there is a marked shortage in feminist work that tries to contest and displace the dominant cultural meanings of penetration and delineate alternative ones. In this respect, pornographic fiction by women and lesbian, gay male, and trangendered community discourses are far more advanced,[27] reframing and rearticulating sexual penetration in ways that are as yet unavailable to theoretical discourse.

FOUR

The Phallus and Its Vicissitudes

In lesbian pornographic fiction of the eighties and nineties the figure of the dildo has become a marked presence. In fact, dildoes have come to occupy a place of prominence in the arena of lesbian representation, as well as in lesbian sexual practice, provoking in the process a considerable amount of commentary and debate. Heather Findlay observes:

> From the pages of lesbian porn magazines to the meetings of the Modern Language Association, a highly organized discourse has developed around a highly unlikely object: the dildo . . . a number of subcultural products (advertisements, erotic fiction, the sex toys themselves) have consistently drawn from a set of familiar conventions, thus constituting a kind of shared fantasy about lesbian dildo use. (328)

And Sue-Ellen Case concurs:

> Strapping on the dildo has become the premier image of the new wave of lesbian sexual imagery and hermeneutics. Photos and ads of dildos for and with lesbians fill the pages of the underground chic 'zines as well as the slide screens of MLA panels on the lesbian. ("The Student" 38)[1]

As Findlay describes, the debates generated among lesbians by this new centrality of the dildo tend to turn around the question of whether the dildo is a penis substitute, with opponents of the dildo regarding it quite simply as a penis representation (and therefore incompatible with lesbian object choice and female identification), and its pro-sex defenders generally downplaying its referential dimension. As she points out, neither position is quite satisfactory: the anti-dildo camp denies the distance between the two terms (penis and dildo) that is implied by the very notion of representation, while the pro-dildo camp fails to account for the particular allure of the "realistic" dildo and for the fetishistic aura that tends to attach to the figure of the dildoed lesbian, exceeding the bounds of instrumentality.

Findlay herself gestures toward a third position: "If, in answer to the question of whether dildoes represent penises, one camp says 'yes' and the other says 'no,' perhaps a third position might be 'yes, but . . .'" (337). I too believe that the answer is "yes, but," in the sense that dildo imagery in contemporary lesbian iconography, the shared lesbian dildo fantasy that has emerged in the eighties and nineties, engages not with the penis as such but with the phallus and its entire symbolic baggage.[2] Not incidentally, feminist theory in these same decades has grappled with the concept of the phallus, as a significant number of feminist and lesbian scholars have turned to Lacanian psychoanalysis for a theory of gendered subjectivity.

The first part of this chapter will examine some of the ways in which feminist theorists have "taken on" the phallus and try to offer answers to the following questions: what are the attractions of the notion of the phallus for feminist theory? How have feminist scholars interpreted it? To what uses have they put it? How have they critiqued and redeployed it? The latter part will look at the ways in which the phallus is deployed (appropriated, deconstructed) in lesbian pornography, in order eventually to examine the relations between the two modes, theoretical and pornographic, of reinscription.[3]

The Uses of the Phallus

One of the most disturbing aspects of psychoanalysis for feminism has been Freud's derivation of female sexuality and femininity in general from the "fact" of female castration. Female heterosexual object choice, female sexual passivity, women's desire for motherhood and their underdeveloped superego, all these, according to Freud, are ultimately derived from the lack of a penis and the girl's immediate and unquestionable sense of deprivation consequent upon the discovery of the anatomical difference between the sexes, which for Freud is tantamount to the presence or absence of the penis. The problem such a theory presents for feminist thinking is twofold: 1. Femininity is ascribed a secondary, ontologically dependent status and is seen as a fundamentally compensatory structure, founded on lack (this is the gist of the argument presented by Freud's opponents, such as Karen Horney and Ernst Jones, in the psychoanalytic femininity debate of the 1920s). 2. Women's inferior social status appears to be rooted in, and justified by, anatomical inferiority, a fact that both renders futile any feminist critique of male dominance and contains it by subsuming it under the category of penis envy.

The latter problem seems to be remedied by Lacan in the distinction he introduces between penis and phallus—between anatomy and its symbolic functions—a distinction that explains the attraction of Lacanian theory for feminist scholars. The shift away from biology also effects a reframing of the first problem, since under a symbolic construction, a reading of femininity as derived is no longer incompatible with feminist thought, particularly in its contemporary antiessentialist mode that understands gender as a discursive construct; in fact, such a reading may be deemed valuable precisely as a description of the process whereby femininity is socially constructed.[4] The various possible interfaces between Lacanian theory and feminist thought will be explored later in this section.

In Freud's writings the term "phallus" occurs mostly in adjectival form, particularly in reference to the phallic stage. In its few occurrences as a substantive it either refers to the representation of the erect male organ in classical antiquity or is employed almost interchangeably with "penis" (Laplanche and Pontalis, "Phallus" 312–314; Macey 318–320). As David Macey notes, "It is difficult to argue that any conceptual distinction [between penis and phallus] is indicated or intended [by Freud]" (318). Lacan, on the other hand, posits a clear-cut distinction between the penis and the phallus and endows the latter with the functions that Freud may be seen to attribute to the former. For Lacan, the penis belongs in the plane of male anatomy; the phallus, defined as a signifier, is part of the Symbolic order. In fact, Lacan's reading of Freud makes explicit the symbolic dimension latent in the Freudian narrative itself: "Castration may derive support from . . . the apprehension in the Real of the absence of the penis in women—but even this supposes a symbolization of the object, since the Real is full, and 'lacks' nothing" (qtd. in Wilden 271). Thus, while the Freudian theory of the castration complex seems to attribute a natural superiority to the male sexual organ and to derive female sexuality and femininity in general from women's genital deficiency, for Lacan, anatomy no longer explains or founds women's social disempowerment. Similarly, if the meaning of sexual difference equals the presence or absence of the phallus, once the phallus is understood as a signifier, anatomical difference no longer *is* sexual difference but rather comes to represent it (Rose 66).

In this way, the Lacanian reading of Freud "saves" him from the charges of biologism and of privileging masculinity; but its value lies not only in salvaging psychoanalysis for feminism: The conceptual distinction between penis and phallus also provides an analytical tool for characterizing the androcentric bias of Western culture. As Elizabeth Grosz states, "To confuse [the penis and the phallus] is to conflate a Real function with a Symbolic one. Yet it is on the basis of this conflation that women are construed as castrated" ("Phallus" 321). The Lacanian notion of the phallus thus defines the project of feminist theory as that of understanding the process whereby the penis comes to stand for the phallus.

Lacan's complex theoretical mythology assigns the phallus a wide range of meanings and functions that go beyond its role as the mark of sexual difference. In Lacan's thought, the phallus acquires a specifically linguistic dimension, as well as a determining role in the formation of the human subject in general, regardless of gender. The clinical facts, Lacan asserts, "reveal a relation of the subject to the phallus that is established without regard to the anatomical difference of the sexes" ("Signification of the Phallus" 282). The phallus stands for the breaking of the mother-child dyad through the intervention of the paternal law. It is the third term that intervenes in that two-term relation, thus initiating the order of exchange, that is, the Symbolic order (Rose 61–62). In this capacity, the phallus is the prototype of the linguistic signifier or, in other formulations, a "privileged signifier" or "master signifier." Through the rupture that it introduces, it "represents a moment of division . . . which re-enacts the fundamental splitting of subjectivity itself" (Rose 63), and it also represents the being that the subject gives up on entering the Symbolic order. The phallus is the imaginary object of the mother's desire and therefore the eternally lost object to which all desire refers. As such, it stands for the fundamentally substitutive structure of desire. This structure undermines identity itself insofar as masculinity and femininity are defined along the binary axis of having or being the phallus, since as Grosz points out, "One can neither have nor be the phallus in oneself. It is not an attribute or property of a *subject*." The man's penis and the woman's whole body acquire the status of phallus only by being objects of the other's desire ("Phallus" 321). To sum up these manifold functions in a phrase, one could say that the phallus in Lacanian theory serves as the lynchpin that joins together signification and sexuality; it is "the privileged signifier of that mark in which the role of the logos is joined with the advent of desire" (Lacan, "Signification" 287).

The attraction of such a notion of the phallus for feminist thinking lies in its simultaneous universalization and fictionalization of the phallus. Men's privileged relation to the phallus is pronounced illusory, and castration becomes a universal human condition consequent upon the individual's entry into language rather than a specifically female one. As a signifier, the phallus by definition stands in an arbitrary relation to the privilege it signifies and cannot function to ground it ontologically. On the contrary, as Jacqueline Rose points out, it serves to expose its arbitrariness: "The phallus stands at its own expense and any male privilege erected upon it is an imposture" (Rose 69). Lacan's theory, then, is phallocentric, but the phallus that is centered signifies its own undermining. To quote Jacqueline Rose once more:

> The subject's entry into the symbolic order is equally an exposure of the value of the phallus itself. The subject has to recognise that there is desire, or lack in the place of the Other, that there is no ultimate certainty or truth, and that the status of the phallus is a fraud (this is, for Lacan, the meaning of castration). (64)

However, while the complexity of the Lacanian notion of the phallus works to distance it from its anatomical referent, which it so infinitely transcends, it also blunts its edge as a feminist analytical tool: The Lacanian phallus is everywhere and nowhere,[5] and its slipperiness and omnipresence, its almost metaphysical nature, displace and subordinate its gendered meanings, which can no longer be examined independently from the entire theoretical edifice.[6] Yet, not all feminist appropriations of the concept of the phallus subscribe to the entire Lacanian system.

One of the most radical and productive feminist appropriations of the notion of the phallus (and one of the earliest) is also probably the most selective appropriation and the least committed to the Lacanian text.

Feminist Readings of the Phallus

In her "The Traffic in Women" Gayle Rubin does not engage with Lacan's complex theoretical apparatus but rather adopts his general principle of conceiving psychoanalysis "as a theory of information rather than organs" (188), and combining it with Lévi-Strauss's theory of kinship, she puts it in the service of a feminist analysis. From this perspective, psychoanalysis provides an invaluable description of the process whereby the modern Western kinship system reproduces itself and "the traces left in the psyches of individuals as a result of their conscription into systems of kinship" (188). In this process of conscription, the Oedipus complex plays a central role, since it performs the function of organizing the child's libido and gender identity "in conformity with the rules of the culture which is domesticating it." Thus, the Oedipus complex may be regarded as "an apparatus for the production of sexual personality," that is, an apparatus for the production of gender and heterosexuality (189).

According to such a structural anthropological reading, the phallus is the distinctive feature that differentiates the two sexual statuses, "man" and "woman," and carries the meaning of their inequality. If kinship systems are based on the exchange of women between groups of men, the phallus, which Lacan characterizes as a symbolic object of exchange, is that which distinguishes giver from gift, exchanger from object of exchange. "It is the embodiment of the male status, to which men accede, and in which certain rights inhere—among them the right to a woman" (Rubin, "Traffic" 192). The rearticulation of Lacanian theory with its Lévi-Straussian roots clarifies why while men *have* the phallus, it is women who *are* the phallus. The phallus is the symbolic token with which one can "get" a woman. Therefore, women not only lack this token, they are its equivalent. As Rubin puts it, "In the cycle of exchange manifested by the Oedipal complex, the phallus passes through the medium of women from one man to another. . . . In this family Kula ring, women go one way, the phallus the other" (192). According to this interpretation, the Oedipal crisis is precipitated by the child's discovery of the rules of the sex-gender system: the incest taboo, gender division, gender hierarchy, and compulsory heterosexuality. For the girl, this discovery entails recognition of her membership in a low-status group, and acceptance of her castration means acceding to the place of a woman in a phallic exchange network: "She can get the phallus—in intercourse, or as a child—but only as a gift from a man. She never gets to give it away" (195). If, for Freud, "when a girl declares that 'she would rather be a boy,' we know what deficiency her wish is intended to put right" (i.e., the lack of a penis) (Freud, "Sexual Theories" 218), Rubin, highlighting the high psychic price paid by the girl for the attainment of femininity (the repression of active desire, the embracing of masochism), reverses this explanatory scheme and suggests a political understanding of penis envy as the girl's or woman's revolt against the status of object of exchange.

Rubin, then, reads the psychoanalytic narrative of the phallus and its vicissitudes as a political allegory, a description of "how phallic culture domesticates women" ("Traffic" 197).[7] Yet it is a narrative that is unaware of what it is describing and therefore needs to have its repressed political implications spelled out. Rubin's reading, however, disregards Lacan's major theoretical constructs and draws only on the very outline of his thought in order to perform a highly non-Lacanian reading of Freud.[8]

Most feminist critics who engage with Lacan do commit to his entire theoretical apparatus and are consequently faced with the problems it poses for a feminist analysis. If the major promise of Lacanian theory for feminism lies in the distinction it posits between penis and phallus, there too lies its chief source of trouble, since, as much as Lacanians assert the separability of the two terms, the phallus cannot but lean on the penis. As Jane Gallop points out, "[The signifier *phallus*] *also* always refers to *penis*. Lacanians might *wish* to polarize the two terms into a neat opposition, but it is hard to polarize synonyms" (126). After all, the nonpsychoanalytic denotations of "phallus," as derived from its Greek origin, are either "penis" or "representation of the penis," and these denotations cannot simply be obliterated. A term can of course acquire a specialized technical usage distinct from its ordinary one, in which case a certain link, often metaphoric, normally exists between the two.[9] If this were the case with the term "phallus," one could simply look for its specialized referent in Lacanian theory and then keep it apart from the referent "penis." But such a strategy does not yield very promising results, since what Lacan says by way of defining the term "phallus" is that the phallus is a signifier ("the signifier intended to designate as a whole the effects of the signified," "the privileged signifier of that mark in which the role of the logos is joined with the advent of desire," "the signifier of the desire of the Other" [Lacan, "Signification" 285, 287, 290]).[10] In other words, Lacan does not give a referent for "phallus," only a list of signifieds. The reasonable conclusion seems to be that in Lacanian usage, "phallus" refers not to an independent referent that bears some kind of metaphoric or symbolic relation to the penis but to the penis itself in its signifying capacity.[11] If that is the case, it makes little sense to insist on a hard and fast distinction between penis and phallus, since as Jane Gallop puts it, "*Phallus* cannot function as signifier in ignorance of *penis*" (128).

Lacanians insist that the penis is an organ and the phallus is a signifier; however, organs are never devoid of symbolic power, and signifiers are never devoid of materiality. The attempt to cut loose the object and the symbolic meanings attached to it and to reify the latter in an autonomous term results in the bizarre theoretical chimeras of an organ that does not signify and a signifier lacking materiality. Thus, paradoxically, the same theoretical move of disarticulating the symbolic from the biological, that is so important for feminist politics, becomes both obfuscatory and politically regressive when taken to its logical extreme and terminologically reified; since, as Gallop points out, it is the putative or wishful separation of the symbolic phallus from the penis that allows Lacanians to consider the phallocentrism of culture as "a structural fact of language that need have no relation to oppression of women by men" (126).

Further, as she goes on to note, the attempt to keep the two terms apart, "to remake language to one's own theoretical needs, as if language were merely a tool one could use," runs counter to the Lacanian view of language, according to which no speaking subject possesses the power to generate meaning. And if this power to control language, which can belong only to the Other, is identified in Lacanian theory with the notion of the phallus, then "the Lacanians' desire . . . to control the meaning of the signifier *phallus*, is precisely symptomatic of their desire to have the phallus," a desire which is by definition unattainable (126).

Gallop's conclusion seems to be that the separation of phallus and penis is both impossible and vital. On the one hand, it marks a crucial feminist goal; on the other hand, when asserted unproblematically, it fulfills a politically regressive function in its occlusion of the interdependence of the two terms:

> The penis is what men have and women do not; the phallus is the attribute of power which neither men nor women have. But as long as the attribute of power is a phallus which can only have meaning by referring to and being confused with a penis, this confusion will support a structure in which it seems reasonable that men have power and women do not. And as long as psychoanalysts maintain the ideal separability of phallus from penis, they can hold on to their phallus in the belief that their phallocentric discourse need have no relation to sexual inequality, no relation to politics. (127)

The feminist project that she advocates from her heterosexual feminist perspective is that of "liberating" the penis from the phallus for the sake of articulating a female heterosexual desire that does not stand under the sign of the transcendent phallus.

Kaja Silverman shares Gallop's skepticism regarding the possibility as well as the political desirability of a clear-cut distinction between penis and phallus. Interrogating a number of Lacanian texts that deal with the phallus, she uncovers the ties that bind the phallus to the penis. Thus, Lacan's allusions in "The Signification of the Phallus" to Pompeian art "unveil the phallic signifier as a penile representation" (Silverman, "Lacanian Phallus" 88), and this iconic link is made explicit in "The Subversion of the Subject and the Dialectic of Desire in the Freudian Unconscious," where he defines the phallus as the specular image of the penis (Silverman, "Lacanian Phallus" 89–90). The allusion to specularity sends Silverman back to Lacan's essay on the mirror stage, which stresses the disparity between the child's actual dependence and lack of bodily control and the wholeness and perfection of his mirror image, an image which, when internalized, forms the core of his Ideal-I. By analogy, she deduces that "the path leading from the palpable, three-dimensional penis to its mirror representation is idealization" (90). Silverman also draws attention to several instances of conflation of the two terms, such as Lacan's use in "Signification of the Phallus" of the paradoxical expression "a real phallus," a use that occurs, significantly, in the context of a discussion of sexual difference and female lack. She concludes that "as long as the phallus is designated the 'image of the penis,' and the penis a 'real phallus,' there can never be less than an analogical relation between those terms, a relation which often gives way to complete identification" (99).

Silverman attempts to counter this tendency toward conflation by making the obverse analytic move, that is, by revealing the plurality latent in the concept of the phallus itself. She splits the phallus into three component elements: the imaginary phallus, the symbolic phallus, and the phallus as signifier of privilege. The imaginary phallus, which signifies wholeness and sufficiency, is the one that the subject either has or does not have (the phallus of sexual difference); the symbolic phallus signifies the being that must be sacrificed to language and is that which no subject can ever be; and the phallus as signifier of privilege represents the paternal position or Name-of-the-Father. This deconstruction of the phallus enables her to highlight "the semantic transformation which occurs midway through the Oedipal complex as Lacan recounts it, when the male subject accedes to the paradox of not being able to be the phallus, yet of none the less 'having' it," and to explain this resemanticization as a moment of slippage between the symbolic phallus and the imaginary phallus, namely, "the redefinition of the lack induced by the entry into language as a penile lack, which itself translates in a seemingly automatic way into a lack at the level of power and privilege" (100).

Looking for that which promotes the idealization of the penis and assigns it the symbolic functions it comes to possess, Silverman finds the answer in the paternal law or Name-of-the-Father. It is the paternal law that holds together the three aspects of the phallus and allows their condensation. Silverman's project, therefore, is to expose this condensation as contingent, and this she does by extending her exegesis to Lacan's later writings. Drawing on Lacan's revised account of the subject's entry into language in *The Four Fundamental Concepts of Psychoanalysis*, she points out that this text suggests a retroactive understanding of the Name-of-the-Father as merely "one of the signifiers that impart a retroactive significance to the lack induced by language, rather than as a timeless Law that will always preside over the operations of desire" (Silverman, "Lacanian Phallus" 112). Consequently,

> in opening up a temporal and psychic space between primal repression [the repression that occurs with the entry into language] and paternal metaphor, *Four Fundamental Concepts* also

makes it possible for us to see not only that the phallus does not represent the agent of primary repression, but that it may not always be the primary, or even the earliest, signifier of desire. (113)

Silverman thus manages to solve the problem posed by the double role of the phallus—as the marker of both sexual difference and the subject's entry into language and desire—*inside* the Lacanian framework, by exploiting contradictions within the Lacanian corpus and invoking the authority of the later formulation. This formulation allows her to pry loose the three aspects of the phallus, pronounce the symbolic phallus a substitute for a more original "mark," and demote the paternal metaphor from its role as agent of primal repression (i.e., vital for the very constitution of subjectivity). When the symbolic phallus and the imaginary phallus (the phallus of sexual difference) are disarticulated, sexual differentiation ceases to be secured by the very structure of subjectivity, and it becomes possible to imagine "other forms of subjectivity than those constituted by the normative Oedipal complex" (Silverman, "Lacanian Phallus" 105).

Lesbian Phallus/Lesbian Fetish

One subset of feminist theoretical engagement with the phallus consists of attempts to employ psychoanalysis to articulate lesbian desire and subjectivity. Interestingly, two such attempts turn to Freud's theory of fetishism for a model of lesbian desire. In a sense, an appropriation of fetishism by women is analogous to an appropriation of the phallus, since, like the phallus, fetishism enjoys the status of an exclusively male attribute, and the theory of fetishism presupposes female castration.

In "Three Essays on the Theory of Sexuality," Freud defines fetishism as a sexual overvaluation of a part of the body or an inanimate object (153). His later essay "Fetishism" explains this overvaluation as stemming from the fact that the fetish is a substitute for the mother's imaginary penis "that had been extremely important [to the boy] in early childhood" (152). Since the perception of women's "castration" arouses in the boy anxiety of his own possible castration,[12] he reacts to it by disavowal, that is, by simultaneously accepting the reality of female castration and retaining his belief in the female phallus.[13] This dual mental attitude, which involves a splitting of the ego, is afforded by the substitution of the fetish for the phallus:

> Yes, in his mind the woman *has* got a penis, in spite of everything; but this penis is no longer the same as it was before. Something else has taken its place, has been appointed its substitute, as it were, and now inherits the interest which was formerly directed to its predecessor. ("Fetishism" 154)

The *over*valuation of the fetish is explained as the displaced *proper* valuation of the phallus. The shoe, the fur, the nose are overvalued; the phallus is not. In this way, Freud's theory of fetishism exposes the status of the phallus in psychoanalysis as the proper and originary locus of value.

It is true that the phallus at stake is "not just any old phallus," as Elizabeth Grosz reminds us, but the mother's phallus, which "endows her with power and authority" ("Lesbian Fetishism?" 42), but this begs the question of what makes the penis into the signifier of power and authority, such that the little boy must assume its possession by the mother whom he perceives as powerful. This question lends support to Teresa de Lauretis's suggestion that the maternal phallus is in fact none other than the paternal phallus, only missing (*Practice* 224), since where if not in the figure of the father could the penis acquire the signification of power and authority? The fact that the phallus is the proper locus of value not only for the child but for the adult male as well is borne out by Freud's remark that the fetish "saves the fetishist from becoming a homosexual, by endowing women with the characteristic which makes them tolerable as sexual objects," that is, a substitute phallus (Freud, "Fetishism" 154). In the ensuing paragraph, Freud admits that he is in fact unable to account for male heterosexuality; since women lack that which would make them "tolerable as sexual objects," it is unclear how heterosexual men who are not fetishists resolve the difficulty.

In fact, Freud provides two only seemingly complementary explanations for the traumatic effect that the sight of the female genitals has on the boy. One is the importance of the mother's phallus for the little boy, an importance that implies the equation of the phallus with power and authority; the other is his natural narcissistic attachment to his own penis, threatened by the information of women's lack. But why should women's lack of a penis prompt the boy to make the inference that his own member might be taken away as well? The only possible reason could be that his imaginary is dominated by what Thomas Laqueur calls a "one-sex model," a model that regards men and women as two versions of the same body, the more perfect version being the male.[14] The repudiation of sexual difference is, then, not merely the end result of the psychic mechanism of fetishism *but its founding cause*, standing at the root of the castration anxiety that gives rise to disavowal. The anxiety, presumed to be the normal male response "at the sight of a female genital" (Freud, "Fetishism" 154), indicates that the moment of the supposed discovery of sexual difference remains caught in an imaginary of sameness, of *hommosexuality*, to use Irigaray's term, an imaginary that is not only that of the male child or the adult man but informs the very theoretical economy of psychoanalysis.

Over against the fundamental inconceivability of female fetishism in orthodox psychoanalysis, Elizabeth Grosz attempts to elaborate precisely such a notion, suggesting lesbianism as the closest equivalent to male fetishism. As Grosz notes, female fetishism is an oxymoron, because the girl has no reason to disavow the mother's castration; unlike the boy, such disavowal "will not protect her against the acknowledgment of her own castration" ("Lesbian Fetishism?" 47). Girls can, however, disavow their own castration, and such disavowal may take three alternative forms: heterosexual narcissism, hysteria, and the masculinity complex. The female narcissist compensates for her castration by phallicizing her whole body (i.e., valuing it as if it were the phallus); the female hysteric rebels against the passive feminine position by phallicizing a part of her body, the hysterical zone, into which her sexuality is displaced; and the woman "suffering" from a masculinity complex refuses altogether to accept her castration and consequently to perform the requisite transformations of sexual object (from mother to father), sexual organ (from the clitoris to the vagina), and sexual aim (from active to passive).

Grosz claims a likeness between the lesbian with the masculinity complex and the fetishist on two counts: both disavow women's castration, although in the case of the masculine lesbian this castration is her own; and both substitute for the missing phallus an object outside their own body. However, as Grosz acknowledges, there is also one major difference between the masculine lesbian and the fetishist: "Her love-object is not an inanimate or partial object but rather another subject" (51). This is a substantial difference indeed, so substantial that one might wonder whether it does not overshadow the points of resemblance. The inanimate or partial nature of the fetishist's object is the very defining core of fetishism; therefore, conceiving an intersubjective relation as a form of fetishism is inherently contradictory. Grosz admits that she is not sure what is to be gained by describing a form of female homosexuality as fetishistic. The gain might be that of appropriating an exclusively male perversion, a perversion predicated on a privileged relation to the phallus, but her theoretical move also carries some significant drawbacks. First, it does not seem politically advantageous to claim the same status and the same etiology for an attraction to women and an attraction to shoes.[15] It obscures the symmetry between same-sex desire and cross-sex desire and tinges lesbian object choice with a compensatory streak. In addition, it obfuscates the issue of lesbian fetishism proper—the libidinal investment in leather and other s/m related garments and equipment, dildoes, male drag, and so on—since if lesbianism itself is fetishistic, how can such a twofold fetishism be conceptualized? Grosz's theoretical move thus gets in the way of a critical reevaluation of the theory of fetishism itself, a reevaluation that would accommodate an anthropological understanding of fetishism as a historically contingent cultural phenomenon.[16] Such a reevaluation would have to come to grips with the notion of overvaluation that is at the heart of the theory of fetishism and its reliance on the phallus as the proper locus and anchor of value.

In her book *Practice of Love*, Teresa de Lauretis also turns to fetishism for a model of lesbian desire and subjectivity; yet unlike Grosz, whose intervention consists in highlighting the similarities between fetishism and the masculinity complex as both are conceived by Freud, de Lauretis elaborates a notion of fetishism that is founded on Freud's notion yet departs from it in significant ways. She takes her cue from Leo Bersani and Ulysse Dutoit's reading of Freud's essay on fetishism. Bersani and Dutoit point out the fetishistic character of Freud's entire theory of desire, in the sense that it posits a primary object of desire, whose absence is repudiated, and for which all other objects "are merely derivative substitutes" (de Lauretis, *Practice* 222). In this they capture a fundamental feature of psychoanalysis as an economy of substitution and representation, for which "the objects of our desires are always substitutes for the objects of our desires" (Bersani and Dutoit 66). Contra this theoretical fetishism, Bersani and Dutoit suggest an understanding of fetishism as irreducible to an economy of substitution. This is how they describe the fetishist's relation to the fetish: "(1) He knows that it is not a penis; (2) he doesn't want it to be only a penis; and (3) he also knows that *nothing* can replace the lack to which in fact he has resigned himself" (69).

Their stress on the gap between the fetish and what it substitutes for, and on the singularity of the fetish that is irreducible to the phallus, leads them to propose fetishism as a model "for all substitutive formations in which the first term of the equation is lost, or unlocatable, and in any case ultimately unimportant" (Bersani and Dutoit 71). This cutting loose of desire from its anchoring to the phallus holds an obvious promise for the theorization of lesbian desire (and female desire in general), which accounts for de Lauretis's declaration, following Bersani and Dutoit, that "what is wrong with psychoanalytic theory may also be an insufficient degree of castration, and hence its holding on for dear life to the paternal phallus" (*Practice* 226). Yet, paradoxically, her own theory of lesbian perverse desire also departs from the model outlined by Bersani and Dutoit in not regarding the lost founding object as unimportant. In fact, while her theory frees lesbian desire from a foundational relation to the phallus, it does posit a unique lost object at its root: the female body. Thus, whereas the initial analogy she draws between the lesbian and the fetishist relies on the happy resignation both display to the absence of the phallus, by positing a unique founding object for lesbian desire, she slips back to the orthodox model of fetishism, making the female body for the lesbian the equivalent of the penis for the Freudian fetishist.

De Lauretis endows what she terms "the lesbian fetish" with many of the traditional functions of the phallus: "It is at once what signifies [the lesbian subject's] desire and what her lover desires in her," it is both an imaginary and a symbolic object, and it serves as a mark of the (sexual) difference between the lovers (*Practice* 228). However, unlike the orthodox phallus, it is shorn of any relations to the penis or to the father. Its affinity to the Freudian fetish may consist in its contingent relation to the lost object, although the lesbian fetish, unlike the Freudian fetish, is not determined through a metonymic relation to the site of the missing penis but constituted by specific cultural and subcultural discourses. For de Lauretis, the fetish is both a signifier of desire and a desire-provoking attribute (the short hair of the butch touching the shirt collar, the big hips of the femme). The function she assigns it in the structure of interpersonal relations distances it from the traditional fetish, which functions as an erotic signal for the subject alone, unintended by—and often unbeknown to—anyone else.

De Lauretis gestures toward the more conventional sense of the term "fetish" when she discusses the attachment of Stephen Gordon, the mannish lesbian heroine of *The Well of Loneliness*, to men's clothes and other masculine accoutrements. But while Stephen is irresistibly tempted by such items, they do not displace her female love objects, nor do they characterize them; unlike the Freudian fetishist, the fetish for her is an attribute of the self rather than an attribute of the object or an object in its own right. Whereas the novel offers an understanding of Stephen's masculinity in terms of an innate masculine physical-mental essence, de Lauretis suggests that the signs of masculinity are a fetish for Stephen, a fetish that both replaces and represents the wish for a lost (absent) female body. This body is the body that Stephen herself never had and whose lack functions as a narcissistic wound that later comes to be figured as castration. Thus, rather than treating Stephen's body and her gender expressions as continuous, as the novel does, de Lauretis interposes between them both a castration and its fetishistic displacement: Stephen's masculine embodiment/lack of a female body equals castration,[17] while her masculine gender expressions are a fetish that substitutes for the missing female body. This entails some paradoxical theoretical outcomes, since if in psychoanalytic theory "the relation of narcissism to the castration complex is predicated on the valued presence of the phallus in the subject's body image," here it is the phallic body image that inflicts a narcissistic wound (*Practice* 241).

Yet, as valuable as the paradoxes generated by de Lauretis's model may be for a critique of psychoanalysis or for an attempt to stretch its boundaries, this model also invites some objections. First, it is less parsimonious than both the inversion model proposed by the novel and Freud's theory of the masculinity complex. Second, and more importantly, by interpreting female masculinity as a fetish, de Lauretis effects an analytical conflation of gender and sexuality. This conflation is one of the structuring principles of psychoanalysis; but while Freud's masculinity complex subordinates object choice to gender identity, de Lauretis subordinates the mannish lesbian's gender identity to her sexuality by assigning her gender expressions a sexual meaning. This move has the advantage of claiming a lesbian sexual specificity and refuting an understanding of the lesbian as an imitation male or a failed male. Yet, while gender is always to a certain extent sexual, denying it the status of a separate analytic axis has impoverishing effects. Can female masculinity be said to be always and only a (culturally conditioned) signifier of the subject's desire for the female body? Does gender identity always follow object choice? Can it not be vice versa? And what about female masculinities that do not align with a desire for the female body, for example, butches or FTMs who are attracted to gay men (whether cisgender or transgender)?[18] A further objection is brought up by Elizabeth Grosz, who points out that "de Lauretis seems to be proposing the possibility of a specific 'lesbian psychology,'" a distinctive etiology and structure of lesbian desire that distinguish it from heterosexual desire (Grosz, "Labors of Love" 290). As Grosz observes, such a concept of lesbian psychology is at odds with fluidity in object choice.

Unlike Grosz and de Lauretis, Judith Butler does not hesitate to appropriate the phallus itself for lesbian use.[19] In an essay titled "The Lesbian Phallus and the Morphological Imaginary," her theoretical gesture consists in coining the phrase "the lesbian phallus" and justifying its legitimacy. Butler does not propose to elaborate a theory of lesbian sexuality or subjectivity in which the phallus/fetish is a central term. Rather, she starts from the assumption that since "lesbian sexuality is *as constructed as any other form of sexuality within contemporary sexual regimes . . . the phallus persists in lesbian sexuality as a structuring principle*" ("Lesbian Phallus" 85). By "phallus" she refers to the cultural signifier "phallus," whatever its significations. She does not offer a formulation of what the lesbian phallus *is*, since her whole point is that the recirculation of the signifier "phallus" in a lesbian context opens the way for it to signify in ways not circumscribed by the Lacanian scheme or dominant culture. Butler's project is to affirm the potentially infinite resignifiability of the phallus, not to fix its meaning in a lesbian context.

The justification for putting forth the notion of the lesbian phallus involves an exegetic move. Juxtaposing Lacan's "The Signification of the Phallus" with his essay on the mirror stage, Butler reads the phantasmatic rewriting of the penis as the phallus as a symptom of the specular idealization of the body described in "The Mirror Stage" and concludes that "the phallus appears *as symbolic only to the extent that its construction through the transfigurative and specular mechanisms of the imaginary is denied*" ("Lesbian Phallus" 79). Having restored the phallus to its imaginary origins, she highlights the way in which the Lacanian text performatively secures for the phallus the status of the privileged signifier of the Symbolic order and origin of signification, through a series of negations that attempt to cut its ties both to anatomy and to the Imaginary. Yet, as Butler points out, the very privileged status of the phallus in contemporary culture opens it to resignification:

> If the phallus is a privileged signifier, it gains that privilege through being reiterated. And if the cultural construction of sexuality compels a repetition of that signifier, there is nevertheless in the very force of repetition, understood as resignification or recirculation, the possibility of deprivileging that signifier. (89)

Further, if as a signifier the phallus is open to unorthodox repetition, as an idealization of morphology, which no body can adequately approximate, it becomes a "transferable phantasm." Highlighting its imaginary nature undermines its naturalized link to masculine morphology, and opens the way for its lesbian reterritorialization (86). Such reterritorialization has significant structural consequences: It subverts the mutual exclusiveness of being the phallus and having the phallus, since the positions of being and having reverse in the course of a lesbian exchange; it promotes a crisis in the very meaning of having the phallus, since "if a lesbian 'has' it, it is also clear that she does not 'have' it in the traditional sense" (88); and finally, it undermines the ties of the phallus to patriarchal power: "When the phallus is lesbian, then it is and is not a masculinist figure of power; the signifier is significantly split, for it both recalls and displaces the masculinism by which it is impelled" (89).

As mentioned, Butler purposely refrains from providing a definition of the phallus in order to leave room for its proliferative resignifications. She states generally that in a lesbian context, "what comes to signify under the sign of the phallus are a number of body parts, discursive performatives, alternative fetishes, to name a few" (89). However, her list of examples for what could symbolize possession of the phallus in such a context—"an arm, a tongue, a hand (or two), a knee, a thigh, a pelvic bone, an array of purposefully-instrumentalized body-like things"— does suggest an implicit definition ("Lesbian Phallus" 88). It includes, as Mandy Merck points out, "only those parts of the woman's body which can readily stimulate another woman to orgasm" (Merck, "Lesbian Hand" 133). The common denominator of sexual instrumentality reveals an implicit definition of the phallus as the capacity to give a woman sexual pleasure. This is interesting, since throughout the text,

Butler seems to be engaging with the Lacanian notion of the phallus, which emphasizes its symbolic function, coupled with a generalized feminist notion of the phallus as a "masculinist figure of power." Her shift here to an entirely different definitional criterion suggests an understanding of the phallus that is not only sexual, and not only corporeally grounded, but which also betrays a specifically lesbian sensibility. She assembles a list of body parts that are analogous to the penis neither in their capacity to penetrate, nor in their capacity to receive sexual pleasure, nor in their signification of desire, nor in their function in generation, nor in their phallomorphism, but solely in their capacity to give a woman sexual pleasure. The fact that of all the properties of the male sex organ she selects this trait as the one that carries "phallicity" indicates that in a lesbian context sexual agency is defined as the ability to give another woman an orgasm—that this ability stands at the heart of lesbian sexuality and subjectivity.[20] In this sense, Butler's phallus is indeed a *lesbian* phallus, a phallus that conveys lesbian sexual specificity.[21]

The Signification of the Dildo: The Phallus in Lesbian Pornography

The major manifestation of the phallus in lesbian pornography is the dildo. The dildo takes us back from the psychoanalytic phallus to the original meaning of the phallus as penile representation. Yet, unlike the phalli of classical antiquity, the dildo has migrated from the realm of representation to the realm of things or, if you like, from the realm of symbolic objects to the realm of instrumental ones. In fact, the dildo occupies an intermediary ground of quasi-object, quasi-representation, a representation that is put to work; and this ambiguous ontological status is the source of its troubling effects, both its subversive resignificatory potential and the discomfort it arouses in its feminist opponents.

The dildo that has gained prominence in contemporary lesbian representations is the strap-on dildo. Handheld dildoes can also be encountered in erotic imagery and erotic fiction, but they are far less prevalent and as Sue-Ellen Case notes, it is *strapping on* the dildo that "has become the premier image of the new wave of lesbian sexual imagery and hermeneutics" ("The Student" 38; see also Lamos 109). This in itself calls for a not strictly instrumental reading of the dildo, since what is eroticized and symbolically charged is not the dildo itself as a pleasure-giving tool but the dildo attached to the crotch of a woman, that is, the phallically endowed woman. The fact that the dildo figures mostly in butch-femme and daddy-boy scenarios is a further indication that its function is not merely instrumental but linked to lesbian deployments of masculinity.[22] Strap-on dildos also figure centrally in transgender porn, but there they function to mark their wearers as not only masculine but also male, complementing other corporeal signifiers of maleness. For this reason, I will limit myself here to discussion of the dildo in the context of lesbian porn; queer and transgender porn will be discussed in chapter 6. In this section, I would like to examine the functions of the dildo (as well as other phallic manifestations) in lesbian pornography and to check what kind of relations it maintains with both the phallus of heterosexual pornography and the psychoanalytic phallus.

The Split Phallus

My main text for inquiring into the signification of the dildo is a cinematic one. The benefit of focusing on a cinematic text is that it allows for an examination of the dildo as a visual object, the way it functions in a scopic economy, the kind of gaze directed at it. This cinematic text is a ten-minute pornographic vignette, one of the three segments that make up a video appropriately titled *Clips*. Released in 1988, *Clips* is one of the first videos by Fatale, a small San Francisco based lesbian production company. Founded in 1985, Fatale was for many years the major producer of pornographic videos for a lesbian audience.[23] I have chosen to focus on this early representation despite its poor technical quality, and even though nearly all lesbian porn produced since includes strap-on sex, because its deployment of the phallus is characterized by an exceptional degree of reflexivity that I have not found in later lesbian video porn.

The third clip, "In Which Fanny Liquidates Kenny's Stocks," presents two characters, a butch and a femme (the femme played by then-co-owner of the company Debbie Sundahl, whose screen name is Fanny Fatale). The film opens with the butch sitting in the living room, reading the business section of the paper, with the TV reporting on the stock market. The femme enters the room in sexy lingerie and seats herself in the armchair in front of the TV. The two characters are stereotypically styled, the femme dressed in a flowing sheer negligée, lacy underwear, stockings, and a garter belt; the butch is dressed in a striped shirt, braces, and trousers. Taking hold of the remote control, the femme switches to the video channel and watches the succession of female figures on the screen,[24] while pensively sucking on a crystalline dildo with which she proceeds to masturbate. The butch, apart from a few quick glances, ignores the sexual spectacle aimed at her and continues reading the paper. Yet, as the femme gets more and more involved in her autoerotic pleasure, the butch becomes increasingly interested. She begins to undress but does not intervene in the action, remaining in the spectator position. Eventually, the femme comes, displaying an impressive female ejaculation. Only at that point do the two begin to interact physically: The butch calls the femme over and unzips her pants, revealing her realistic strap-on dildo. The femme fellates her and stimulates her to orgasm by pressing her shoulder to the butch's crotch. The film ends with a shot of the butch fucking the femme with the dildo.

While the film represents an erotic interaction based on a very clear-cut and exaggeratedly—even parodically—performed gender division, it nevertheless presents a very atypical deployment of the phallus in a butch-femme encounter. First of all, in the traditional butch-femme dynamic the dildo is an exclusive attribute of the butch and signifies both her masculinity and her sexual agency, her ability to give sexual pleasure to the femme. The film, on the other hand, features two dildoes: the crystalline handheld dildo of the femme and the realistic, flesh-colored, strapped-on dildo of the butch. These function very differently in the sexual and scopic economy of the film. The crystalline dildo is the more spectacular. It appears almost luminous and functions as the major prop in the sexual spectacle that the femme puts on for the butch. Like the femme's attire, it is glamorous and seductive, and in this it is very much a femme's dildo. It is also a femme's dildo in that it functions in the narrative to signify the femme's control of her own sexuality. On the other hand, it plays no role in the physical interaction between the two women, while the butch's dildo stands at the very center of that interaction. However, while the femme's dildo is effectively employed as an instrument of sexual gratification, the butch's dildo functions only secondarily in an instrumental capacity—it is used for penetration only at the very end of the film, after both women have climaxed—and its major function is as a fantasy object and the focus of erotic ritual or, in other words, as a fetish. It is important to note that the butch's dildo functions as a fetish not only for the femme and the spectator but for the butch as well. Since a dildo is an insensate prosthesis, "the subject's

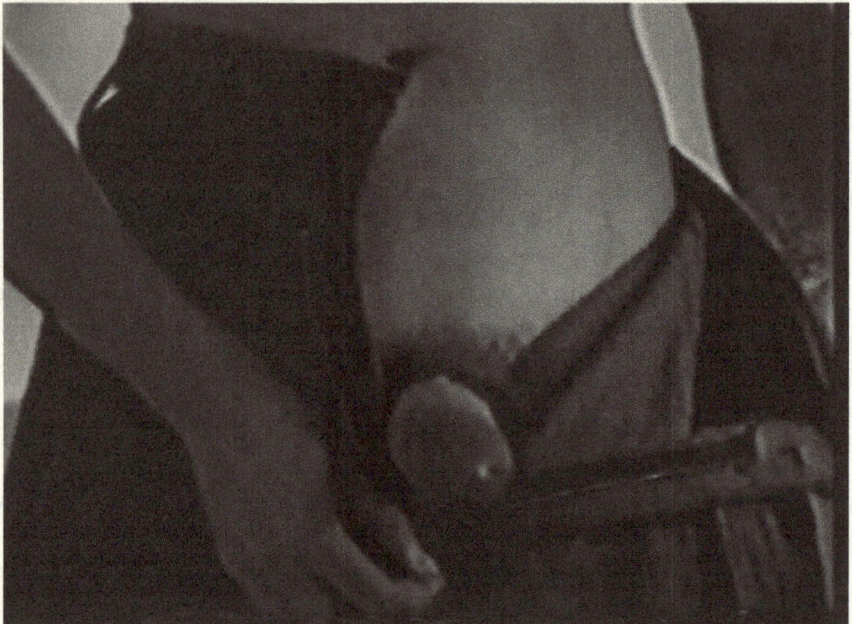

Figure 4.1. Butch striptease. Still from *Clips* (Fatale, 1988). © Nan Kinney, 1988.

pleasure [in penetration] is purely speculative, purely porno-graphic" (Lamos 116). This is particularly poignant in acts of fellatio, when the subject's gratification cannot be said to derive from giving pleasure to the insertee, but is evidently scopophilic and fetishistic in nature.

The shot that establishes the fetishistic status of the butch's dildo is the close-up of her crotch when she unzips her pants to reveal the dildo she is wearing underneath. This is a ten-second-long close-up of the butch's pelvis, in which the only motion is that of her hands slowly unzipping her fly, followed by the slow downward movement of the released cock that finally comes to rest at a ninety-degree angle to her body. The shot is marked by a quality of erotic contemplation, which arrests the flow of the action, a quality that corresponds to Laura Mulvey's description of the element of erotic spectacle in narrative film (27). Yet while Mulvey identifies erotic spectacle with the figure of the woman, the representational codes at work in the eroticization of the butch are those of the representation of the male body, and the eroticization of the dildo betrays more specifically the influence of gay male pornography with its eroticization of the male member. This shot, together with an analogous one of the butch unbuttoning her shirt, constitutes an instance of alternative striptease, butch striptease; and the dildo becomes via the conventions of gay male porn the object of a fetishistic gaze, a gaze that in classical Hollywood cinema was reserved for the female figure and that Laura Mulvey's critique of the pleasures of Hollywood cinema characterized as structurally male.[25]

While Mulvey described the fetishization of the woman as resulting from the convergence of three looks—that of the camera, that of the male protagonist, and that of the spectator—here we find Fanny's look converging with ours on the figure of the fetishized dildo. In cinematic terms, the femme's dildo is fetishized as well, particularly in a close-up of it moving in and out of her mouth, in which it seems almost glowing (in fact, as Fanny's masturbation occupies two-thirds of the film's running time, her dildo gets more screen time than the butch's dildo); but while the fetishistic gaze at the butch's dildo is followed by an act of adoration that it appears to compel—the femme comes to her on her hands and knees and takes it in her mouth—the femme's dildo does not provoke similar adoration. It does not function as an erotic object in its own right but rather as an instrument of autoerotic pleasure.

The status of the dildo as fetish raises the theoretical questions invoked in the previous section concerning the very possibility of female fetishism, and the nature of the relation between the fetish and the phallus. As noted, the causal relation Freud posits between fetishism and castration anxiety defines fetishism as an essentially male psychic mechanism. In addition, the fetish is supposed to represent the missing organ metonymically, not realistically (Findlay 331, 334), a criterion that seems to disqualify the dildo. However, as Heather Findlay points out, the image of the bedildoed woman evokes in fact the figure of the phallic mother, a figure that predates the discovery of sexual difference (333). Thus, in terms of its function, the dildo, like the fetish, represents the disavowal of female castration.[26] As Findlay goes on to note, this disavowal is also acted out in the film on the narrative level in the act of fellatio that succeeds the unveiling of the dildo. Although both the actors and the spectators know that Kenny comes as a result of clitoral stimulation, "for the sake of the fantasy we believe [the pleasure] is phallic" (334).

Reading the dildoed butch as a pre-Oedipal phallic mother is an elegant theoretical solution, yet in explaining dildo fetishism as a disavowal of female castration it fails to account for the marked affinity between the fetishization of the dildo and the fetishization of the erect penis in heterosexual and gay male porn. Quite obviously, the figure of the dildo in the nascent genre of lesbian video porn draws on the figure of the erect penis in the established tradition of straight porn and exploits its erotic valences.[27] Linda Williams asserts that in the new lesbian pornography "the dildo is a fetish if ever there was one" ("Pornographies" 255), yet she also regards fetishism as the defining characteristic of the representation of the penis in heterosexual pornography.[28] For Williams, the penis itself, and particularly the ejaculating penis, which has become a sine qua non of hardcore porn, is a cinematic fetish. To read the penis as a fetish is, of course, to employ the Freudian concept of fetishism in a very unorthodox fashion, and Williams justifies this usage by invoking the (implicitly Lacanian) distinction between the penis and the phallus:

> In its Freudian sense this fetish is peculiarly literal: in place of the psychic compromise that invests pleasure in a relatively different signifier ... the money shot offers a real penis substituting for the mythic phallus Freud's little boy fears to have lost. Indeed, these close-ups of remarkably long, perpetually hard, ejaculating penises might seem to be literal embodiments of this idealized fantasy phallus which Freud says we all—men and women—desire. (*Hard Core* 116)

But if the pornographic penis attempts to embody the fantasy phallus, which is itself, as Judith Butler notes, an idealization of male morphology, then the often remarkably long and certainly perpetually hard dildo is an even more perfect approximation of the phallus than the erect penis.[29] Lesbian dildo fetishism, through its mimetic relation to penile fetishism, thus serves to expose the cultural fetishization of the male member itself.[30] If fetishism is defined as overvaluation, then the idealization of the penis as the phallus is a form of fetishism. And Freudian psychoanalysis both plays a major role in the cultural fetishization of the penis and functions to occlude this fetishization by taking the overvaluation of the penis for granted.[31]

The dildo does not only embody the phallus, thus eliding the difference between phallus and fetish; in relocating the phallus to the terrain of a lesbian exchange, it also resignifies it. If the phallus is the signifier of both desire and difference, the (butch's) dildo functions in the same way. Yet, while the phallus connotes a notion of sexual difference that is stable and grounded either in anatomy or in a symbolic order that is deemed immutable, the dildo signifies gender fluidity (Smyth 157). It creates difference and polarization not grounded in any natural difference, and it is precisely this denaturalization of gender difference that it represents. To quote Sue-Ellen Case:

> The butch is the lesbian woman who proudly displays the possession of the penis, while the femme takes on the compensatory masquerade of womanliness [i.e., of castration]. . . . This raises the question of "penis, penis, who's got the penis," because there is no referent in sight; rather the fictions of penis and castration become ironized and "camped up." ("Toward" 291)

The dildo is not the only manifestation of the phallus in the film; another phallic signifier is the "cum shot" or the "money shot." As Linda Williams explains, the genre of film pornography is motivated by the drive for maximum visibility, both of the mysteries of the female body and of the sexual event; more specifically, it is motivated by the desire to obtain an involuntary visual confession of uncontrollable bodily pleasure. Yet this drive is paradoxically thwarted by the fact that penetration prevents visibility. The solution found in the seventies, which has turned into one of the trademarks of the genre, is the "money shot," the shot portraying external male ejaculation. According to Williams, the money shot is a fetishistic substitute for that which cannot be seen and particularly for the invisible female orgasm. But while it is positioned as the climax of most heterosexual pornography and supposed to represent the "ultimate truth" of sexual pleasure, it provides incontrovertible, visual, quantifiable evidence only of the "truth" of male pleasure. Further, while it is seen to symbolize phallic power and potency, "it can only figure satisfaction as failing to do what masculine sexual ideology frequently claims that the man does to the woman: to occupy, penetrate, possess her" (*Hard Core* 113–114; see also "Pornographies" 242–244).

Clips presents a female version of the cum shot in the form of the spectacular female ejaculation displayed by Fanny. Here we have an external, quantifiable female orgasm, more compelling in its visual effect than most male cum shots. This shot not only offers an equivalent of the male cum shot, but at the same time it also solves the problem

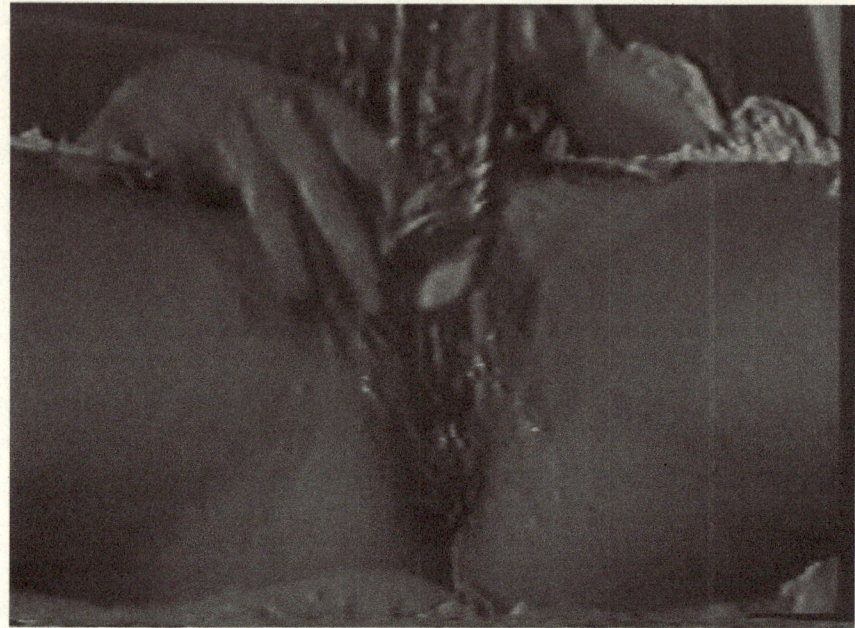

Figure 4.2. The femme phallus and the female cum shot. Still from *Clips* (Fatale, 1988). © Nan Kinney, 1988.

of the visualization of female sexual pleasure, a major stumbling block for mainstream porn. If the conventional money shot works to signify female pleasure through fetishistic displacement, the female money shot functions more directly as an index of female orgasm. However, the indexical quality of female ejaculation is still not tantamount to that of male ejaculation, since it involves a relatively unfamiliar type of female orgasm. Thus, the female cum shot provides evidence of a pleasure few women can identify with, while on the other hand, as Cherry Smyth remarks, in "the lesbian viewer who has never achieved such an awe-inspiring feat" it may induce feelings of inadequacy (156). Also, on a more basic level, the unfamiliarity of female ejaculation creates a problem of legibility, which turns the shot, at least for some viewers, from an index of sexual pleasure to a riddle to be deciphered or even a visual gag.

Not only does the film appropriate the cum shot by offering a female version of it, it also reverses the heterosexual visual economy in assigning the cum shot, the symbol of phallic power and potency, to the femme, whereas the butch, who owns the phallus (both in the concrete sense—she is the one with the strap-on dildo—and more generally as the usurper of the signifiers of masculinity), comes invisibly; she does not even remove her pants, and recognizing her orgasm requires a certain degree of interpretive proficiency.[32] The butch makes do with a parodic allusion to the cum shot as she stops in front of the camera to open a can of beer.

To sum up, the film dismantles the phallus to its various concrete and symbolic components—the dildo as its plastic representation, the cum shot as the visual guarantee of potency and pleasure, penetration, the desiring gaze—and distributes these between the two partners. Each is assigned a different phallus, so to speak, in accordance with her type of sexual subjectivity. The femme's dildo signifies both her seductiveness and her control of her sexuality but remains circumscribed in a narcissistic and autoerotic relation. The butch's dildo signifies the power to possess and give pleasure, but this signification is undercut by the fact that its promise is not fulfilled within the scope of the narrative. If in conventional heterosexual porn female masturbation functions as foreplay and normally gives way to penile penetration as offering true satisfaction, here the butch refrains from intervening, and the femme achieves orgasm single-handed. Her satisfaction is not dependent on the butch's phallus. The butch has the visible phallic prosthesis, but the femme has the visual evidence of pleasure: the cum shot. Both own the desiring "phallic" gaze, but in the femme it is disarticulated from the power to possess sexually and translated into autoerotism (she masturbates as she watches images of sexual or vulnerable women), and in the butch there is a certain gap or lapse between look and act.

This "splitting" of the phallus between the butch and the femme partners is reminiscent of Sue-Ellen Case's notion of the butch-femme pair as a "coupled-subject," which she suggests in "Toward a Butch-Femme Aesthetics." For Case, the butch and the femme together offer an alternative feminist subject position "outside the ideology of sexual difference" (283). But while in her formulation the butch "proudly displays the possession of the penis, while the femme takes on the compensatory masquerade of womanliness" (291), *Clips* subverts the traditional butch-femme model and disperses the signifiers of sexual subjectivity *between* the partners.

The film maintains the phallus as an indispensable signifier of difference and desire, but the recontextualization of the phallus within a lesbian exchange works to deconstruct it, undoing the categorical difference between phallus and fetish, splitting the phallus into its component elements, and dislodging it from the heterosexual division of labor enshrined in the psychoanalytic paradigm, a division of labor that aligns masculinity with the phallus, activity, and desire on the one hand and femininity with castration, passivity, and object status on the other. In the film, these alignments are systematically undone and rearticulated, bearing out Butler's observation that

> the simultaneous acts of depriviliging the phallus and removing it from the normative heterosexual form of exchange, and recirculating and repriviliging it between women deploys the phallus to break the signifying chain in which it conventionally operates. If a lesbian "has" it, it is also clear that she does not "have" it in the traditional sense; her activity furthers a crisis in the sense of what it means to "have" one at all. ("The Lesbian Phallus" 88–89)

The recontextualization of the phallus in a butch-femme interaction both undermines the unproblematic anchoring of its symbolic valences in male anatomy and exploits these symbolic valences for the benefit of eroticism between women, appropriating the phallus as a lesbian fetish.[33]

What links are there between the feminist theoretical engagement with the psychoanalytic concept of the phallus in and the deployment of the phallus in lesbian pornographic representation? First, both seem to be in agreement that the notion or the figure of the phallus needs to be reckoned with and cannot be simply left out of an account or a representation of female sexual subjectivity. The centrality of the dildo in lesbian sexual representation testifies to a growing need to signify sexual subjectivity within the dominant sexual semiotics, that is, in terms that are culturally intelligible beyond the bounds of the lesbian subculture.[34] Second, lesbian porn seems to be in agreement with feminist theory concerning the inherent difficulty of the ideal separability of penis and phallus. Resorting to the dildo, a penile representation, to signify sexual desire and agency implies skepticism concerning the ability of the phallus to signify independently of the penis.

On the other hand, the function of the dildo in lesbian sexual representation reflects an implicit performative conception of the phallus. According to such an understanding, the phallus is no more than the rituals and posturing that signify its possession and culturally constitute it. Getting your cock sucked equals having the phallus, whether that cock is made of silicone or flesh and blood. What matters is the performance of the ritual of cock-sucking. However, once that ritual is relocated to the terrain of a lesbian exchange, the phallus, whose possession is signified by the ritual, comes to signify differently. This understanding is very much in line with Judith Butler's insistence that the privileged way the phallus operates in our culture "is not independent of its perpetual reconstitution"; that "inasmuch as the phallus signifies, it is also always in the process of being signified and resignified"; and that this resignification means "signifying in ways and in places that exceed its proper structural place within the Lacanian symbolic and contest the necessity of that place" ("The Lesbian Phallus" 89). The major resignification that the dildo effects consists, of course, in severing the connection between the phallus and the male body.

While Butler does not mention the dildo, except for an oblique reference to "body-like things," her theorization of the lesbian phallus seems informed by contemporary lesbian sexual practice. The film we have discussed both bears out her claim regarding the inevitable resignification of the phallus in a lesbian context and gives scope to a conceptualization of the lesbian phallus that goes beyond her formulations. Since, as we saw, *Clips* suggests not only that the positions of "being" and "having" the phallus can be reversed and occupied successively (as Butler proposes), but also that both partners in the erotic interaction can "have the phallus" at the same time. Furthermore, by "splitting" the phallus into its various symbolic and concrete components and redistributing them in different configurations between the partners, the film uncovers the multiplicity inherent in the notion of the phallus but veiled by its supposed monolithic irreducibility. Thus, it shows that if the phallus can be resignified through its lesbian reterritorialization, it is because it has never been the "one" that it pretends to be.

For Jane Gallop, writing from a heterosexual feminist perspective, the goal vis-à-vis the phallus is to liberate the penis from the phallus for the sake of articulating a female heterosexual desire that does not stand under the sign of the phallus. The project of much contemporary lesbian porn, on the other hand, seems to be the appropriation of the phallus, an appropriation increasingly effected by recourse to a penile representation: the dildo.[35] The dildo, of course, both refers to the penis and displaces it, but its symbolic efficacy relies on its representational power. This suggests that the lesbian and the straight feminist projects in the sphere of sexuality may not necessarily overlap. While both aim at an eventual disarticulation of penis and phallus, the routes they take are diametrically opposed, the one attempting to shear the penis of its symbolic attributes, and the other attempting to lay hold of these symbolic attributes by invoking the figure that signifies them.[36]

From "Taking On" the Phallus to Penis Envy

Finally, it is important to note that other pornographic texts may give rise to different observations and concerns. Literary texts in particular tend to provide more insight into the experiential aspect of lesbian dildo fetishism. Lesbian pornographic fiction depicts a whole range of forms of consciousness and subjectivity effects related to the dildo. Thus, for example, Pat Califia in a self-reflexive narrative provides a description of the experiential complexity and ambivalence of sucking a dildo:

> Sucking a dildo is so perverse, evoking a series of emotions and images that ought to be confusing, but that make perfect sense at the time. I am sorry that the instrument that moves in my mouth is not flesh, because then I would be able to give my daddy pleasure beyond the visuals.... I am also (more selfishly) sorry because a real cock would come long before my daddy will get tired of this game and withdraw ...
> On the other hand, I am glad this is a dildo and not a cock, because I don't have to worry about STDs and because its presence means I am with a woman, which is consistent with my sexual identity, allowing me to sample the pleasure of oral violation without violating my sense of myself...Then there is the point in time where I lose awareness of my daddy's gender, or even my own. It is an infantile state. I am sucking, and this is what I must do to live. It is all that life is. ("Daddy" 67)

If, looking at lesbian moving-image pornography, Linda Williams can declare that "the point about this dildo is not only that [the lesbian sadomasochist] puts it on but also that she takes it off" ("Pornographies" 256), some fictional and nonfiction accounts of dildo use stress, on the contrary, the way in which the dildo may not be so easy to take off.

Thus, Jacob Hale, discussing the remapping of the body that often takes place in s/m practice, notes that "inanimate objects—dildoes—sometimes take on some of the phenomenological characteristics of erogenous body parts." He illustrates this with the following story:

> When Powersurge [a leatherdyke event] defined a woman as someone who could slam her dick into a drawer without hurting it, a common response among some butch leatherdykes and some ftms was to say that it sure would hurt if their dicks got slammed into a drawer.

He adds, "A dildo may not be a dick only in the conception, it may be a dick phenomenologically as well" ("Leatherdyke Boys" 230).

One of the paradoxical effects of dildo play is that this subversion of the phallus may sometimes slip back into penis envy. Thus, for instance, Robin Sweeney reports:

> There are times I'm shocked when I reach down and I find out I don't have an actual dick. Once I started to cry when we were fucking like this, and Daddy asked me what was wrong. I got angry and told Daddy that I couldn't be a boy if I didn't have a cock, didn't she know that? (99)

So while Williams asserts that "the point of this play with the phallus is . . . neither that the dildo is a penis manqué nor that it is believed in as a substitute for the 'real thing,' but rather the proof that there is no 'real thing' based in biology" ("Pornographies" 256), as subjectivity aligns itself with practice, the "point" of the play with the phallus may not be so easily determined or fixed.

FIVE

Sexuality beyond Gender

Gender Performativity in Lesbian Pornography

Another way in which women's pornography—and lesbian porn in particular—tackles the problem of female sexual subjectivity is by offering a performative understanding of gender. In other words, if sexual subjectivity is incompatible with femininity as it is constructed, one way around this impasse is to demonstrate that women are not bound to femininity and can "do" masculinity just as well. Such an understanding of gender in effect reformulates, perhaps even sidesteps, the question of female sexual subjectivity, since by disrupting the fictitious coherence of sex and gender it severs the link between female embodiment and any particular form of gendered subjectivity.

Before moving on to examine the ways in which pornographic texts construct gender as performative, I will first discuss the notion of performance itself in its multiple contemporary theoretical usages, focusing on the most elaborate and sophisticated theoretical formulation linking gender and performance, Judith Butler's theory of gender performativity.

What Is Performance?

The term "performance" figures as a central concept in an array of contemporary discourses across several disciplines, from performance art and theater studies, to anthropology, sociology, psychology, linguistics, and literary criticism.[1] The signification of the term differs from field to field, as well as from thinker to thinker, but the various concepts are also interrelated, often derived from one another. Broadly speaking, the concepts of performance developed by the social sciences are figuratively derived from the notion of theatrical performance, in other words, the term "performance" serves to highlight those features of social action—such as role playing or the scriptedness of social interactions—that it shares with the theater.[2] Alternatively, such concepts convey the recognition of a continuum between the theater and other social behaviors like rituals, ceremonies, play, and other forms of public behavior.[3] At the same time, with the emergence of performance art in the 1960s, the theatrical notion of performance has been broadened in a way that tends toward eroding the distinction between theater and "normal behavior." Thus, while behavior in general has been explained by means of the theatrical analogy, theater has stretched out toward everyday behavior. And consequently, the distinction between figurative and literal usages of the term "performance" has nearly collapsed.

Since the various notions of performance evince a large degree of resemblance and overlap, it is possible to put together a kind of compounded definition of performance by assembling those elements that figure in several definitions. Such a definition would include the following components: 1. *action* or doing; 2. *repetition* or redoing[4] (which entails either 3 or 4); 3. a preexisting *script* or protocol that guides the action; 4. a notion of *representation* or mimesis, one which implies the binary oppositions: imitation/origin and simulation/reality; 5. an *audience* that receives and interprets the performance; 6. a *"frame"* that marks the performance *as* performance and sets it apart from other activities and from everyday life; (which entails) 7. the actor's *consciousness* that s/he is performing rather than simply behaving and possibly also *agency* of the actor. Minimally, a concept of performance must include action and repetition. As regards the other components, some notions of performance stress the consciousness and agency of the actor, while others privilege the role of the audience, and others still stress the importance of framing. Such privileging of one component may lead in turn to downplaying the role of the other components or leaving them out altogether.

So far, I have not discussed the linguistic notion of performance, which while it falls within the minimal definition of performance I have offered, forms a separate branch, not derived from the figure of the theater. The theory of linguistic performativity developed by J. L. Austin in his book *How to Do Things with Words* distinguishes a certain category of utterances that, though they belong to the indicative mode, do not describe a state of affairs but rather *perform* an action. Some of the examples provided by Austin for such utterances are "I promise," "I bet," and "I do" (in the context of a marriage ceremony). Such utterances he names "performatives," "speech acts," or "illocutions." While Austin begins by defining performatives as a distinct class of utterances with a specific grammatical form, he goes on later in his book to elaborate a more comprehensive understanding of linguistic performativity that recognizes the inherent potential of every utterance to perform an action in the world. This generalized understanding accounts for the many uses and elaborations Austin's notion of performativity has generated, of which Butler's theory of gender performativity is one.

Butler's Theory of Gender Performativity

Judith Butler's theory of gender performativity, which she first outlined in the last section of *Gender Trouble* and went on to explicate, modify, and elaborate in subsequent works, is by now widely disseminated, and the notion of gender performativity has been assimilated into the critical vocabulary of feminist, queer, and cultural studies. And while I believe that there is no need to expound it again here, I would like to explore its relations to the theatrical and linguistic tropes that inform it and to argue for restoring the theatrical frame to the concept of performativity.[5]

The central insight embodied in the notion of gender performativity is that it is not some internal essence that our behavior reflects and expresses; rather it is an illusory effect produced and maintained by acts of signification, both linguistic and corporeal:

> Acts, gestures, and desire produce the effect of an internal core or substance, but produce this *on the surface* of the body, through the play of signifying absences that suggest, but never reveal, the organizing principle of identity as a cause. Such acts, gestures, enactments, generally construed, are *performative* in the sense that the essence or identity that they otherwise purport

to express are *fabrications* manufactured and sustained through corporeal signs and other discursive means. That the gendered body is performative suggests that it has no ontological status apart from the various acts which constitute its reality. (Butler, *Gender Trouble* 136)

Butler's notion of performativity in *Gender Trouble* simultaneously invokes theatrical, sociological anthropological, and linguistic notions of performance. In the preceding quote, the stress on gender as produced through signification, and on the opposition between the ostensible expressive function of signification on the one hand and its actual function of "fabricating," "manufacturing," or "constituting" on the other hand,[6] indicate that the operative sense is that of linguistic performativity. But Butler also invokes the theatrical connotations of "performance" through her stress on bodily acts and gestures, her definition of gender as "a corporeal style" (139), and her use of such terms as "drama"[7] and "parody" (137–138). All these indicate that the theatrical frame is at work as well, even without taking into account the exemplary status Butler accords drag as an instance of gender performativity (and which she later claims to be misleading). Still other formulations make allusion to sociological and anthropological notions of performance.[8]

In the works that follow *Gender Trouble*, Butler elaborates and modifies her notion of gender performativity in a way that downplays or even rejects the theatrical frame in favor of the linguistic frame. Based on Austin's notion of linguistic performativity—but extending it significantly—Butler offers an understanding of gender as produced by acts of signification, both discursive and bodily, that in fact produce what they claim to be "describing" or expressing. The rejection of the theatrical model in favor of the linguistic one came largely in response to a common construal of Butler's argument as claiming that gender can be reduced to gender performance, where the latter is conceived on the model of drag, that is, theatrical performance. Butler attempted to counter this reading by offering an explicit distinction between *performance* and *performativity*, relegating the theatrical connotations to the former while founding the latter on the notion of linguistic performativity, namely, the capacity of discourse to produce what it names. This attempt to purge the theatrical from her concept of performativity appears to stem from the fear that the theatrical trope centralizes the subject, as Butler makes clear in the following passage:

> The misapprehension about gender performativity is this: that gender is a choice or that gender is a role, or that gender is a construction that one puts on, as one puts on clothes in the morning, that there is a "one" who is prior to this gender, a one who goes to the wardrobe of gender and decides with deliberation which gender it will be today. This is a voluntarist account of gender which presumes a subject, intact, prior to its gendering. ("Critically Queer" 21)

Austin's account of linguistic performativity also runs the risk of privileging the subject as the origin of the authoritative speech act, but Butler does not draw on the Austinian notion directly but via Derrida's critique of it, a critique that stresses the *citational* status of the performative utterance.[9] Following Derrida, Butler understands the efficacy of the performative to lie in its citation or reiteration of norms:

> Performance as bounded "act" is distinguished from performativity insofar as the latter consists in a reiteration of norms which precede, constrain, and exceed the performer and in that sense cannot be taken as the fabrication of the performer's "will" or "choice." ("Critically Queer" 24)

The norm's authoritative power is reinforced through the very process of reiteration. In the case of gender, the reiteration fosters the illusion of a stable gender identity and an inner gender core expressed by gender performance; the norm compels constant repetition in order to disguise its workings and naturalize its effects. From the other end, the subject is compelled to cite the gender norms that constitute her/him in order to qualify as a viable subject. Yet this very mechanism of repetition opens the way for resistance, since gender norms can be cited in unauthorized ways that work to undermine their power and expose their regulatory nature. Citation involves both repetition and recontextualization, as what is cited is transplanted from one context to another; therefore, citing the norm has the potential to resignify it.

Such unauthorized repetitions have a twofold function: subversive and productive. The subversive function is to undermine the norm by denaturalizing it and exposing the political constraint that produces the semblance of stable, coherent, and binary genders. The productive function, which figures far less prominently in Butler's texts but is there all the same, is exemplified by the proliferation of gender configurations beyond the binary norm, as well as by the rearticulation of kinship terms to create a system of alternative kinship for those outside the heterosexual family, in her analysis of the film *Paris Is Burning* ("Critically Queer" 28–29).[10] Resignification is not merely a practice of subversion and destabilization; it constructs new subjectivities and forms of sociality. To sum up, the notion of gender performativity accounts both for the efficacy of gender norms and their ability to lend a semblance of ontological solidity to the effects they produce *and* for the innate *inefficacy* of these norms that makes them vulnerable to practices of resignification and enables their subversion.

As we have seen, the distinction Butler introduces between *performance* and *performativity* revolves around the notion of the subject. However, I would like to argue against the theoretical move reflected in this distinction on two counts. First, debunking the humanistic subject does not necessitate banishing the theatrical from the concept of gender performativity; second, this banishment incurs a theoretical cost. As noted in the first section of this chapter, sociological and anthropological notions of performance employ the theatrical model *figuratively*, that is, they highlight those features of social action that it shares with the theater. A figurative use of this kind need not import all the features of the "vehicle" into the "tenor"; therefore, it is possible to base a notion of gender performativity on the theatrical trope without thereby admitting into it the elements of volition, consciousness, or preexisting subjectivity. Such a notion can stress the elements of script, audience, and framing (or context) rather than the agency of the performer. After all, if the notion of linguistic performativity could be adapted in a way that debunks the subject from its position as origin of discourse, why can't a similar adaptation of the theatrical model—one that does not assume an actor who intentionally and consciously plays a role—be possible?

I insist on this point because I believe that there is a loss involved in rejecting the theatrical model. What gets lost is the singular suitability of the theatrical trope for describing the embodied character of gender. Butler suggests that the embodiment of gender norms and the performative use of discourse both "converge as modes of citationality" ("Critically Queer" 22), thus making "citationality," that is, the linguistic trope, into the higher order principle that subsumes and explains gender performance. But understanding gendered acts as speech acts, involves considerable adaptation and reduction, particularly an elision of the dimension of bodily experience, a dimension that the theatrical trope does bring out.

And, indeed, Butler herself does offer precisely such an account of gender performativity based on the theatrical trope in an essay entitled "Performative Acts and Gender Constitution," published shortly before *Gender Trouble*. In this essay, far from taking the theatrical trope to presume a subject, she employs a "theatrically-based" view of acts to criticize the view that sees social agents as constituting social reality (276). Butler, on the other hand, offers an understanding of the social agent as an object of constituting acts and employs the theatrical model to illustrate it:

> The act that one does, the act that one performs, is, in a sense, an act that has been going on before one arrived on the scene. Hence, gender is an act which has been rehearsed, much as a script survives the particular actors who make use of it, but which requires individual actors in order to be actualized and reproduced as reality once again. ("Performative Acts" 277)

The theatrical analogy serves her here to convey the ambiguous position of the gendered subject as neither fully determined nor enjoying radical freedom but rather possessing a limited agency whose scope is figured as the space demarcated between script and interpretation:

> Actors are always already on the stage, within the terms of the performance. Just as a script may be enacted in various ways, and just as the play requires both text and interpretation, so the gendered body acts its part in a culturally restricted corporeal space and enacts interpretations within the confines of already existing directives. (277)[11]

In my discussion of gender performativity in this chapter I will revert back to these earlier formulations by Butler. That is, I will deliberately pause at the moment before she found it necessary to split off performance and performativity and banish the theatrical frame from an understanding of gender. The notion of performativity that I will employ is one that restores to the concept its theatrical dimensions and that hovers productively between theatricality and citationality. This choice reflects the theoretical considerations noted previously, yet it is also motivated by the fact that in the fictional texts I will be discussing, the sense of gender as citational and resignifiable emerges, as we shall see, precisely through the operation of a theatrical frame or a theatrical awareness.

Gender Performativity, Gender-Bending, and the Sexual Arena

Several elements of Butler's theory of gender performativity—the notion of gender as practice and effect rather than essence, the stress on gender codes and gender norms as resignifiable through recontextualization, and the valorization of gender fluidity and plurality—correspond to (and are most likely informed by) the more popular notion of "gender-bending" or "gender fuck," a notion that has enjoyed wide currency in lesbian and queer culture since the 1980s.[12]

Much lesbian and queer porn features and celebrates gender-bending and seems committed to an enterprise of transcending gender or breaking free from its fetters, namely, defying the norm of sex-gender coherence and redefining gender as fluid and multiple rather than stable and binary. Gender-bending is not specific to the sexual arena; it can take place in performance (especially drag and other types of performance informed by drag), in photography (e.g., some of Cindy Sherman's and Del LaGrace's work), or in various subcultural spaces and practices. However, within lesbian and queer culture since the 1980s, sex has been recognized as a privileged site of gender-bending, that is, we find a new stress on and awareness of sex as an arena where gender boundaries can be transgressed, where one may "play" and experiment with cross-gender behaviors and identities.

It is worth noting that though Butler herself does not focus on sexual practice per se as a site of gender performativity,[13] all the examples she provides, both in *Gender Trouble* and in later works, for the subversion and resignification of gender norms involve practices and identities drawn from the queer world, most notably drag and butch/femme identities. So that if we employ a broader understanding of "sexuality" as denoting also identities and cultural practices within sexual subcultures, we can say that Butler does single out nonnormative sexuality as a privileged site of gender resignification. In her 1999 preface to *Gender Trouble* Butler explicitly links queer sexual practices to the subversion of gender:

> The text asks how do non-normative sexual practices compel the question: what is a woman, what is a man? If gender is no longer to be understood as consolidated through normative sexuality, then is there a crisis of gender that is specific to queer contexts? ("Preface," xi)

And in what comes closest to a directive, she concludes the essay "Imitation and Gender Insubordination" with the hypothesis that perhaps the way to expose the performativity of gender is by "working sexuality *against* identity, even against gender . . ." (318). Thus, while Butler on other occasions expresses skepticism concerning the aspiration to transcend gender through sexual practice, she too suggests the notion of queer sex as a privileged site of gender subversion.

Two factors most likely contribute to the emergence of sex as a site of gender play. One is the contemporary tendency to think of sex itself in terms of play. Since the "sexual revolution" of the 1970s, various strands of sexological and libertarian sexual discourse promote a vision of sex as a form of recreation that involves imagination, creativity, and experimentation. The other factor is the recognition of the erotics of gender, that is, our libidinal investment in gender divisions and roles. The latter point is raised by Pat Califia in her 1983 essay "Genderbending: Playing with Roles and Reversals," where she states:

> I have come to the conclusion that this situation [gender polarization] exists because it is eroticized. Strict gender division is so important to the majority of people's sexual pleasure that they want to disguise it as nature or biology, so nothing will threaten to change it. ("Genderbending" 178)

Califia comes curiously close here to Catharine MacKinnon's claims about the eroticization of women's inferiority, but she veers in a different direction, opening a space between eroticized gender polarization and sexism: "There's nothing inherently oppressive about getting off on polarized roles during sex. Butch/femme homosexuals can select the things that are rewarding and gratifying about the male/female gender system and leave behind the ugly aspects of institutionalized inequality" ("Genderbending" 179).

As this quote signals, in contemporary lesbian culture the emergence of the notion of sex as a site of gender play is closely related to the reclamation and political rehabilitation of butch-femme roles that took place in the 1980s and 1990s. Significantly, in their fin-de-siècle version, butch and femme appeared more as styles and less as essentialized identities and figured primarily in erotic contexts.[14] The revalorization of butch-femme entailed both recognition of the erotics of gender and recognition of the progressive political implications of these identities or styles as instances of destabilizing/resignifying (or, in more common parlance, "bending") gender. It is these political implications that Judith Butler affirms when she names butch and femme "parodic identities," that is, identities that reveal the imitative structure of gender itself. And in a similar vein, Sue-Ellen Case upholds butch and femme roles as providing an alternative compound subject position for women, "lending agency and self-determination to the historically passive [female] subject [by] providing her with at least two options for gender identification and with the aid of camp, an irony that allows her perception to be constructed from outside ideology" ("Toward" 292).

How Gender Is Bent: Gender Performativity in Lesbian Pornography

As noted, gender-bending is a prominent theme in contemporary lesbian pornography. For lack of any authoritative definition, I will define gender-bending as involving three components:

- Cross-gender performance—in our case, performances of masculinity, either straight or gay—by biological women. Such performances work also to denaturalize performances of femininity either by the same persons or by their partners.
- A sense of performance or "play," that is, consciousness of performing for an audience (be it only one's partner or oneself) and/or a sense of assuming a role or acting according to a script.
- A sense of transgression or liberation vis-à-vis the gender system and one's assigned place in it.

Cross-gender performance is crucial to the very notion of gender-bending, as it undermines the norm of sex-gender coherence and its illusion of naturalness. Some index or awareness of the performative dimension is necessary in order to avoid a construction of the performance as the natural expression or extension of a given gendered essence (I am referring here to the two elements of the general definition of performance suggested earlier that I have termed "frame," that which marks the performance as performance and sets it apart from other behaviors and from everyday life, and "consciousness," the actor's consciousness of performing rather than simply behaving). The transgressive or liberatory impetus marks both the motivation for and the significance of gender-bending as an implicitly political project.

Works of erotic fiction depict—and eroticize—gender-bending within the context of a sexual exchange. Pat Califia prefaces her theoretical discussion of gender-bending in the piece cited earlier with a first-person narrative of purchasing male garments, getting into male drag (strap-on dildo, jockstrap, chaps, and leather jacket) in front of the mirror, and having sex with a woman partner in this attire. Her leatherman drag is described as an erotic turn-on for both her partner and herself, and she remains in her male role throughout the sexual interaction. The process of donning male attire is described as producing a concomitant change of consciousness: "I don't feel like a woman anymore." This temporary change of gender identity is first and foremost a change of body image; as Califia says, "The [bodily] semiotics have shifted." The dildo becomes a cock, and even the long hair "doesn't mean femme; it means hippie biker" ("Genderbending" 175).

While the cross-gender performance Califia describes is voluntary and deliberate, this does not undermine the authenticity of the psychic transformation. Further, this performance does not necessarily fall under the voluntarist account of gender rejected by Butler, where a subject "goes to the wardrobe of gender and decides with deliberation which gender it will be today" ("Critically Queer" 21), because the fact that Califia can temporarily "put on" masculinity does not entail that other gender performances are equally available to her, and that this (albeit cross-gendered) performance is not in some way culturally or psychically determined.

The sense of transgression and liberation that attends gender-bending is prominent in Califia's account. Interestingly, the transgressiveness is underscored in relation to the most innocent of the series of acts depicted, which, however, takes place in the public sphere involving the gaze of the outside world, the act of purchasing a jockstrap. Califia does, nevertheless, mention the transgressiveness of usurping the (presumably sexual) pleasures of masculinity that have been denied her as a woman.

Significantly, Califia's cross-gendered performance—like any gender performance for that matter—requires a validating audience, whether this audience is her sexual partner or even her own self in front of the mirror, acting as performer and appreciative audience simultaneously.[15] Finally, Califia stresses the fluidity of her gender performance and the contingence of her gender play with her partner. She notes that in the next encounter the sexual roles (top/bottom) will probably be reversed, and with them presumably the gender roles (she will be a "slut" and her partner the one with the cock), and that she and her partner can also interact sexually as two men as well as two women. This fluidity again underscores the performative dimension; the availability of different roles and different scripts reactivates the theatrical trope.

S/M and Performance

In lesbian pornography, gender-bending often takes place in the context of s/m eroticism. This is hardly surprising in view of the theatrical structure of s/m. Most discussions of s/m, whether by practitioners or cultural commentators, invoke the theatrical trope.[16] Thus, Pat Califia in an essay that forms an early contribution to the feminist debate on lesbian s/m, states: "The key word to understanding S/M is fantasy. The roles, dialogues, fetish costumes, and sexual activity are part of a drama or ritual." And similarly: "The S/M subculture is a theater in which sexual dramas can be acted out and appreciated" ("Feminism and Sadomasochism" 168). These descriptions convey an understanding of s/m as involving a structure of representation, a performative doubling. To go back to the definition of performance that I have elaborated in the beginning of this chapter, we can see that all its components are present in s/m eroticism. The fantasy, stressed by Califia, functions as a preexisting *script* that shapes all aspects of the interaction: the roles, costumes, dialogues, and sexual activity. In addition, both the interaction (the s/m scene) and the phantasmatic script it enacts are *representations*, in the sense that they draw on, imitate, or re-present—usually in a hyperbolic mode—various social power relations or situations that emblematize such relations. However, it would be more accurate to understand s/m as an intertextual practice that draws on cultural topoi rather than as a direct representation of social experience.

The *audience* in s/m, unless the interaction takes place in a public play space, is often restricted to the performers themselves.[17] In this s/m resembles children's play more than theater proper, the performance taking place not for the benefit of an outside audience but for the performers' pleasure alone. Yet the participants do indeed function as audience for one another, in the sense that they evaluate and appreciate one another's performance, and that the performance of each is responsible for creating and maintaining a space of suggestion for the other. The interaction is usually very clearly *framed* by means of a contract or a preliminary negotiation that sets its boundaries both in temporal and spatial terms and in terms of the range of activities that the interaction may include. The transition into and out of play mode is often signaled by verbal or nonverbal cues or change of costume. The highly stylized and scripted nature of the interaction clearly sets it off from ordinary behavior.

Consciousness of performing is also clearly involved in s/m. As Lynda Hart asserts, lesbian sadomasochistic practices enact what performance theorist Herbert Blau terms the first "universal" of performance, that is, the consciousness of performance. Paraphrasing Blau, she explains: "Although all 'acts' are performances, in a performative act the participants must be aware of themselves as actors in the very moment that they are performing" (Hart 151). Hart goes on to fine-tune this observation, noting that all performance vacillates between forgetting and remembering oneself, and further, that there is something "in between forgetting and remembering that haunts all performance." As for the type of consciousness at stake in s/m, she observes that "the s/m performer takes up a position in relation to her 'self' and the role she plays that is much more akin to the Brechtian gestus [than to the realistic acting method]" (151).

S/m is also performance oriented in another sense that my discussion so far has omitted, that is to say, in the sense of performance as execution or accomplishment. S/m players, whether acting as top or bottom, share an ethos of performance that entails a commitment to excellence in their respective roles: the top is expected to control the interaction, take responsibility for the bottom's well-being and pleasure, and lead her to respond; the bottom is expected to be able to "take" what is meted out to her but also to know her own limits. Their performance is evaluated, both by themselves and by the other players or observers, not only in terms of its mimetic quality but also against a standard of perfection. Of course, the striving toward excellence, and the constant evaluation of performance, foster an awareness of the roles *as* roles rather than as a natural expression of an essential self, so in this way, the two senses of performance do converge.

As demonstrated by Califia's essay, in the context of the feminist debate on s/m the theatrical trope has often been invoked in response to accusations that s/m is a form of violence and oppression. Califia not only stresses the imitative character of s/m, the electiveness of the roles, and the distance between the player and the persona she assumes, she also takes care to clarify that the performers' investment in the performance does not imply uncritical identification with the role and the script by characterizing the performance as parodic: "S/M is more a parody of the hidden sexual nature of fascism than it is a worship of or acquiescence to it" ("Feminism and Sadomasochism" 170). This latter assertion has been a frequent point of contention. Thus, for example, Tania Modleski, who undertakes a political assessment of s/m practice on the basis of her reading of *Coming to Power*, the first anthology on lesbian s/m, comments that "in the actual s/m rituals described in the anthology playfulness and parody seem to be entirely lacking, perhaps because, as Bersani notes, parody is an erotic turn-off" (Modleski 154).

Modleski is correct in her observation that s/m play usually takes itself very seriously and has to in order for the interaction to be erotically effective. Yet she seems to miss the sense in which Califia, and other defenders of s/m, employ the term "parody." This sense resembles Butler's (subsequent) usage of the term, when she speaks of drag and butch-femme as "parodic identities" (*Gender Trouble* 137). Butler characterizes this type of parody as a humorless one, more akin to Fredric Jameson's definition of pastiche as "blank parody, parody that has lost its humor" (138). Her notion of parody refers to an imitation that is neither intentionally parodic nor necessarily perceived as such by those who perform it. It is parodic because its very existence works to denaturalize hegemonic identities and exposes their contingency:

> Parodic proliferation deprives hegemonic culture and its critics of the claim to naturalized or essentialist gender identities. Although the gender meanings taken up in these parodic styles are clearly part of hegemonic, misogynist culture, they are nevertheless denaturalized and mobilized through their parodic

recontextualization. As imitations which effectively displace the meaning of the original, they imitate the myth of originality itself. (138)

These formulations suggest that in Butler's account the parodic function is structural, independent of either intention or reception. The very occurrence of unauthorized repetition, repetition outside the bounds stipulated by hegemonic gender norms, functions as parodic commentary on the norms themselves, especially on their claim to naturalness. Reception comes back into the picture when Butler addresses the question of what makes a parody subversive. In order to have a subversive effect, a performance needs to be recognized as parodic, hence, its subversiveness depends on context and reception and is therefore always contingent and difficult to calculate.[18]

To go back to the subject of s/m, though s/m play may be neither motivated by a satirical intent nor characterized by lightness and playfulness, it is parodic in that the power exerted by the top over the bottom does not reflect real-life privileges, hierarchies, or power differentials. S/m imitates relations of domination or force—gendered, racial, parental, institutional, and so on—where no such relations obtain. Even in those cases where s/m roles do reflect and refer to actual status or power differentials between the participants (e.g., a white top and a black bottom, or a male top and a female bottom), the hyperbolic character of s/m involves an accentuation and exaggeration of the hierarchy in a way that far exceeds its socially acceptable manifestations in everyday life, hence, works to denaturalize social power.[19] As in Butler's example of the drag queen whose exemplary performance of femininity denaturalizes gender and highlights its imitative structure, s/m play underscores the performative dimension of all social roles and denaturalizes the power vested in them. Like drag or butch/femme styles, s/m is an instance of unauthorized performativity.[20] And like drag or butch/femme, it is often criticized as either trivializing what it imitates (real women in the case of drag, real oppression in the case of s/m) or as an envious imitation that idealizes its object (heterosexual relationships in the case of butch-femme, actual domination in the case of s/m).

The latter charge is made by Leo Bersani, who—contrary to Califia's assertion that s/m is *not* a worship of or acquiescence to fascism—claims that s/m reveals "the continuity between political structures of oppression and the body's erotic economy," and that "if bondage, discipline, and pain are such extraordinary sources of pleasure, very few people will be willing to limit the enjoyment of that pleasure to weekend parties" (Bersani, *Homos* 90, 91). The problem with this claim is that it seems oblivious to the possibility that the pleasure of play, even highly erotically cathected play like s/m, might hinge precisely upon its status *as* play; and far from being enhanced, such pleasure might altogether vanish were the same practice to take place outside the realm of "play." While Bersani's criticism assumes that s/m play aspires to approximate reality and threatens to spill over into it, another prevalent critique faults s/m precisely for its lack of "realness." As a structured interaction observing an elaborate protocol, s/m is found lacking when sex is evaluated according to a standard of authenticity and spontaneity. Thus, s/m is condemned either for being too theatrical or for not being theatrical enough.[21]

As Lynda Hart observes, the distinction between performance and reality is at the crux of the feminist controversies over lesbian s/m. Hart contends that it is not so much the issue of violence that triggers the controversy as it is the ambiguity between the real and the performed that characterizes s/m practice and on which its eroticism depends (149). Yet, as she points out, this controversy relies on an untenably naive notion of representation:

> To a certain extent, the controversy about whether s/m is "real" or performative is naive, since we are always already in representation even when we are enacting our seemingly most private fantasies. The extent to which we recognize the presence of the edge of the stage may determine what kind of performance we are enacting, but willing ourselves to forget the stage altogether is not to return to the real, as s/m opponents would have it; rather, this will to forget is classical mimesis, which, as Derrida points out, is "the most naive form of representation." (91)

In its theatricality, s/m underscores the performative dimension of all sexuality, thus admitting and making explicit what "straight sex" (Hart's term for all "sexual acts that claim to being unmediated by culture and ideology") disavows (148). As Hart observes, the performative dimension is foregrounded by s/m terminology itself—the notion of "doing" a scene as opposed to the notion of "having" sex. While the latter assumes that there is such a thing as "sex" and that it preexists the performance, the former assumes that sex is made in and through the performance.

Yet, the "real" is not banished altogether from Hart's account. On the contrary, she assigns it a central place in s/m practice but as the object of an impossible yearning, as the "impossible-real." This yearning to break through to the "real" is what motivates the attempt to push the bottom's limits to the breaking point. And, as Hart asserts, it is on the anticipation "that the 'scene' will cross over into the 'real'" in this way that its eroticism depends (91). Thus, while s/m highlights the performative or representational quality of all experience, it is also "a performance that yearns for an experience that is beyond the closure of representation, and it seeks that beyond through the apparently paradoxical method of discipline, regulation, prescription" (159). Hart's position, then, undermines the real/performance binary, in which critiques such as those of Bersani and Modleski are grounded, while admitting the constitutive role that the *desire* for the "real" plays in s/m eroticism.

In view of the highly performative character of s/m that I have outlined here, it is no coincidence that most instances of gender bending in lesbian pornography are lodged in an s/m context. Within the field of s/m, gender is one more erotically charged role, one more vector of play. And since play identities do not observe any simple correspondence with everyday ones, s/m facilitates, even encourages, gender-crossing. This is true primarily of lesbian s/m. In the straight s/m subculture gender-crossing seems to be far more marginal and consists usually of feminizing the male bottom (e.g., by "forced" cross-dressing) rather than masculinizing the female top,[22] whereas gay male leather culture tends, as I have previously noted, to establish a universal standard of masculinity for both tops and bottoms. Both straight and gay male s/m "bend" the gender system in the sense that they contest the equation of domination with masculinity and submission with femininity: straight s/m makes it possible to combine femininity and domination, and gay male s/m recodes submission as masculine. Yet, beyond the resignification of power and powerlessness, both tend to be invested in an essentialist notion of gender.

We can see, then, that while s/m provides an apparatus that is congenial to practices of gender bending and, correspondingly, to a performative conception of gender—Jacob Hale even refers to s/m as "gender technology" (228)—it is only within the arena of lesbian or queer s/m that this potential is significantly explored. That this is so makes sense in view of the quest of lesbian sex culture to articulate a female sexual subject position. One way to dispel the equation of femaleness with lack of sexual subjectivity is to define femininity (as Butler does) as a forced performance and to highlight the performativity of gender, especially in the sexual arena. And since s/m play underscores the performative dimension of all social roles and denaturalizes the power vested in them, it provides a particularly suitable apparatus both for denaturalizing gender hierarchy and for exposing—and making use of—the performativity of gender itself.

Further, s/m roles, "top" and "bottom," can be read as both allegorizing the gender division (though, as previously noted, gender is not their only model) and substituting for it, thus making it redundant. This latter line is the one Parveen Adams takes in her essay "Of Female Bondage" when she states that "the lesbian sadomasochist has separated sexuality from gender and is able to enact differences in the theatre where roles freely circulate" (264). If, as Gayle Rubin notes, in normative sex the only roles allowed are "man" and "woman" ("Thinking Sex" 14),[23] the "theater" of s/m substitutes for gender difference a variety of roles and axes of difference. And in the context of lesbian s/m, where no physiological "sexual difference" can purport to structure the sexual encounter, those other differences—differences not claiming any ontological solidity or embodied authority—take its place.

The Leather Daddy and the Femme

One of the prominent forms of gender-bending in lesbian erotic fiction, mostly of the s/m variety, is daddy-boy (or daddy-girl) play. Daddy-boy as a fantasy and a type of role-play is inherited from the gay male leather culture, where it substitutes a manhood initiation model for a master-slave model. Yet while, in the gay male context, the roles are congruous with the assigned gender of the participants and work to reconcile same-sex desire with an ethos of masculinity, once they are imported to an all-female context, they are ipso facto resignified, and their primary signification becomes that of gender-crossing. Even the lesbian variation of daddy-girl play transgenders at least one of the participants.

In a story entitled "Daddy," Pat Califia depicts first an s/m scene with the narrator as "little girl" and her partner as "daddy" and then, switching roles, a scene in which the narrator is "daddy" and her partner is in the role of "boy." The collection *Doing It for Daddy*, edited by Califia and containing stories by both lesbians and gay men, is wholly dedicated to the topos of daddy-boy/girl. This collection features two chapters from Carol Queen's erotic novel *The Leather Daddy and the Femme*. Though *Leather Daddy* ventures beyond the realm of strictly *lesbian* erotica, taking the daddy-boy topos to the terrain of cross-gender queer sexual exchange,[24] it is nevertheless located on the perimeter of the field of lesbian erotic writing and furnishes one of the best examples of gender-bending or gender performativity in this field. (The blurb on the front cover hails it as "an erotic classic for the gender revolution.")[25]

Leather Daddy plays for the first couple of pages on the ambiguous gender of its protagonist Randy/Miranda. Her female identity is disclosed to the reader only shortly before it is discovered by Jack, the leather daddy she has picked up on the street by masquerading as a gay boy. Her queerness, however, is established regardless of her gender by reference to the Act-Up and Queer Nation stickers on her leather jacket.[26] The initial ambiguity of her gender signals the complexity of her gender and sexual identity. In an anthologized version of one of the chapters, Randy is introduced as "a bisexual cross-dressing femme switch with a taste for leather daddies" ("Ganged" 38). "Femme," a category of lesbian gender, which traditionally referred to both dress, mannerism, erotic preference (for butches), and sexual behavior,[27] is found here in highly unorthodox contiguity with other categories of gay nomenclature, like "cross-dressing" (in this context, wearing male drag), "switch" (i.e., switching between the sexual roles of top and bottom), and "leather daddy" (the top in a gay male s/m relationship premised on age difference and based on an initiation model rather than a master-slave model). Randy's identity is so plural that it can only be described through an act of linguistic hybridization, bringing together categories that are seemingly incongruous and losing their definitional purity in the process.[28]

Randy is looking for a playmate who would embrace all aspects of her complex gender and sexuality, and in Jack she finds one: After having sex with him as a boy, when she finds him undeterred by her femaleness, she switches to femme drag and has sex with him as a woman, while the next morning she straps on her dildo and fucks him. Randy's initial cross-gendered performance, her boy performance, which disrupts the fictitious coherence between her gender and her biological sex, functions also to denaturalize her subsequent feminine performance. And as though to assure us that the performative frame is still in place even when Randy switches to a gender role that *is* congruent with her biological sex, she introduces her transformation from "boy" to "femme" by saying to Jack, "I want to play a new game" (5). "Femme" and "boy" are equally performative, a fact underscored by Jack talking about her "boy drag" (4) and Randy's narrative voice describing putting on her feminine persona as "getting femmed out" (6).

Randy's gender performance is represented as voluntary to a large degree but not wholly so. Thus, while she often deliberately takes on the appearance of a boy in order to cruise gay men, in the opening episode of the novel she is not purposely masquerading as a boy but rather mistaken for one (her boyish appearance elicits a look of interest from Jack when her car stops next to his motorcycle at the traffic light), a mistake she capitalizes on. Her gender presentation is also represented as the outward manifestation of an inner quality or "energy" that though transient rather than stable (as gender identity is supposed to be) is nevertheless authentic, for example: "When boy energy gets into me I look like an effete young Cambridge faggot looking to go bad" (1). Her gender performances might even be construed as manifesting two aspects of an essential self. Thus, Randy phrases her problem as that of expressing, and gaining recognition of, such a double self: "I love being a boy, but I don't like having to be two separate people to get what I want. I really want the men I fuck to turn me over and see *the whole me*: the woman in the boy, the boy in the woman" (5, my emphasis).

On the other hand, these "selves" are depicted in purely performative terms, in expressions such as "boy-drag" or getting "femmed out." Randy transforms from one self to another through change of clothes and makeup, and the appropriate psychological attributes soon follow upon the apparel in what could be seen as an almost parodic demonstration of Butlerian insights: "I get so very narcissistic when I'm femmed out," she reports (6). Her self-image, in both her femme and boy incarnations, is self-consciously mediated through cultural imagery—and particularly through gay cultural imagery—whether it is the "adventurous gay boy in a South-of-Market alley" (3) she fantasizes herself to be, or the "*Vogue* model who'd stumbled into a Tom of Finland painting," or the way that in her femme incarnation she pronounces the word "Daddy," "lush with irony, like a '40s burlesque queen" (6). In this sense, Randy's gender is, to use Butler's term, entirely parodic, "an imitation without an origin" (*Gender Trouble* 138). Neither ensuing from her biological sex, nor necessarily in conflict with it, her gender performances are repetitions of what are already cultural clichés, repetitions that open them to recontextualization and resignification. Moreover, as we have seen, the very gender categories operative in the novel are not the heterosexual ones (man/woman) but rather categories of queer gender, such as femme, boy, and daddy. In other words, these are already categories that cite and parody hegemonic gender categories, that is, whose performativity is underscored from the outset.

The link between the gender play and the sexual interaction that provides its setting is explained by the erotics of gender. To paraphrase Pat Califia quoted earlier, gender is sexy, and gender play forms a kind of foreplay to sex or enhances sexual play. Thus, Randy in her transformation to femme is turned on by her own reflection in the mirror ("I wanted to reach for my image in the mirror, take her apart and fuck her"). She is also turned on by Jack's embodiment of gay hypermasculinity of the Tom-of-Finland kind: "He was every bit the spectacle I was, body modified and presented to evoke heat, to attract sex" (6).[29] Gender presentation and gender roles function as props in the game of sex, and the construction of sex as "play"—"Do you still want to play?" asks Randy after her transformation—facilitates an understanding of gender in similar terms: "I want to play a new game," she declares to Jack before switching genders. On the other hand, while gender performance acts as a sexual turn-on, sex itself functions as a means of going beyond gender altogether: on their first night, after they both orgasm, Randy and Jack are described lying together "in a tangle of sweaty limbs, not man and woman, just animals, two sated animals" (9). Sex transports them to a place beyond gender, and since, as Butler reminds us, there is no [human] subject position outside gender, this transcendence of gender is aptly figured as a departure from the realm of the human.

Another interesting point is that the correlation between gender role and sexual practice is far from obvious and predictable. When asked by Jack what her name is, Randy answers that the one he picked up (the cock-sucking boy) is Randy, and the one he fucked (the femme) is Miranda. But as Randy notes to herself while fucking Jack—who maintains his virile identity throughout—he is submitting to her in just the same way she has submitted to him, a fact that destabilizes the notion of binary, gender-determined sexual roles ("Fuck sex differences, fuck 'men are . . .' and 'women are . . .'" she exclaims, 18). There is also the question of which of her gendered personas is the one that fucks him, a question that the text leaves undecided, since neither her appearance (naked with a strap-on dildo) nor her interior monologue provide clear-cut indications; her gender identifications during the act seem multiple and complex.

The radical potential of daddy-boy play between biological women is underscored by C. Jacob Hale in his groundbreaking article "Leatherdyke Boys and Their Daddies: How to Have Sex without Women or Men." In it Hale explores "how leatherdyke genderplay functions as a means of gender interrogation, solidification, resistance, destabilization and reconfiguration" and suggests a notion of "multiple, context-specific, and purpose-specific gendered statuses" (223). According to this notion, it is misguided to assume that "a person has a unitary gender status across cultures with varying gender categories . . . even if some of the cultures in question are subcultures" (232). Thus, when two biological women engage in daddy-boy play in which they intelligibly and convincingly perform masculinity for each other in accordance with community gender codes, they form a "culture of two" within whose bounds their status *is* male. Hale describes his own experience of participating in such a "culture":

> When I was a boy with my dyke daddy, in that culture of two I was a boy. I was not an adult woman playing a boy's role or playing a boy, nor was I an adult woman doing boy in some other way. Daddy's participation was necessary for me to be a boy with her. I was a boy with her by engaging in a gender performativity that made sense to both of us as a *boy's* gender performativity. (229)

Hale reinforces the ontological solidity of such performativity by describing the ways in which boy-daddy play "can facilitate female-to-male transitioning paths" through providing a kind of laboratory situation for exploring various forms of masculinity (226). The radical thrust of his argument lies in the fact that for him, a leatherdyke boy's performativity in the context of daddy-boy s/m play and an ftm transsexual's gender performativity in a broader social context are different only in their scope of enactment, not in essence.[30] In this sense, Hale's argument undermines the distinction between gender play and gender reality along the lines charted by Butler's theory. Yet, in contradistinction to Butler, Hale's account does not pit performativity against identity and does not posit the subversion of identity as an ultimate goal. Rather, it offers a more complex understanding of gender identity as multiple and situational and stresses the function of performativity in reconfiguring and solidifying gender identity.

Gender Performativity and Sexual Subjectivity

How does the performative understanding of gender address the problem of female sexual subjectivity? If femininity has been constructed as antithetical to sexual subjectivity, performativity—by denaturalizing gender and unveiling the fictitiousness of sex-gender coherence—"frees" women from compulsory femininity, thus removing the barrier to sexual subjectivity. Moreover, texts such as *Leather Daddy* that feature gender performativity *within the sexual arena* offer a vision of sexuality not constrained by either sexual or gender identity. This vision partakes in the new queer cultural formation, where sexuality is queered by flouting any identitarian norms—hetero- or homonormative—and queer identity is performed precisely through the defiance of these norms in the sphere of sexuality (as in other spheres).

In this sense, as I noted in the beginning of this chapter, a performative understanding of gender displaces the whole problematic of female sexual subjectivity. Since the theory of gender performativity is opposed to any notion of "*the* female subject," it is also incompatible with any substantive and monolithic notion of female sexual subjectivity. From a performative perspective, there is no necessary correspondence between female embodiment and any particular form of gendered subjectivity, hence, one cannot speak of female sexual subjectivity, only of multiple and contingent configurations of sexual subjectivity for women. Furthermore, for Butler, the notion of gender performativity entails a conceptual shift from interiority to surface significations so that, insofar as subjectivity remains an operative term, it is defined as an effect of signification. In fact, the very notion of sexual subjectivity might be problematized and resisted as a regulatory ideal, as indeed it is by Foucault, whose critique of the subject informs Butler's theory.

And yet, a notion of sexual subjectivity can be compatible with the performative perspective, if we conceive of it not as a "thing" to be acquired but as a norm that is open to resignification and recontextualization. In fact, the very phrase "*female* sexual subjectivity" already implies a resignification of the term "sexual subjectivity" through its juxtaposition to and qualification by the adjective "female." Performativity casts the question of female sexual subjectivity in terms of signifying practices (i.e., representations whether public or internal); hence, it directs our attention to the discursive norms that either facilitate or bar being constructed as a sexual subject, as well as to practices that reinscribe these norms. With sexual subjectivity understood as a surface effect of signifying practices, we are back at the question of what representational and phantasmatic strategies can produce effects of sexual subjectivity for women.

Performativity and Its Pitfalls

So far we have noted how lesbian pornography, especially of the s/m variety, constructs gender as performative as part of an implicit project of transcending or breaking free from gender. However, this very enterprise, especially as it relates to "queer" as a nongendered identity category, has come under feminist critique. Thus, Butler in "Critically Queer" poses a number of poignant questions concerning the viability of the very project of transcending gender *through* sexuality:

> If we seek to privilege sexual practice as a way of transcending gender, we might ask, at what cost is the analytic separability of the two domains taken to be a distinction in fact? Is there perhaps a specific gender pain that provokes such fantasies of a sexual practice that would transcend gender difference altogether, in which the marks of masculinity and femininity would no longer be legible? Would this not be a sexual practice paradigmatically fetishistic, trying not to know what it knows but knowing it all the same? (27)

Biddy Martin, too, expresses concern regarding the stress laid by queer theory (she addresses Eve Sedgwick's work in particular) on the distinction between gender and sexuality, thus making sexuality "seem strangely exempt from the enmeshments and constraints of gender" ("Sexualities without Genders" 16). But Martin extends her critique to warn against the implicit tendency she finds in much queer work of equating gender with femininity and sexuality with masculinity, an equation which, added to the tendency to conceive gender "in terms of fixity, miring, or subjection to the indicatively female body," makes the masculine position the emblem of mobility and advocates cross-identification as the truly liberating strategy for women (13):

> The result is that lesbians, or women in general, become interesting by making a cross-gender identification or an identification with sexuality, now implicitly (though I think not intentionally) associated with men, over against gender and, by extension, feminism and women. (16)

In other words, the association of gender with women and the association of sexuality with men are culturally overdetermined. Hence, for women to attempt to transcend gender through sexuality implies, ipso facto, making an identification with masculinity or with men. From this perspective, gender-crossing is not an achievement but a capitulation; it is not subversive or liberating but forms rather an overdetermined choice for women and might even involve an antifeminist stance.

It is possible to dismiss Martin's critique as yet another version of the cultural feminist notions of woman identification and male identification, which conflate gender identification with political allegiance to one's own or the opposite gender group. Yet, Martin does not condemn cross-identification as such but rather calls attention to its construal as the only liberating choice for women and deplores the fact that antideterminist accounts of gender "depend on the visible difference represented by cross-gender identifications to represent the mobility and differentiation that 'the feminine' and 'the femme' supposedly cannot" (13). In a sense, Martin's complaint about the reliance on visible differences touches precisely on the inability to separate performativity from performance. The notion of gender performativity (or the antideterminist account of gender, in Martin's words) depends on the ability to render the "performed" nature of gender (i.e., gender as a role or compulsory social performance) visible. And its performed nature can be made visible only through defamiliarization, as in Butler's example of the drag queen's imitation of femininity, which makes us aware of the imitative structure of gender itself, hence, the privileging of cross-gender performance. In other words, Martin's critique demonstrates that Butler's attempt to distinguish between performativity and performance, and to cleanse performativity of any theatrical associations, is impracticable.

However, while the privileging of cross-gendered formations and manifestations is accounted for by the need to render performativity visible, this does not undercut the force of Martin's argument concerning the equation of gender with femininity and sexuality with masculinity, hence, the quest to transcend gender as tantamount to a flight from femininity and the attempt to do so through sexuality as ineluctably entailing an identification with masculinity. This line of thinking and its implications will be explored further in the next chapter.

The notion of gender performativity and the equation that emerged between performativity and gender-crossing has also come under attack from a different quarter, namely, transgender scholars and activists. Jay Prosser offers the most developed and forceful version of this critique in the first chapter of his book *Second Skins: The Body Narratives of Transsexuality*. Based on readings of several queer theorists, most notably Butler and Sedgwick, Prosser argues for the existence of an implicit symbolic equation between transgender, performativity, and queer. He argues that "queer studies can be seen to have been crucially dependent on the figure of transgender," since the trope of crossing that is central to "queer" as theory, but also I would add as identity, is often "impacted with if not explicitly illustrated by the transgendered subject's crossing" (21). Queer theory, he claims, has idealized transgender as a queer transgressive and destabilizing force, in effect turning transgender into "a kind of archetypal queer gender" (30). Prosser is troubled by such an appropriation of transgender since it ignores—or worse, brands as politically regressive—those transgendered subjects who are not queer, notably transsexuals, and fails to account for the transsexual desire for sexed embodiment as *telos*. While Martin worries about the queer privileging of gender-crossing on account of its implications for "femininity played straight," meaning, its reinforcement of the association of cisgendered femininity with fixity and constraint, Prosser objects to it on account of the appropriation of transgender as a figure for gender performativity, an appropriation which disregards the investment many transgendered subjects have in the sexed body and in a stable bodily "home." This latter critique is less pertinent to the question of female sexual subjectivity, but it corroborates Martin's description of the symbolic nexus of "queer," performativity, and gender-crossing and lays the ground for the discussion in the next chapter of the resignification of gender-crossing in the queer world in the wake of the transgender movement.

SIX

Female Sexual Subjectivity in a Queer World

In this chapter, I would like to examine how some of the phantasmatic strategies I have identified, especially cross-identification with gay male masculinity, the resignification of sexual receptivity, and the performative understanding of gender enacted through gender-bending, have continued to play out in the context of two cultural and political processes: the growing currency of "queer" as an overarching identity category that women have increasingly aligned themselves with and the rise of the transgender movement and especially the increased presence and cultural visibility of transmen. To do that, I will look at two cultural phenomena in the sphere of sexual representation: the topos of cross-gender queer sex in literary fiction and transgender porn, both textual and visual.

Cross-Gender Queer Sex and the Limits of Resignification

In my previous reading of *The Leather Daddy and the Femme*, I have treated the text simply as an exemplary instance of gender-bending within the orbit of lesbian erotica without problematizing the aspect of cross-gender eroticism. I would now like to take another look at *Leather Daddy*, together with two other works constructed around the topos of cross-gender queer sex (i.e., sex between women attracted to women and men attracted to men within the queer arena),[1] and to examine this topos as indicative of the vicissitudes of the quest to articulate female sexual subjectivity in lesbian pornography.[2]

In a sense, the topos of cross-gender queer sex is a direct and logical extension of the gender-bending trend in lesbian porn and especially of the proliferation of daddy-boy fantasies. If two women can have sex *as* gay men, there seems to be no reason why a woman shouldn't have sex *as* a gay man *with* an actual gay man. Moreover, such a configuration seems like the ultimate proof of the performativity of gender, a proof that even in the realm of sex, where of all gendered interactions the body plays the most central role, gender is, ultimately, not determined by the sexed body. Cross-gender queer sex seems to make the point more emphatically than lesbian daddy-boy play, since it radically blurs the distinction between gender play and "normal" gender performance. The gay man and the dyke-boy interacting as daddy and boy are both self-consciously performing according to a pre-set script *and at the same time* enacting their authentic gender identities; and the mutuality of the performance works to place the two performances of masculinity on par ontologically, despite their differential access to a corporeal "ground."

As a fictional topos, cross-gender queer sex appears then to offer a utopian vision of a sexuality that transcends (assigned) gender and of gender as autonomous of bodily sex. It is worthwhile, therefore, to look more closely at its textual manifestations in order to see to what extent this utopian promise is actually delivered on. Beside *Leather Daddy*, I will examine here two other texts, Pat Califia's "The Surprise Party" and Helen Sandler's *Big Deal*. Looking together at these three texts, whose publication dates span a period of a little over a decade, reveals the changes that took place along that time period both in the formulation of female masculinity and in the manner in which affinities between women and men under the aegis of queerdom are conceived.

"The Surprise Party," published in 1988, is probably the first story to introduce the theme of cross-gender queer sex. The plot depicts an s/m scene on the theme of police arrest between a butch s/m dyke and three gay leathermen who, masquerading as cops, "abduct" and "rape" her. The text is constructed around a slippage in the ontological status of the fictional reality: while at first the protagonist appears to have fallen prey to sexual harassment by homophobic policemen, by the end of the story it turns out that their leader is a "good buddy" of hers, and that the whole encounter has been "a surprise party for [her] birthday." As the plot unfolds, more and more cues invite the reader to interpret the interaction in terms of s/m rather than violence.

Unlike *Leather Daddy*, in "The Surprise Party" the reality of gender difference, accentuated by the same-sex preference of both parties, is a central concern of the text.[3] Beyond the standard s/m themes of humiliation and submission, the story depicts a process of mutual exploration of this core difference, which is described primarily in corporeal terms:

> Their nearly-naked bodies were alien to her. Their lips were too flat, shoulders too broad, nipples too small and flat, their muscles came in long plates, and they were covered with fur everywhere.... They even smelled strange—had a tang about them that women did not. (229)

To this essential physical foreignness is added the incompatibility in sexual practice and expertise, which gives rise to performance anxieties:

> He could get good head everywhere. She knew she hadn't enough practice to be as good as the boys who went to the glory holes, fell to their knees, and stayed there for hours, taking eight inches and more down their throats until dawn. (219)

What enables the characters to bridge this gap is the common language of s/m, which provides a shared system of signs and norms, within whose framework gay men and lesbians can communicate sexually. Bodies and practices are immediately translated to symbolic terms, and it is on this symbolic terrain that the encounter takes place. The fact that a process of abstraction and symbolization is constantly at work on both sides is made clear by such details as the protagonist referring to her situation as a "fetishistic nightmare" or Don's choice of the epithet "fascist" for his boots when he commands her to lick them. The concreteness of the body, with its plethora of unfamiliar sensory information, is mediated by a set of cultural signifiers.

A central aspect of s/m that helps overcome the gender barrier is the performance ethos mentioned earlier. After Joe and Mike confess to Don their inexperience and poor performance record with women, he tells them: "Well, you're going to fuck one now.... I don't want any excuses, and I don't want any piss-poor performance. This isn't the back seat of your daddy's car, and you ain't in high school any more"

(231). The performative imperative, to which Don appeals,[4] can enable both parties to transcend any particular circumstance such as gender and turns the incompatibility in practice and experience into another challenge to be withstood.

Whereas Randy in *Leather Daddy* is in no way troubled by her attraction to gay men, Califia's protagonist is highly ambivalent about her attraction to men, and her concern over its implications for her lesbian identity forms a major preoccupation of the text. The status of the whole encounter is one of a forbidden fantasy coming true, and it comes true, significantly, in the context of dramatized violence. In her role of unwilling victim, the protagonist's participation in the interaction is distanced as much as possible from any exercise of free will, all the more so since the consensual frame is revealed only toward the end of the story.

The story hovers ambivalently between a sense of shared (queer) identity[5] and shared (s/m) eroticism, on the one hand, and a sense of insurmountable differences and gender antagonism, on the other. And while it is the first that forms the very condition of possibility of the interaction, the latter is the key to the disturbing intensity and erotic power of the text. Thus, for example, police harassment belongs to the realm of shared gay experience, common to both gay men and lesbians. In this respect, the "scene" the story depicts functions as a mutual act of exorcism. Reenacting the scenario of humiliation and abuse—and eroticizing it—works to co-opt male heterosexual power as a fetish for queer (male and female) sexual pleasure. Moreover, the protagonist is humiliated in the scene not only as a dyke but as an s/m dyke, a feature of her sexuality that is shared, of course, by the three men, serving as the very ground of their mutual play but also providing a shared background of persecution. On the other hand, while the homophobia of the "cops" is obviously fake, their misogynist treatment of the protagonist is in keeping with their actual gender positioning and could signify a gay man's identification with straight men under a gender-separatist topos.[6] Such an identification, with its concomitant male chauvinism and woman hatred, is suggested by the text for instance when Don says of lesbians: "Arrogant bitches. No man is good enough for'em" (223), thus aligning himself with straight men's offense at lesbian indifference.

Much of the force of the story resides in the fact that the "cops" are male and their "victim" female, and that the participants' play gender corresponds to their real gender. The correspondence between the top/bottom roles and the actual gender division in the story undercuts somewhat the performative dimension of the interaction. As noted earlier, the parodic function of s/m depends on the fact that the power exerted by the top over the bottom does not reflect real-life privileges, hierarchies, or power differentials. When the power differential within the scene corresponds to the one that obtains between the participants in the outside world, the structure of domination may not be denaturalized. The electiveness or reversibility of the roles and a distance between actor and persona are necessary for the performance to function as a parody of social relations.[7] In "The Surprise Party," although both parties are social outcasts of a similar kind, the top/bottom division is nevertheless overdetermined by gender.

Thus, in this text the cross-gender encounter both accentuates gender differences to the point of equating difference with antagonism and outlines the possibility of transcending these differences through the common language of s/m. Cross-gender queer sex figures as an ambiguous site where gender differences are both affirmed and overcome. On the one hand, the story makes clear that wanting to be a man and being a man are not the same thing (231), yet on the other hand, the s/m ritual works as a sort of initiation rite, through which, by withstanding her trials, the protagonist eventually attains a kind of manhood, and even the bodily differences seem to be ultimately obliterated by the joint immersion in cum, sweat, and tears.

Helen Sandler's erotic novel *Big Deal* narrates the sexual adventures of Lane and Carol, a butch-femme couple in which Lane, the younger butch, has sex with gay men. Lane's adventures with gay men begin with an initiation by her best friend Jack and progress to a threesome with Jack and an older friend of his, group sex in Russell Square at night, and anonymous sex in the darkroom of a gay male club. Each of these encounters is cast as a kind of trial and involves accordingly a high degree of anxiety for Lane. In the first two encounters she is scared and unsure whether she can "go through with it" at all. The cruising and darkroom experiences, which involve anonymous sex, also bring up the risk of rejection by the men into whose all-male territory she has trespassed, and this risk is heightened in the darkroom where she is passing as a man without Jack to protect her. In the Russell Square scene, there is indeed a hint of rejection by one of the men who, discovering her to be a woman (conveniently enough after they all came), advises her to watch herself since "not everyone's so understanding as us" (*Big*

Deal 139). This man also reprimands the guy who has just fucked her for his gender transgression.

Like Randy and the nameless protagonist of "The Surprise Party," Lane in her sexual interactions with gay men is mostly in a receptive and subordinate role. This position is justified by the initiatory context—Lane is "in training" by Jack—and while this training seems at first to be of a technical nature, a training in anal receptivity, it gradually turns out to be a comprehensive initiation into gay male sexuality. Interestingly, for Lane anal penetration is experienced not as feminizing but as masculinizing; she feels transformed by the act "from butch top to gay bottom" (17), that is, the loss of power is combined with a sense of transgendering.[8] This experience relies on gay male culture's construction of the insertee's role as virile that I have discussed in chapter 3, the notion that "taking it" from a real man is a masculine thing to do. And in fact, it seems that for Lane as a butch top, bottoming is only conceivable in a gay male context (and not, for instance, with her femme lover), since under the aegis of the gay male code that defines bottoming as virile, being topped by someone more powerful and masculine than her does not undermine her masculinity but rather affirms it. The notion of "taking it like a man" recurs several times in this context, and in the encounter with Jack's older friend, Matthias, Lane is even declared "a boy" for the night and referred to with masculine pronouns. It is as though, like a rite of passage, the gay male sexual practices she engages in effectively turn her into a boy.

The difference between the intense problematization of cross-gender queer sex in "The Surprise Party" and its relatively unproblematic status in *Leather Daddy* and *Big Deal* is probably attributable to the cultural changes that took place in the ten years that separate the publication of the first from the latter two. The emergence of queer identity as a joint identity seemingly oblivious to gender, and the increasing visibility and acceptance of bisexuality in the gay world have facilitated conceiving a lesbian (or queer) identity that can accommodate cross-gender sex.[9] The very topos of cross-gender queer sex takes place under the auspices of "queer" as an overarching, genderless identity category that organizes sexual attraction around a deviant erotic community, and it reflects the growing embrace of a queer identity by lesbians and lesbian-affiliated bisexual women, a process that began in the late 1980s with "Queer Nation" and gained momentum in the 1990s. As I noted, the term is already invoked in Califia's 1988 story, where Don employs it—half jokingly and still drawing on its pejorative connotations—to assign the protagonist and her gay male "assailants" to the same identity category and asserts: "Queers have sex with other queers." And in Sandler's 1999 novel, when a gay male friend charges Lane that she's not gay since she has sex with men, she rebuffs him saying that having sex with gay men just means she's queer (193). By this time, cross-gender queer sex has indeed been pronounced a queer and queering practice, for example, by Doug Sadownick in a 1991 essay whose title, "The Birth of Queer Nation and the Death of 'Gay' and 'Lesbian,'" heralds the queer era.[10] In fact, it may even be argued that part of the phantasmatic allure of sex with gay men is derived from its function as a badge of queerness.

However, granting that the topos of sex with gay men is a manifestation—perhaps the most radical one—of the larger phenomenon of women embracing queer identity, I believe that this drive toward a non-gendered/gay-male-oriented formulation of identity should be understood in relation to the quest for female sexual subjectivity. In chapter 2 I have noted lesbians' phantasmatic investment in gay male sexuality manifested in the consumption and occasionally the writing of gay male porn; the topos of cross-gender queer sex seems to go one step further and insert the female subject into the fantasy itself, where she gets to actually partake in gay male sexuality. The mise-en-scène remains the same, but the text represents a kind of second-order fantasy in which the subject checks whether she can inhabit this phantasmatic terrain.

To recap, the turning toward gay men as phantasmatic objects is related to the adoption of the gay male model of sexual subjectivity in lesbian pornography and in the lesbian sex culture in general.[11] As I noted in chapter 2, the lesbian sex culture that has emerged in the 1980s is in many ways modeled after the gay male one: Definitions of erotic identity, erotic styles, sexual attitudes, sexual etiquette, ideals, and fantasies are largely derived from the gay male subculture and the gay male cultural imaginary;[12] and this tendency is even more pronounced in the realm of fiction, where fantasy is unimpeded. This extensive borrowing from gay male sexual culture should be understood, I argued, in the context of the attempt to articulate female sexual subjectivity.

Gay male pornography since the seventies has at least partly unraveled the cultural knot linking sexual receptivity and nonsubjecthood. It reconceives receptivity as manly endurance—an ability to "take it"— and as an assimilation of the phallus, namely, the agency of the penetrating partner. The symbolic system of s/m, which lesbians have inherited from gay men, reinscribes the subject/object binary in strictly positional terms—top and bottom—thus highlighting the potential instability or fluidity of these roles and their performative character. Also, since s/m is *about* the possession and domination of one individual by another, penetration is dislodged from its privileged status as the ultimate token of possession and domination and becomes merely one practice among others. Striving to reinscribe themselves as sexual subjects, lesbians have adopted these cultural forms, attitudes, and symbolisms and profited from the symbolic realignments they afford. Mediating desires traditionally coded "feminine" through a (gay) male subject position affords not only to sever them from biological determinism but also to reinscribe them as transgressive, hence, consistent with and expressive of sexual subjectivity.

And yet, our three texts are also indicative of the ways in which adopting the gay male model of sexual subjectivity may be problematic for women. Even in *Leather Daddy*, whose protagonist blithely switches between her femme and boy incarnations, the utopian vision of a sexuality that transcends gender reveals some fissures upon closer inspection. As we have seen, the first two chapters of the book operate on a principle of perfect symmetry: in the first Randy is the submissive partner, while in the second she is the aggressor. All potentials are acted out. However, in the fourth chapter, "Ganged," this idyll of fluid gender and polymorphous perversity gives way to a certain anxiety about real differences. Jack orders Randy to come "butched up" as much as she can, and when she appears in boy drag with her breasts bound down and "packing a small one," he complains that she looks like a dyke. When she answers, "Jack, there's hardly any difference in this town!" he retorts: "Oh yes there is," asserting the existence of an irreducible (and specifically gay) sexual difference (*Leather Daddy* 31). He takes Randy to a private party for a play session with a number of top men, where she is expected not only to perform satisfactorily but also to "pass" as a boy. These two performances are related, since Randy's sexual proficiency supports the reality effect of her maleness. They are also related on a more fundamental level since, as Nancy Chodorow points out, while femininity is conceived as a natural condition, masculinity is conceived as something to be achieved. And yet, despite the fact that Randy "did good," as she is eventually assured, it turns out that she has been discovered by Jack's buddy, Demetrius, who felt her up while she was unconscious, and her "sweet little dick just seemed to come off in [his] hand"

(44). In spite of her performance Randy is a flawed male, a castrated male. Her phallus is—quite literally—insecure. True, this castration is presented in a comic light rather than a tragic one, but still there is a trace of failure about it: the physical insecurity of her phallus casts doubt on her symbolic possession of it. Randy proves herself performance-wise, yet the shadow of a doubt remains to haunt her achievement precisely at the point where the relation of the phallus to the penis is at stake. In this the text seems to signal the limits of the fantasy, implying that playing in the court of gay men must at some point entail running against the phallocentrism of gay male culture.

A closer look at the first two chapters also reveals a certain streak of anxiety beneath the utopian façade. There are several moments during their first date when Randy fears rejection by Jack. First she fears he'll kick her out when he finds out she's not a real boy; later, when she switches to her femme persona, she risks rejection once more; and the next morning, when she straps on her dildo and surprises him in the shower, she's anxious that her nonrealistic dick would turn him off or that he'll refuse being flipped by a girl. None of this happens, of course, because we are in the ideal realm of porn, but these textual moments attest to the anxiety that attends the fantasy of sex with gay men, an anxiety that gains admittance into the fantasy itself. In fact, fear of rejection seems to be endemic to this fantasy and is the flip side of the pleasure of transgression, the thrill of trespassing into gay male territory. As we have seen, the thrill of transgression and the fear of rejection are also a recurrent motive in *Big Deal*, and even the protagonist of "The Surprise Party" who is spared the burden of agency by her status as helpless "victim" is not exempt from some degree of performance anxiety.

The predominance of the narrative structure of initiation and trial, with its inherent power differential, and the themes of recognition and rejection that keep surfacing in all three texts suggest that the adoption of the gay male model of sexual subjectivity seems ultimately to call for male ratification. Thus, paradoxically, the project of articulating female sexual subjectivity ends up replicating the traditional gesture of seeking male endorsement. It is this need for ratification that lies at the heart of the fantasy of cross-gender queer sex, and it finds expression not only in the core fantasy of sex with gay men but also figures recurrently in the texts in the form of various challenges and the performance anxiety they evoke. To give head as proficiently as a gay man, to endure as much as a gay man, to satisfy a gay man who can have "the real thing" using a dildo, and finally, to be able to "pass" as a gay man, all these are challenges that bespeak the same need for endorsement of one's sexual subjectivity. And since the model for this sexual subjectivity is derived from gay men, ratification is ultimately sought from them.

The topos of cross-gender queer sex also raises broader questions concerning the ultimate usefulness of the gay male sexual imaginary for the project of articulating female sexual subjectivity. Gay male culture since the seventies has managed to break the equation of homosexuality with effeminacy by coding both the subject and the object position in male-male desire as masculine, thereby dissolving the symbolic equation of sexual receptivity with both femininity and nonsubjecthood. However, this resignification does not challenge the traditional equation of subjectivity with masculinity. Thus, when lesbians adopt this alternative symbolic, it allows them to inscribe themselves as sexual subjects even when occupying the object position— and even when enjoying penetration—but only to the extent that they align themselves with masculinity, an alignment that is evident, to varying degrees, in all the texts belonging to this topos and in fact forms the premise of the cross-gender encounters they depict.

This latter observation calls to mind Biddy Martin's criticism of queer thought, discussed in the previous chapter, for positing sexuality as a means of escaping gender and prescribing gender-crossing for women. The very same tendencies that Martin is worried about can be seen to operate in the fictional texts featuring cross-gender queer sex: Their protagonists transcend the limitations of gender and become interesting by making a cross-gender identification that is both enacted and tested through sex with gay men. And this identification is implicitly constructed in the texts as identification with sexuality itself, free from the constraints imposed on it by gender divisions. As Martin observes, the danger of this symbolic constellation lies in the rejection of "'the feminine' played straight" as a form of miring and entrapment, while masculine positions reassert their status as the emblem of mobility.

Masculinity, Trans Bodies, and Pornographic Reinscriptions

The rise of the FTM movement in the 1990s brought about the emergence of FTM porn toward the end of the decade. Pornographic representations of transmen by transmen seem to fulfill a function of "self-constitution through representation," as Bobby Noble terms it (310). The growing popular participation in the production of explicit images reflected in the tide of amateur porn in recent years indicates the extent to which explicit sexual representation has become one of the central practices of the contemporary performance of identity.[13] This kind of pornographic self-constitution becomes all the more crucial for subjects stigmatized for their sexuality or their failure to conform to norms of gender and/or embodiment. The transgendered body "supposed to be a site of shame and impossibility" (Noble 309) is constructed in FTM porn as both masculine, sexually functional, and desirable. Jay Prosser in his chapter on transsexuality in photography points out the way in which photographic portraits and self-portraits of transsexuals function as "testimony to the truth of posttransitioned sex," but he notes also the capacity of the visual media to "realize the image of the 'true' self that is originally only apparitional," a capacity manifested by pre-transition or mid-transition portraits (207, 211). For the pre-transition transsexual, he claims, the photograph may be more referential of the self than the body. Relying on the referential character of photography, transsexual portraits work to establish the gender realness of their subjects.[14] Transgender video porn, I would argue, works in a similar way by constructing the transmale subjects it represents as both male in their embodiment and masculine in their sexual performance. Their gender emerges specifically out of their sexual performance, hence, may be termed a "sexual gender," to borrow the phrase from Noble. In this construction of masculinity through sexual performance FTM porn employs many of the same strategies, which, as I have shown, lesbian porn borrowed from the gay male sex culture.

For example, *Alley of the Tranny Boys* (Dir. Christopher Lee, 1998), the first feature-length porn film starring a full cast of transmen, locates itself squarely in the phantasmatic terrain of gay male porn, especially of the leather variety. The film draws heavily on gay male leather culture, its symbolisms and imaginary, and adopts some of the aesthetics, settings, and scripts of 1970s gay male porn. Shot entirely in black and white, it employs a seventies retro aesthetic that, by lending the film a rough feel and invoking the iconicity of classic leather masculinity, furthers the macho portrayal of the characters, enhancing their masculinity through a combination of performance and setting. The film features, for instance, one episode that begins with street cruising and evolves into an s/m abduction scene; another in which a group of men watch

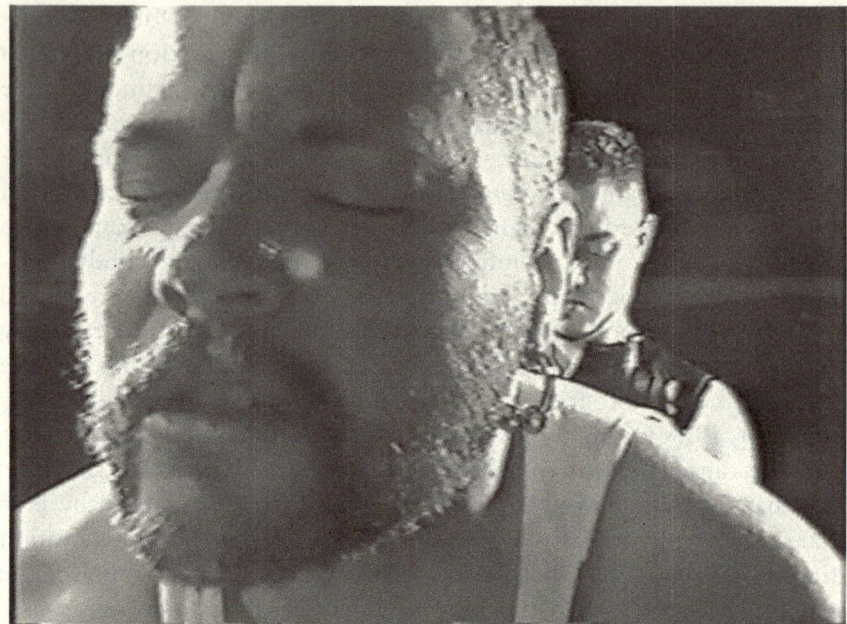

Figure 6.1. Receptivity as hypermasculine. Still from *Alley of the Tranny Boys* (Christopher Lee, 1998) ©Jae Carranza, 2012.

porn together in a hotel room and then go on to suck each other's cocks; and yet another in which a cop surprises two gay men having sex in a hotel room and the two overpower, tie up, and rape him. By harking back nostalgically to the origins of gay male porn, *Alley* not only codes the masculinity of its protagonists as gay or queer but aligns it with a classic and lost gay male masculinity.

The opening episode depicts an act of anal penetration between two transmen. Both partners, and especially the bottom (Buck Davis), are characterized as highly masculine. Davis, muscular, hairy, and heavily built, is dressed in jockstrap and tank top and leans on the footrest of a gym bench. The sex is rough and involves hard thrusting. Throughout the act, close-ups of penetration are interspersed with close-ups of Davis's straining mustachioed and bearded face, and the major sound on the soundtrack is his low-pitched grunts. By superimposing all these signifiers of masculinity (both bodily and cultural), the insertee's position is represented as strictly virile, and the coding of both the act and its participants within the idiom of gay male leather works to reinforce their maleness. Thus, Angel, the top, is the only transman shown barechested who has not had top surgery (in most of the film his chest is covered, but in two of the episodes he appears shirtless). His ambiguous embodiment is counterweighed by his sexual dominance, and the masculine signification of his sexual dominance is bolstered by the masculinity of his partners.

We can see, then, that similar to lesbian daddy-boy and s/m porn, FTM porn has recourse to the gay male recoding of receptivity as masculine endurance. Yet while in lesbian porn, recoding the insertee's position works to pave the way for female sexual subjectivity by undermining the view of penetrability as incompatible with subjectivity, FTM porn employs the same strategy for a different purpose, namely, to establish the masculinity of nongenetic men.[15] Transsexual porn star Buck Angel is the most notable example of pornographic performance of hypermasculinity by a transman. While performing in a variety of genres, he also became the first FTM to be featured in an all-male porn film produced by an exclusively gay porn company (*Cirque Noir*, 2005). Angel is pansexual in his choice of screen partners and polymorphous in his sexual repertoire, but he has taken the recoding of receptivity as masculine a step further by featuring vaginal penetration as his distinguishing specialty and dubbing himself "the man with a pussy." Recently turned into a filmmaker as well, Angel works in the genre of docu-porn, and in 2011 he created the documentary project *Sexing the Transman*, produced in two versions: a mainstream (though sexually explicit) documentary version and a hardcore version titled *Sexing the Transman XXX*, which has since turned into a three-volume series.

Docu-porn is a popular genre in contemporary feminist porn,[16] presumably owing to its capacity to counter the possible objectification of the performers and underscore their agency as well as the desire to present nonnormative sexuality as politically informed and an integral part of dissident lifestyles. In FTM porn, docu-porn also follows in a long tradition of documentaries about transmen (e.g., *You Don't Know Dick, Boy I Am, Gendernauts*, as well as others that document individual stories). While mainstream documentary films about transmen refuse to indulge the voyeuristic desire to see the unclothed refigured body and usually avoid overly detailed discussions of sexual practice, a docu-porn film like Angel's adopts a different stance, opting to indulge voyeurism rather than thwart it, thereby affirming the desirability of FTM bodies and the viability of FTM sexuality.

Each volume of *Sexing the Transman XXX* consists of several sections, each featuring a different transman. Every section opens with a short interview in which Angel questions his subject about his gender transition and sexuality, followed by a lengthy performance of masturbation. The interview and the masturbation segments complement each other, the latter functioning as a kind of demonstration of what the subject has narrated about his sexuality. All the interviewees are asked about their attitude to their vagina, how they feel about penetration, and whether that has changed following their gender transition. And the masturbation parts all include self-penetration either by dildos or fingers. Even one of the interviewees who states that he does not particularly crave penetration is shown using a dildo during his masturbation scene. Angel seems to have a clear agenda, both in his own pornographic performances and in the sexual representations he produces of others, of showing that transmen can own and enjoy their vaginas and enjoy penetration without being any the less men for that.

The choice to focus on masturbation in the *XXX* version seems to hinge on the confessional status of this practice. Thus, the masturbation sequences form a direct continuation of the interview both in temporal and spatial terms and in the sense that the verbal confession is followed by a "confession of the flesh."[17] Since it does not involve a partner who brings his or her own sexual preferences, and since it is less susceptible to scripting than other sexual practices, masturbation is taken to reflect one's genuine sexuality. Hence, the inclusion of vaginal penetration in the masturbatory repertoire of Angel's interviewees works to establish it as an integral part of their authentic sexuality. In addition, the fact that the penetration at stake is self-penetration deflects the whole problematics of domination associated with penetration. When transmen incorporate vaginal penetration in their autoerotic activities, the implication is that the practice is freely chosen simply for the erotic pleasure it yields.

The choice of masturbation as the sexual performance that the film focuses on has also the interesting consequence of reinforcing the masculinity of the men it features, since it is specifically in gay male porn that "jack off" forms an independent pornographic category (rather than serving as a teaser and prelude to sex as in straight porn). However, in terms of the masturbatory practice itself and the way in which it is shot, the masturbation scenes most resemble similar ones that can be found in lesbian porn or women's educational porn (which unlike female masturbation scenes in straight porn are less performative, focus

Figure 6.2. Deterritorializing the vagina. Still from *Sexing the Transman XXX* (Buck Angel, 2011). © Buck Angel, 2011.

more on clitoral stimulation, and feature convincing orgasms). The absence of a cum shot as visual evidence of pleasure is also dealt with similarly to lesbian porn through a focus on facial expressions during orgasm. In general, during the jerk-off scenes the camera alternates between genital close-ups and facial close-ups, occasionally managing in very low-angle shots to fit both face and genitals into the frame. In this way, not only is the expressive power of the face fully exploited to convey sexual pleasure, but in addition it may be said that the hardcore scenes, despite their focus on genitalia, strive to not let go of the men's subjectivity established in the preceding interview sequence.

While gay male culture recodes penetrability in cisgender male bodies, transgender porn disrupts not only the marking of bodies as feminine by sexual penetration in general but also the way in which vaginal penetration in particular marks bodies as female. As Bobby Noble comments about Buck Angel's work, "The contradiction—that a "pussy" does not always equal a "woman" or "woman with a vagina"— suggests that sexual "genders" articulate bodies despite sex not because of it" (310). Angel himself, in a short text he wrote for *The Feminist Porn Book*, articulates the educational agenda of his porn as one of challenging people "to examine how our society defines gender on the basis of genitals alone" (285). The deterritorialization of the vagina, and its reterritorialization in the terrain of maleness, takes place partly through acts of renaming: One of the questions that Angel poses to his interviewees is how they refer to their vaginas, and the answers include terms like "front hole" and "bonus hole." Jacob Hale discusses this kind of resignification of sexed bodily zones practiced by FTMs as a technique for recharting the body that enables one to change the personal and social meanings of the sexualized body or even "to change our embodiments without changing our body" (230). As he indicates, this technique is practiced also among butch leatherdykes, for whom, for instance, a dildo may take on the phenomenological characteristics of a dick, and he acknowledges that some FTMs derive such practices of "retooling" from the leatherdyke cultures in which they formerly participated. In other words, Hale points out the continuity between gender play in the context of lesbian s/m sexuality and the resignification of sexed bodily zones by FTMs as part of their gender transition.

This continuity between lesbian gender-bending practices and representations and FTM practices and representations is very evident in the realm of porn. The same erotic identities and styles, and the same phantasmatic scripts (ultimately derived from gay male porn), circulate in both lesbian gender-bending porn and FTM porn, and as I already noted, both perform the same recoding of sexual receptivity. *Alley of the Tranny Boys* demonstrates the *continuum* between gender-bending and transgender, when in two of the episodes it features a mixed cast of FTM transsexuals whose bodies show evidence of hormonal and/or surgical modification, together with a couple of performers who could more properly be described as transgendered or genderqueer, whose bodies (more fully clad than those of the others) show no such signs and who sport painted mustaches. The latter two, who could also be read as drag kings since their gay male masculinity is more performative than that of the others, engage sexually both with each other and with the transmen, the interactions centering on the strap-on dildos all of them wear. One of these episodes depicts an s/m fantasy, in which a cop bursts into a hotel room in which two gay men are having sex. The two turn the tables on him, and the scene ends with the "cop" being vaginally fisted by one of them. In this episode, one of the "drag kings" plays the cop, and the other plays one of the surprised gay men. Thus, we have one transsexual man and two female-bodied fags enacting a gay-male fantasy scenario, with neither the participants' bodily configurations giving any indication as to their roles in the scene nor

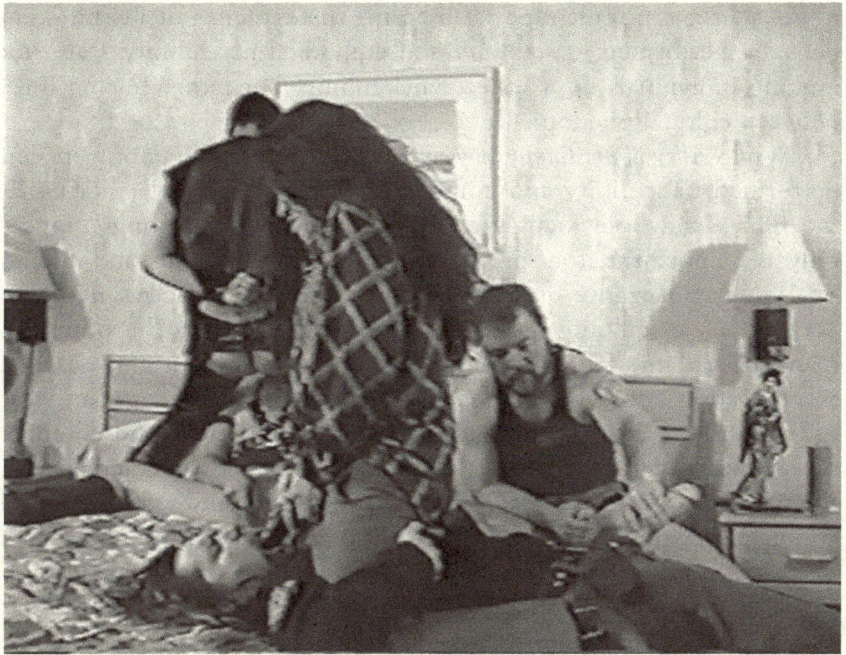

Figure 6.3. The transmasculine continuum. Still from *Alley of the Tranny Boys* (Christopher Lee, 1998). © Jae Carranza, 2012.

the all-male roles precluding a manifestly female sexual practice. The same scene might have equally been played by an all-female cast in a leatherdyke context, and its mixed cast underscores the continuum between performed masculinity (gender-bending) and embodied masculinity (FTM transsexuality).

In *Female Masculinity* Judith Halberstam offers a discussion of the affinities between butch and FTM identities that is tangential to mine. Pointing out that "the distinctions between some transsexual identities and some lesbian identities may at times become quite blurry," Halberstam nevertheless refuses the notion of "a masculine continuum" since it implies that bodily alteration indicates a higher degree of masculinity or gender dysphoria (150–151). Instead, she suggests that "the lines between the transsexual and the gender-variant lesbian inevitably crisscross each other and intersect" (164). While my discussion like Halberstam's rejects "the fiction of clear distinctions" (153), I do find the notion of a continuum useful. Since my focus is on practices and representations, not identity, in observing the existence of a continuum between performed masculinity and embodied masculinity, I am not ranking individuals on a scale of masculinity but rather tracing links between cultural phenomena.

While *Alley of the Tranny Boys* works to blur the distinction between performed masculinity and embodied masculinity, the very fact that the film as a whole focuses on FTMs, and the "drag kings" appear only as supporting actors, privileges embodied masculinity and implies a teleological narrative of the kind that Halberstam criticizes, in which performing masculinity is the first step toward actually "becoming" a man. Halberstam's criticism has emerged as an intervention in—as well as a reflection on—what she terms the "butch/FTM border wars," that is, the tensions and conflicts around identity definitions and community boundaries that arose as a consequence of the public emergence of FTM transsexuals in the 1990s. These tensions crystallized both around conflicting appropriations of contemporary and historical figures, such as Brandon Teena or Billie Tipton,[18] and around issues of inclusion and exclusion (e.g., admittance of FTMs to women-only events, their lesbian partners' community membership, etc.). As significant numbers of former lesbians began to identify as transmen, many lesbians felt betrayed, and moreover, the growing visibility and vogue of FTM transgenderism was felt to threaten or at least problematize butch identity.[19] While FTM activists and scholars accused certain lesbian critics of symbolically erasing trans identity by representing transmen as confused or self-hating lesbians, Halberstam criticizes a tendency in FTM discourse to dismiss butchness as an early stage of transsexual identity (or a failure to develop one).

What I am trying to get at, however, is less about the blurred line between butch masculinity and trans masculinity and more about the way in which a stylistic and erotic preoccupation with gender-bending that characterized some areas of lesbian culture in the eighties and nineties was gradually succeeded by the proliferation and growing visibility and vogue of trans and genderqueer identities, more or less within the same subcultural milieu. This cultural shift seems to be poignantly exemplified by the gender transition of Pat—now Patrick—Califia. As an author who dealt extensively with lesbian gender-bending and manifested hir phantasmatic engagement with gay male sexuality by writing both gay male porn and stories like "The Surprise Party," Califia's own eventual gender transition could be construed as the outcome and culmination of such phantasmatic investment (conversely, expressions of phantasmatic investment in masculinity in hir fiction might be retroactively interpreted as intimations of a "core masculinity" that found its proper manifestation in the later choice to live as a man). In this respect, it is interesting to look at Califia's own account both of hir eventual decision to transition and of hir former choice not to do so. Both accounts are found side by side in the second edition of Califia's book *Sex Changes*, first published in 1997, a few years before hir transition.

As a lesbian writing about transgender, Califia felt compelled to position herself in relation to the book's subject by discussing her own experience of gender dysphoria in the introduction. She explains, "There are many levels of gender dysphoria, many aberrant accommodations other than a sex change. Feminism, for example" (5–6). Among these "aberrant accommodations," she lists both lesbianism and s/m (which provides a safe venue for cross-dressing and gender play). Califia accounts for the decision *not* to undergo sex reassignment as arising from a combination of political qualms ("In the end, I decided that I could not separate my personal ambivalence about being female from the misogyny and homophobia of the surrounding culture") and pragmatic considerations (a negative cost-benefit evaluation of the outcomes of sex reassignment, especially in terms of the attractiveness and functionality of the post-reconstructive body) (*Sex Changes*, 4–6).

In the preface to the second edition of the book, published in 2003, three years after he began living as a man, Califia explains his gender transition in following way:

> For most of my adult life, I had kept my gender dysphoria at bay by creating a male persona in the bedroom. But I reached the point where I wanted this crucial aspect of myself to be more than a sexual fantasy, and I needed to be able to see a male face and body when I looked in the mirror every day. (xii)

Interestingly, Califia's account of the reasons for the decision to transition is much more laconic than the account of the previous decision not to transition, and the familiar language of dysphoria—"inner turmoil and profound discomfort," "growing despair and frustration"—figures prominently in it (xii). The two accounts are, however, compatible, offering two slightly different versions of the same narrative of self and demonstrating how a change of emphasis can yield a different narrative outcome. Califia cites aging as a determining factor in the decision to transition, but it seems safe to conjecture that the passage of time has facilitated this decision also in the sense that cultural conditions have changed, making life as an FTM a more viable and desirable option. At any rate, while in the earlier self-narrative the political and identitarian aspects of gender are intricately entangled, and sexuality figures as a major site for living out gender identifications, in the later narrative the political dimension recedes to the background, and sexual performativity gives way to the stability of embodiment.

Califia is not only emblematic of the continuum between lesbian gender-bending and transmasculinity, but more specifically, because of the prominent role s/he played in the feminist sex wars, hir very life history illustrates some of the threads that connect the sex wars of the 1980s and the transgender movement that emerged in the 1990s. Califia hirself identifies pro-sex feminism as one of the factors that contributed to the development of a new phase of transgender activism (*Sex Changes*, 226). S/he and other scholars also note the way in which the exclusion of transsexual women from lesbian feminist organizations and events acted as a catalyst for trans activism.[20] In this relation, it is notable that some of the figures most identified with the antiporn and anti-s/m agenda, such as Sheila Jeffreys, have also been vocal opponents of the inclusion of transwomen in lesbian feminist culture.

Another connecting thread Califia points to is s/m culture's contribution to the sense of ownership of one's body and the claiming of the right to modify it as an act of self-expression that characterize the transgender movement. At least some transgender theorists, for example, Jacob Hale and Susan Stryker, were personally involved in queer leather culture and attest to the ways in which their experience in it shaped and informed their performative understanding of gender. Stryker describes the "radical sexuality underground" as having provided her with a set of technologies (i.e., s/m and drag) and performative spaces that enabled her to realize her cross-gendered identifications before she ever considered engaging with the apparatus of transsexuality (150–151). Similarly, Hale points out the "uses of leatherdyke genderplay as ftm transitioning technologies" ("Leatherdyke Boys" 224). In particular, he discusses the ways in which boy-daddy play "can facilitate female-to-male transitioning paths" by providing a kind of laboratory situation for experimenting with various forms of masculinity (226). Both Hale and Stryker provide insight into the move from performativity to embodiment by demonstrating how medical technology can be conceived as simply another means for producing gender reality effects, which enables a broadening of the social sphere of enactment of one's gender identifications. As their formulations demonstrate, the drive toward transgendered embodiment need not entail an essentialist model of gender identity and might be grounded in a sophisticated performative understanding of gender.

David Valentine suggests an understanding of transgender identity and community as products of an imaginary. Valentine points to the function of the category "transgender" in securing the distinction between gender and sexuality, thus cleansing gay identity of gender variance in the interest of accommodationist gay and lesbian politics. However, the question that I would like to raise is: might it be that at least for female-born persons the imagining of "transgender" has to some extent displaced the project of imagining female sexual subjectivity for which masculine performativity had acted as a trope? If the notion of gender performativity as proposed by Butler seemed to hold out the promise of completely disarticulating anatomical sex, gender identity, and object choice, it turns out that a performative understanding of gender does not necessarily make femaleness any easier to inhabit and does not contravene the pull toward sex-gender coherence or gender stability. Gender-bending practices can be seen as a means for gender transition rather than an end in itself, and the need for coherence reasserts itself in the drive toward transgendered embodiment.[21]

On the other hand, at least in the case of FTM transsexuals, gender reassignment results in an ambiguous body that still does not comply with the edicts of heterosexual coherence, making transmen into "one site of political and corporeal incoherence where embodied sex, gender presentation, erotic object choice, and desire organized around sexual acts do not align normatively or within grids of intelligibility" (Noble 307). When such bodies put themselves on display, as they do in FTM porn, they do not only disrupt gender essentialism and heteronormativity; they also take part both in the construction of alternative masculinities within the realm of pornography[22] and in a resignification of the female body that might be available to cisgender women too (Buck Angel states that he promotes "the idea that having a vagina is powerful, no matter who it is attached to" [285]).

Queer Intertextuality

"The fiction of clear distinctions" is untenable not only in regard to identity but also in regard to sexual representations. Up to this point I have tried to keep the categories of lesbian porn and transgender porn more or less distinct; now however, I would like to complicate matters and show that the boundaries between lesbian, queer, and transgender porn are blurred and porous, so that instead of neat and stable groupings, what we find is an intertextual web. For this purpose, I will go back to literary erotica and take a look at a few more stories.

In the first part of this chapter, I examined the topos of cross-gender queer sex. Another story pertaining to this topos is "The Triangle," by Lady Sara, published in 1993 in the collection *Leather Women*. Kris, the protagonist of the story, offers yet another variation on the theme. Like Randy, she is in a relationship with a gay male daddy, but contrary to her she does not seek recognition of a multifaceted or fluid gender identity; she is quite simply "a boy." The text leaves it unclear whether her "boy" status is a play identity, a full-fledged gender identity, or more likely something in between the two. It is evident that she has a strong investment in masculinity, but she does not evince a sense of discomfort with her female body nor with female pronouns, hence, she does not read as an FTM transsexual but rather as genderqueer or transmasculine. Her relationship with her daddy is not problematized in the story in any way; the difficulties arise in her relations with the surrounding environment in her new status. The conflict over recognition is crystallized in her relationship with Surrender, a dominatrix whom she reencounters at a public play party and who makes fun of her newly acquired transgendered identity. Surrender offers Kris a bargain: she would let Kris top her enticing young boy-slave if Kris would first bottom to her. Kris, who aspires to become a daddy herself, accepts the challenge and submits to a particularly harsh scene. The bargain is almost a classic fairy-tale challenge: Undergo a trial and win the beautiful princess as prize, only here the princess is a long-haired boy.

The text constructs an opposition between Kris's loving and benevolent daddy and Surrender, the vicious (step)mother. The good father accepts Kris as "boy," while the bad mother questions her possession of the phallus, that is, challenges her new boy status and addresses her as "missy" during their session together. However, in order to ascend from boyhood to adult masculinity, the mother's recognition must be obtained as well. In this highly unconventional family romance, even though the father *can* confer the phallus on the daughter, it is the mother who must certify the daughter's attainment of it. And while in normative kinship systems, as Gayle Rubin points out, the phallus is the token that can be exchanged for a woman,[23] in the alternative kinship system projected by the story, the phallus is the token that signifies entitlement to a boy in an all-male incestuous lineage.

As in *Leather Daddy*, the confirmation of (female) masculinity involves a trial, yet Kris's trial, unlike Randy's, consists not in passing as a boy but in proving her masculine qualities—endurance, self-possession, dignity—that coexist with female embodiment. Perhaps this is the reason that her trial is much harsher; she has to prove her masculinity in the face of undenied femaleness. For Kris, not to break is to prove her masculinity, and for this very reason Surrender, who refuses to recognize her masculinity, attempts to break her. The scene between the two is fraught with ambivalence: even as Surrender denies Kris recognition of her chosen identity, she nevertheless attempts to gain Kris's recognition, which the latter denies her. Surrender demands Kris to wear her collar (instead of her daddy's) and to kiss her boots, two symbolic gestures that Kris refuses to perform, stressing that she is giving her only her physical submission.

Again, the scene can be read as the mother's losing battle over the daughter's allegiance in the Oedipal triangle, a battle that consists both in an attempt to subordinate the daughter by humiliating her and in a more seductive effort to win her over to the side of femininity. Consider, for example, the deep ambivalence inherent in Surrender's remarks upon ascertaining Kris's arousal in response to the torture:

> "All this tough talk about being a boy, and look at this . . . full of girl-wet, aren't we? All nice and open for Surrender, hmmm? . . . This is no cock, missy . . . and this is not boy cum, all nasty . . . this is nice pussy juice, isn't it, you little butch slut . . ." (Sara 191)

Surrender implies that Kris's sexual arousal—an arousal that attests to (feminine?) masochism—feminizes her, and that it represents a bodily truth that belies Kris's claim to masculinity. Yet on the other hand she also offers Kris a positive identification with femininity, in a kind of prepubescent discursive opposition that describes boys and their bodily fluids as "nasty" and girls and their bodily fluids as "nice."

But the story also lends itself to a different reading. Referred to throughout the story only as "Sir," Kris's leather daddy is described solely through Kris's focalizing consciousness and receives very little physical description. Kris mentions that his cock is very different from her own, but the description of his genitals is rather vague, and though it is implied that his is a flesh cock, on the other hand, when Kris sucks it there is no mention of ejaculation. In other words, there is no clear-cut indication of Sir's maleness, and the story leaves open the possibility that "Sir" could be a butch dyke or a transman. The reading of the story as depicting gender play between leather dykes rather than cross-gender sex is reinforced by the author's prefatory warning: "This story contains . . . a strong suggestion of (if not actual) sexual interaction between women and men. Things are not always as they seem, and some characters are portrayed as they see themselves, not as the world sees them" (167). Under such a reading, it is Kris's transgendered identification that takes center stage (rather than the cross-gender relationship), and her masculine identification is affirmed not by a gay man but rather by another masculine-identified woman. The mock Oedipal triangle remains, but the drama is played out by an all-female cast, and the benevolent father is a butch. Will Kris's transgendered identification remain within the bounds of s/m gender play, or will it eventually seek a broader sphere of enactment, as in the process that Jacob Hale describes having undergone? The answer to this question is of course beyond the scope of the text itself, but the very question underscores once more the continuum between gender play and transgender.

Another story that combines the themes of daddy-boy eroticism and cross-gender queer sex yet with a transgendered twist is "As the Sparks Fly Upward," by Raven Kaldera, published in 2002. Written by a transman and appearing in a collection of transgender porn, the story's unnamed narrator-protagonist is a leatherdyke boy in a relationship with an FTM daddy. The transgressive allure of cross-gender sex is combined for her with a particular attraction to "third gender" persons: "I was beginning to fantasize about breaking that utter taboo for a dyke. You know. People who weren't female . . . or not exactly female, anyway" (210). Though she picks up Trevor, her daddy, on the assumption that he is a cisgender gay man, she is pleased to find that "he was a man who knew more about what it was like to be me than any fag in that bar, and who was guaranteed not to treat me like a girl" (211). But she is drawn not only to queer and transgendered masculinity but also to femininity of the transgendered variety: "I'd never been much for genetic female femmes," she confesses, "but my cock was like a magnet for genderfuck" (211). After all, both transsexual men and transsexual women answer the definition of "people who are not exactly female." Her attraction to transwomen, however, manifests in sexual harassment of young MTFs, for which her daddy devises an original punishment: He delivers her into the custody of an older, dominant non-op transwoman, where she is to learn to respect femmes.

As a counterpart to the daddy-boy relationship, their relationship is constructed as one of mother-son. The two parent figures are constructed in oppositional terms: Trevor has work-roughened hands and rough manners, wears a bush hat, and drives a battered old van. Elaine, on the other hand, is not only meticulously dressed and adorned and equipped with all the trappings of femininity but is also characterized as genteel, complete with a faint British accent; and our protagonist's education with her includes learning gentlemanly behavior and cavalier manners that presumably are out of place between men. The stereotyped characterization of the two "parents" turns them into paradigmatic representatives of the genders they inhabit, regardless of their atypical bodily configurations. Beside refining her manners, our protagonist also has to learn to make love to her "Mama" attentively and respectfully, and here too the sexual dynamic is described in gender-stereotypical terms: to be a good lover, she must restrain her own pressing (masculine) desire to penetrate Elaine and put her partner's sexual needs first.

Unlike the rivalry between the parent figures in "the Triangle," here we have a much more harmonious Oedipal triangle. The "parents" who are ex-lovers cooperate in the "boy's" education, and the "mother" does not challenge the protagonist's masculinity but rather helps to perfect it. Any element of rivalry between the parents is deflected, because the "boy" is never asked to choose between them; at the end of his education, the mother simply delivers him back to the father's care. In this unconventional but functional family, the masculine ideal is female born and the feminine ideal is male born. What's even more interesting and significant is the story's insistence on respect for femininity and femmes as a crucial part of proper masculine socialization. Before her transformation, the protagonist could be described as what Ariel Levy termed a "female chauvinist pig." In a chapter titled "From Womyn to Bois" in her 2005 book, Levy describes and decries the sexism that pervades contemporary "boi" culture, which she claims is not only about a more noncommittal attitude to sex, and a masculine or androgynous identification, but often involves contempt and condescension toward feminine women, as manifested by expressions like "bros before hos." FTMs' celebration of their masculinity sometimes involves a glorification of masculinity in general and a concomitant disparagement of feminine women (often accompanied by a turning toward homosociality and homoeroticism).[24] It is this kind of sexually predatory and trivializing attitude toward (transgendered) femmes that the narrator's daddy condemns, and the narrator's transformation makes the point that the attainment of female masculinity need not involve a denigration of femininity.

The comparison between "The Triangle" and "As the Sparks Fly Upward" is instructive. Both feature a genderqueer protagonist in a daddy-boy relationship, a fascination with cross-gender sex (whether actualized or phantasmatic), and an Oedipal triangle that involves tension between opposite gender models. However, the first appeared in a collection of stories organized around female leather sexuality, the second in a collection of transgender erotica. These different groupings of similarly themed stories, along with the all-trans cast of the second story, attest to the influence of the transgendered movement that has emerged in the interim (i.e., between 1993 and 2002). The divergent foci of the two stories—attaining recognition of non-embodied masculinity versus learning to respect femininity—also reflect agendas born of different historical moments and changed cultural conditions.

"Becoming," another story in the same collection of transgender erotica, combines genderqueer identity and cross-gender sex in a different configuration by adapting the "forced feminization" topos of straight BDSM, in which a male submissive is forced by a female dominant to dress in female clothes and is sometimes also fucked by another man as part of his feminization. "Becoming" offers a takeoff on this theme: its female boy-identified protagonist is instructed by her mistress to take off her men's clothes and put on a sexy feminine costume—pink lace panties and a corset—and is subsequently fucked by another mistress's male slave. Her trial is to learn to be a girl, "because [her] mother certainly didn't do a very good job teaching [her] the first time around," as her mistress asserts (Gino 190). This crash course in femininity, which goes against her core masculine identity ("*Didn't I burn all my Barbie Dolls? Wasn't I the one who refused to wear a dress to graduation?*" she adduces her butch credentials in her mind when confronted with the demand to learn to be a girl [189]), is not actually meant to transform her into a proper girlie girl but functions as a rite of humiliation as it does in straight BDSM. Yet paradoxically, because this is something that is done to men, the forced feminization does not threaten her masculinity but ultimately works to affirm it. And indeed the protagonist is rewarded for her obedience by the gift of a strap-on dildo and the prerogative of penetrating her mistress, thus reassuringly aligning gender and sexual performance with (trans)gender identity.

The forced feminization scene in this story is oddly reminiscent of an analogous one in a story published more than twenty years earlier in the volume *Coming to Power*, the first collection of writings on lesbian s/m edited by members of the lesbian feminist s/m organization Samois. The story "Passion Play," by Martha Alexander, also depicts an s/m scene that revolves around a similar (though more elaborate) process of feminization by means of clothing, cosmetics, and jewelry, although here heterosexual coitus is not part of the script. However, "Passion Play" sets this scene in the context of a relationship that is very different from the mistress-boy s/m relationship of "Becoming." Its two protagonists are characterized as strong and successful professional women, who moreover are identified as politically involved feminists. They are longtime friends and part-time lovers, and their relationship is egalitarian and premised on mutual respect and affection. This emphasis on the women's power, independence, and feminist credentials, as well as on their equal relationship should probably be understood in the context of contemporary feminist attacks on s/m as a violent and patriarchal practice. Yet it is also interesting to see the different way in which the humiliation of feminization is construed. When Meg protests to her friend: "You *know* how much I hate being a 'girl.' It's embarrassing, humiliating..." (Alexander 235), this sentiment seems to suggest lesbian feminist distaste for male-defined femininity just as much as it expresses lesbian gender dysphoria. And while the text tells us that Meg "almost considered wearing women's clothing as a form of cross-dressing, it was so against her character" (239), her gender preferences are never defined in identitarian terms and do not become a focus of the story. Here the forced feminization ritual is not set against a clearly defined masculine identity; rather, the central tensions the story develops and exploits are those between public persona and private desires, politics and sexuality.

As we saw in "As the Sparks Fly Upward," gender-ambiguous bodies lend another twist to the theme of cross-gender queer sex. As sites of corporeal incoherence, such bodies provide divergent axes of identification and desire (gender presentation, embodiment, genital sex, object choice, and sexual practice) that do not align normatively, hence, lending further complexity to the question of likeness or difference and making it hard to categorize attraction as same-sex or cross-sex. A story that demonstrates this is "The Therapist and the Whore," by Giselle Renarde, from a recent collection of transgender and genderqueer erotica. Manny, its protagonist, is an African American butch dyke who lives with her girlfriend and regularly sees a transsexual sex worker. She is conflicted about her own masculine identification, what it means, and how to live it, and her relationship with the transsexual Star is figured as more intimate than her relationship with either her lover or her therapist. Star is depicted as feminine, warm, understanding, and nurturing, but Manny's attraction to her has to do also with her cock, which she likes to suck and be fucked with. This phallic woman who provides feminine nurturance is both like and unlike Manny in different ways: she complements her in a butch-femme dynamic, she is uniquely understanding and supportive of her cross-gender identification by virtue of her own transgender identity, and she also provides the forbidden pleasures of sex with a flesh-and-blood cock. Manny's relationship with her oddly combines transgressive sexuality with the cozy intimacy of drinking tea together in the kitchen.

As I have shown, rather than representing discreet categories, lesbian, queer, and transgender pornographic texts form an intertextual web in which certain themes and phantasmatic topoi circulate, both accruing cultural resonance and modifying their significance as they shift from one context to another. The porous boundaries between queer and transgender porn are manifested by the fact that contemporary queer representations figure trans bodies among the spectrum of identities, bodies, and sexualities they put on view,[25] and on the other hand the transgender spectrum that figures in anthologies like *Best Transgender Erotica* or films like *Alley of the Tranny Boys* includes both performative crossings and bodily ones.

Butches attracted to transwomen, transmen who affirm their pleasure in vaginal penetration, leatherdykes who cruise gay male daddies, and gay men who fall for FTM bears,[26] all seem to suggest a brave new queer world characterized by a total disarticulation of genetic sex, gender identification, body configuration, object choice, and sexual practice. Yet at the same time, these examples also demonstrate that the centrality of the figure of crossing for the definition of "queer," which Jay Prosser has observed in relation to queer theory, obtains for queer porn just as much. While the ethics of contemporary queer and feminist porn is self-consciously inclusive and pluralistic, crossing—whether of gender lines, identity lines, or other normative boundaries—is still a key trope. That transgender subjects continue to function as emblematic of queerness, as Prosser pointed out, is borne out by the fact that the presence of transgendered bodies functions as one of the discursive markers that distinguishes queer porn from lesbian porn.

While Prosser and other transgender critics have protested the use of transgendered bodies to signify queer transgression and fluidity, my point is different. Despite the riskiness of generalization, I would argue that the cultural signification of gender-crossing has shifted over the years: whereas in the eighties and early nineties practices of gender-crossing in the sexual arena were constructed mostly in terms of play, since the rise of the transgender movement they have been increasingly constructed in identitarian terms. Even a category like "genderqueer" that stresses incoherence and gender performance rather than gender embodiment is usually construed in identitarian terms. In other words, a minoritarian discourse of nonnormative gender identities seems to have largely taken the place of a universalist discourse of gender performativity. Even in Halberstam's discussion of female masculinities, the move to cut off masculinity from its exclusive ties to the male body and claim it as the legitimate province of women tends (perhaps inadvertently) toward essentializing masculinity. In affirming non-male masculinities the question of what an investment in masculinity might *mean* has been sidelined, probably since it is felt to put in question or detract from the authenticity or primacy of such masculinity.[27] I have argued that in female-authored porn an investment in gay male masculinity and homoeroticism functions as a phantasmatic strategy that enables women to recode their sexuality and thus gain symbolic access to sexual subjectivity. When such an investment is naturalized and closed off to interrogation and masculine identifications are consolidated in identitarian terms, their function in the project of articulating female sexual subjectivity is obscured.

From this perspective, both FTM porn and the topos of cross-gender queer sex can be seen to indicate the limitations of the appropriation of the gay male sexual imaginary for the project of articulating female sexual subjectivity. The phantasmatic strategy of adopting the gay male model of sexual subjectivity encounters its limits when it folds back into a desire for the "real": to have sex not only *as* a gay man but *with* a gay man; or to be not only *like* a gay man but an *actual* gay man. When phantasmatic identification with gay men turns into a desire for literal becoming, that is, into a drive toward embodied identity, then we are no longer dealing with *female* sexual subjectivity.[29] Similarly, when such identification ends up reprivileging masculinity, women's possession of sexual subjectivity is questioned once again. There seems to be a fine line between employing masculinity as a *signifier* of sexual subjectivity and equating subjectivity with masculinity *tout court*. And while a phantasmatic investment in gay masculinity has played a facilitating role in the articulation of lesbian sexual subjectivity, since the rise of the FTM movement such an investment is increasingly spelled out in identitarian terms and, hence, loses its previous enabling function vis-à-vis the problem of female sexual subjectivity. I realize that in saying this I lay myself open to the charge of stabilizing the categories male/female in a reality in which new forms of subjectivity and embodiment are emerging that contest and erode this dichotomy. Certainly, one solution to the problematic of female sexual subjectivity is to reject not only femininity but also femaleness in favor of a redefined maleness or a hermaphrodite subject position, but obviously, this is a solution of limited applicability. And it is unclear, for example, to what extent Buck Angel's resignification of the vagina is available to cisgender women whose bodies do not provide a similar configuration of cross-gender signals.

Coda

*Pornographic Pedagogy, Explicit Utopias,
and the Future of Female Sexual Subjectivity*

I have always enjoyed screening porn in unlikely places and contexts: university classrooms, academic conferences, public lectures; in small seminar rooms and large lecture halls, in galleries and museums; to art students, gender students, sexologists, feminists, queers, the general public. I enjoy it for its obvious transgressiveness—putting sexual images "on scene" in the public sphere. But more than that, I like showing people images that they are not accustomed to seeing: Annie Sprinkle's five-minute-long orgasm, female ejaculation, butch-femme sex, women fucking men with strap-ons, transfags having leather sex. When I teach academic courses on pornography, such representations make up a small portion of the screenings in the class. The course is constructed around two axes: historical and political. The first traces the history of pornography as a category and a genre, and the second centers on the feminist pornography debate. Alternative images are screened mostly in relation to the second axis, in the concluding section of the course. However, when I look into my motivations for teaching such courses, the opportunity to acquaint students with nontraditional sexual imagery plays an important part in them, and I cannot envision a course on pornography from which such images would be absent.

These images for me are fragments of a sex-gender utopia. As cinematic images they are records of actual practices and performances;

moreover, inasmuch as they are products of contemporary sexual cultures, they represent currently existing sexual identities and practices. However, their utopian aspect lies in their distance from the dominant order of sexual representation: the types of bodies, couplings, gazes, and practices that they put on view have no place in the visual economy of the prevailing sex-gender order, hence, suggest an alternative order not yet in existence that can only be glimpsed through them. In other words, such images are concrete utopias that participate in the project of feminist and queer world-making. They displace the dominant sexual imaginary of mainstream porn substituting for it a different vision of sexuality and gender.

The impersonal spaces of classrooms and lecture halls are an interesting setting for watching porn. These formal blank environments, designed to bear no traces of their occupants, and assuming a collectivity of rational exchange that disavows the body, make no allowance for the bodily response and mimetic spectatorship that pornographic representations call for. In a classroom setting, one's co-spectators are neither self-chosen intimate partners nor total strangers who can be ignored in the darkness as in the adult movie theaters of years past. These conditions of collective viewing—knowing that their responses are observed by their classmates and that soon they will be asked to discuss what they are watching—make for an uncharacteristically self-conscious mode of consumption. This may lead to embarrassment and social inhibition, but it also effects a defamiliarization that fosters reflection.

Watching porn together also turns a class into a special kind of public, creating a partly forced, partly conspiratorial intimacy that excludes strangers (we take care to close the class door to elude the gaze of curious passersby who may be attracted by the sound of groans seeping out into the corridor; a technician coming to fix a problem in the AV system is hurriedly thanked and dismissed without getting to see more than a DVD box or the relatively innocuous beginning of a film). We go on about our business seriously but somewhat furtively, claiming our right to the institutional space of the university while trying to fly under the radar lest someone be outraged by our use of public funds. Just as queer theory classes often create ad hoc queer spaces in the midst of academic institutions, so does the screening of alternative sexual images. Lifted from their marginal niche-market status, and screened in an educational context to a mixed group of young adults who are called to evaluate them for the representational alternatives they offer, these images are granted a legitimacy, a dignity, and a centrality that turn the class itself into a utopian space. And of course, for those students for whom the images reflect their own sexuality, whether in terms of actual practice or phantasmatic investment, such occasions provide validation of a sexuality barred from mainstream visibility. Coming out of class I sometimes feel like a conjurer, having managed to bring into temporary existence a collective mode of relating to sexual imagery that not only accords serious attention to minor sexual representations but also claims this attention without denying the other, more visceral, ways in which such images interpellate us.[1] I also know from students that often discussions begun in class extend into the off-hours and continue not only with classmates but also with partners and friends.

But what about the reception of these utopian images? Are they necessarily perceived as such? The time span of an academic course allows enough time for building a context of reception and an interpretive frame that afford appreciation of the utopian dimension of such representations. In one-off contexts, however, the encounter with unfamiliar sexual images could be experienced as an unexpected and startling assault that results in a sense of alienation and antagonism. People may either walk out or channel their shock and anger into expressions of disappointment (this is not any different from straight porn, not arousing, aesthetically poor, boring, etc.)[2] or charges that the images themselves are violent.[3]

Even when the shock factor is mitigated by gradual exposure to different kinds of porn, the very utopian nature of the images may be experienced as alienating. After all, utopian texts may inspire or they may dishearten when we measure our current reality against the vision they offer and calculate the chances of its realization; they may give rise to hopefulness or they may arouse frustration. And this is all the more true for pornographic utopias that present records of pleasures that seem to be out of one's reach. I have seen women respond defensively to Sprinkle's orgasmic tour de force or to impressive spectacles of female ejaculation. Such performances can be seen to pose a sexual standard that is hard if not impossible to follow, hence, women can perceive such images as no less oppressive than the images of female perfection they are fed by mainstream culture. Surveys cited by Pamela Paul indicate that the more porn people watch, the less satisfied they are with their partners and with their sex life in general. Might not this apply to alternative porn as well? Surely a claim can be made that a brush with utopian sexuality only breeds discontent.

This may be the case in some instances, but since we live in a culture saturated by sexual representations, I believe in the pedagogical value of learning to observe porn and reflect about it, not just use it. Further, I believe in the pedagogical value of alternative porn as a counterweight and antidote to the sexual economy and sexual ethics of mainstream porn, as a reeducation of the imagination. This is why I persist in the curious vocation of screening alternative porn and pointing out its utopian potentialities: the different gender order it envisions and provides a foretaste of.

This book is in a sense an attempt to check whether my convictions concerning the utopian potential and educational value of alternative porn stand up to close examination. Going back to the set of questions and concerns with which I began this book, we have seen that far from replicating the objectification and humiliation that antiporn feminism sees as endemic to the genre, pornographic fiction by women takes advantage of the phantasmatic potential of pornography to construct women as sexual subjects. The readings in chapters 3 and 4 have shown how pornography by women tackles and to a large degree surmounts two of the major stumbling blocks for the articulation of female sexual subjectivity: the privileged role of the phallus as signifier of agency and desire, along with its overdetermined relation to male anatomy, and the notion of sexual penetration as antithetical to subjectivity. These readings bear out the optimism of the anti-antiporn position regarding the ability of feminist appropriations of pornography to produce a reinscription of fantasy in line with feminist projects and aims.

Granted, in terms of their cultural impact, such reinscriptions are no competition for the mainstream pornography industry with its huge resources and ubiquitous presence. However, the fact that appropriations of the pornographic genre by women manage to resignify gender and sexual norms demonstrates that pornographic discourse is not irrevocably tethered to male power and proves the viability of the strategy of representational struggle within the realm of sexual representation itself. And in terms of the current state of the field, the internet has created enabling conditions for the emergence of what Alexander Halavais terms "small pornographies" (as opposed to "big porn"), thereby encouraging the proliferation of alternative pornographic discourses and the formation of counterpublics that produce and consume them. Hence, while the increasingly central role played by the internet contributes to the ubiquity of mainstream pornographic representations, it also facilitates the growth and spread of representational alternatives.

Further, as we have seen, in its capacity to effect such resignifications and to articulate new symbolic configurations, representational practice is often ahead of feminist theory. Thus, for example, the pornographic texts we have looked at not only contest the dominant cultural meanings of penetration but also delineate alternative ones while at the same time debunking genital penetration from its position as the prime mode of sexual possession. Similarly, these texts complement the painstaking feminist critiques of the phallus as the privileged signifier of sexual subjectivity with a bold appropriation of it in the form of the dildo, thereby dismantling it to its various component elements, which are then redistributed in unorthodox ways.

However, my inquiry has also pointed out the limits of pornographic resignifications. New phantasmatic options do not arise ex nihilo but evolve within existing social realities, hence, rely on a restricted repertoire of cultural notions, narratives, and roles. This repertoire furnishes the raw material from which unexpected configurations may be fashioned, but it also delineates a limiting horizon. A case in point is a central phantasmatic strategy that this book has identified and explored in pornography by women: identification with gay male sexuality. My inquiry has traced the enabling effects that such a phantasmatic investment has had for the project of articulating female sexual subjectivity, but it also revealed how the enduring equation of subjectivity with masculinity proves limiting and how some of the trajectories along which this investment has evolved eventually veered away from the project.

The resignificatory potential of pornography is also restricted by the fact that—its utopian aspect notwithstanding—most works of pornographic fiction, and certainly most of the works that I have discussed here, are not "pure fantasy" but rather straddle the gap between fantasy and everyday reality. In other words, they are phantasmatic scripts that already make concessions to the constraints of reality, meeting reality halfway, as it were. Moreover—and here I am willing to concede some ground to antiporn feminism—the promise of pornography for a project of cultural resignification may be partly curtailed by the fact that in order to affect us erotically, it cannot imagine a world too unlike our own.

As for the problem of female sexual subjectivity, it will probably not be resolved once and for all by any one theoretical formulation or phantasmatic strategy. But the contemporary proliferation of phantasmatic reinscriptions gives scope to the hope that at some point the collective reworking of the sexual imaginary will make the question of female sexual subjectivity obsolete as a cultural problematic.

Notes

Introduction

1. Andrew Ross cites surveys indicating that 40 percent of the adult video rentals in the United States in the mid-1980s were by women (173); Jonathan Coopersmith cites a 1998 study showing that almost 20 percent of female internet users logged on to pornographic sites, compared to 45 percent of male users (11); and Pamela Paul cites the 2004 *Elle*-MSNBC.com poll, according to which "41 percent of women said they have intentionally viewed or downloaded erotic film or photos" (116).
2. Paul 4. Both Paul and Gail Dines argue that "most women and some men have an idea of pornography that is 20 years out of date" and describe the unparalleled nature of current conditions in terms such as "seismic change" (Dines xxviii, xi).
3. "Much of what I heard was not just news; it was revelatory. There was a story about pornography that had not yet been told," writes Paul (3).
4. Pamela Paul, for instance, describes Andrea Dworkin and Catharine MacKinnon as "feminist hardliners," implicitly distancing her critique of pornography from theirs, and charges that their position "that all women are victims and that all sex is rape" is alienating for the majority of women (258–259). Similarly, Gail Dines refuses to situate herself within the traditional antiporn/pro-sex division and argues that she is "pro-sex in the real sense of the word" (x).

5. Thus, for example, Annie Sprinkle's work after she quit the mainstream porn industry blurs the boundaries between performance art or body art and alternative porn. The convergence between the project of feminist art and feminist pornography is instantiated by the 1991 anthology *Angry Women*, which consists of interviews with feminist thinkers, writers, and performance artists and includes among them Annie Sprinkle and Susie Bright.
6. A recent example is Charlotte Roche's bestselling *Wetlands*.
7. For example, the video-sharing website queerporntube.com, the commercial Cyber-Dyke network of erotic websites, and the website SuicideGirls that functions like an online community. For a comprehensive survey of the different kinds of pornographic production by women on the internet, as well as the modes of interaction and exchange the net has facilitated, see Jacobs.
8. In her book, *After Pornified*, Anne Sabo provides a broad survey of alternative porn (or as she terms it, "re-visioned porn") by women that covers the work of most of the filmmakers I mention as well as some others, though, as she acknowledges, her book focuses on porn that is heterosexually oriented and overlooks lesbian or queer porn.
9. Some of the instances she lists are the films of Émilie Jouvet, the PostPornPolitics Symposium in Berlin in 2006, the annual Feminist Porn Awards in Toronto, the annual Pornfilmfestival in Berlin, the "Crash Pad" Series, and the website Queer Porn TV.
10. Comella cites the fact that quite a few feminist and queer pornographers, for example, Susie Bright, Tristan Taormino, and Jackie Strano, had worked in such stores before going on to create pornography that was informed by their interactions with customers.
11. The most notable—and quite recent—exceptions are Anne Sabo's book and Ingrid Ryberg's dissertation. Sabo, however, sets out mostly to describe the range of pornographic filmic production by women and does not offer in-depth analysis of individual works; and Ryberg focuses on one filmic text, the *Dirty Diaries* DVD, a collection of twelve pornographic shorts curated by director Mia Engberg. Ryberg offers textual readings of the short films that make up this collection, alongside extended discussions of its production, distribution, and reception.
12. For example, Smyth; Merck, "*More of a Man*"; Kipnis, "She-Male Fantasies"; Straayer, "The Seduction of Boundaries" and "Discourse

Intercourse"; Findlay; Heather Butler; Jacobs; Carnes; Ryberg; Sabo; Waugh; Patton; Beggan and Allison; Fung; Simpson; and Joshi.

13. The few exceptions include discussions of "slash" fiction written by female and queer fans (e.g., Penley, Jenkins, and Kustritz); Tania Modleski's short but insightful reading of one of the stories in the collection *Coming to Power*; Clare Whatling's reading of Pat Califia's *Macho Sluts*; and Esther Sonnet's and Simon Hardy's discussions of Virgin Publishing's Black Lace imprint of erotic fiction by women for women (Sonnet, however, offers only a general discussion of the imprint's ideological discourse of erotica as female empowerment and does not perform readings of the texts themselves) (Sonnet, Hardy).

14. I do not mean to suggest that for literary texts the question of their conditions of production is irrelevant or negligible, only that it is not as ethically imperative as in discussions of pornographic films and photos. The question of the conditions of production of the latter is not only ethically complex, invoking the problematics of choice and agency, but also involves the further difficulty of the radical inability—the documentary promise of pornography notwithstanding—to infer from a representation the conditions of its making.

15. Heather Findlay suggests this concept of a partly conscious cultural labor in relation to the fetishization of safer sex by AIDS activists (338).

16. Cf. Anne Sabo's notion of "re-visioned porn," and the assertion of the editors of *The Feminist Porn Book* that "social identities and ideas are formed in the act of viewing porn, but also in making and writing about it" (Penley et al. 15).

    This conceptualization also resonates with Michael Warner's notion of counterpublics as engaged in collective world-making. Borrowing Nancy Fraser's definition of counterpublics as "parallel discursive arenas where members of subordinated social groups invent and circulate counterdiscourses to formulate oppositional interpretations of their identities, interests and needs," Warner notes that a counterpublic "can work to elaborate new worlds of culture and social relations in which gender and sexuality can be lived" (Fraser 122–123; Warner, *Publics* 57).

17. Cf. Jacob Hale's assertion that queer theory lags far behind community discourses of sexual minorities ("Leatherdyke Boys" 223).

18. This is precisely the way Gloria Steinem's distinction between pornography and erotica, a distinction popular among some feminists, functions. Steinem sees erotica as about "a mutually pleasurable sexual expression" and pornography as about "violence, dominance and conquest" (qtd. in Paul 121).
19. A further function of the distinction is noted by Jane Juffer, who points out that explicit sexual representations targeting a female audience are often labeled "erotica" as a marketing strategy (7).
20. Probably the best-known dismissal of "the female subject" is the one performed by Judith Butler in *Gender Trouble*. See also Adams and Minson, "The Subject of Feminism."
21. Granted, the notion of sexual subjectivity does not enjoy the wide currency of popular categories such as homo- and heterosexuality; however, it does possess theoretical currency, and I would contend that its sphere of influence extends beyond the theoretical discourses in which it is deployed.
22. For Foucault, of course, sex itself is a cultural construct, not a natural entity laden with symbolic functions. As he asserts, "The notion of 'sex' made it possible to group together, in an artificial unity, anatomical elements, biological functions, conducts, sensations, and pleasures, and it enabled one to make use of this fictitious unity as a causal principle, an omnipresent meaning, a secret to be discovered everywhere . . ." (154).
23. Foucault himself, in one of his rare references to the specificity of women's relation to sexuality, notes the saturation of the female body with sexuality through the mechanism he terms the "hysterization of women's bodies" (104).
24. For definitions of the notion of sexual citizenship and a discussion of women's incomplete sexual citizenship, see Richardson.
25. This threefold claim is characteristic mostly of MacKinnon and Dworkin. For a critique of this "hyperdetermination of the ontological claim," see Butler, "The Force of Fantasy."
26. Cowie includes in this category "films, stories, plays, television" ("Pornography" 149).
27. See Freud, "Creative Writers and Day-Dreaming."
28. See de Lauretis's important caveat that not *any* film is phantasmatically accessible to *any* viewer ("On the Subject of Fantasy").
29. This latter effect is exemplified for instance by the way in which Tom of Finland's homoerotic drawings in American physique

magazines formed "image reservoirs from which gay men were able to construct new codes for dress and behavior" and "began to constitute a placeless community for gay men before physical communities existed" (Blake 353).
30. The continuities between queer and transgender formations will be explored in chapter 6.
31. For descriptions and critiques of this process, see Warner, *Trouble with Normal*, and Duggan, "New Homonormativity."
32. Cf. Sonnet's characterization of this discourse in relation to the Black Lace imprint of erotic fiction (Sonnet 171).

Chapter 1. Between Sexual Commodities and Sexual Subjects

1. This chronology of the debate is based mostly on Hunter.
2. Similarly, in 1992, the Supreme Court of Canada employed antiporn argumentation in a ruling that upheld the Canadian obscenity law on the grounds that sexually explicit speech is comparable to "hate speech" because it degrades women (Hunter 28).
3. Additional writings include Boyle 2010, Sarracino and Scott, and Tankard Reist.
4. Several such surveys—reflecting different positions on the debate—exist, for example, Easton, *The Problem of Pornography*, and Duggan and Hunter, *Sex Wars*. In addition, *Feminism and Pornography*, edited by Drucilla Cornell, is a comprehensive anthology of writings from both sides of the debate.
5. As Gayle Rubin points out, MacKinnon has been a relative latecomer to the antiporn movement but, following the Minneapolis and Indianapolis ordinances, has come very much to represent it ("Sexual Traffic" 44).
6. Other major figures in the antipornography camp are Diana Russell and Susan Griffin.
7. Wendy Brown designates MacKinnon "the unquestioned theoretical lodestar of the feminist antipornography movement" (78).
8. The term "anticensorship" seems to originate in the title of FACT (Feminist Anti-Censorship Taskforce), founded in 1984, and was later adopted by Feminists Against Censorship in Britain. It implies a stress on opposition to the legal regulation proposed by antiporn feminists but usually signifies a broader critique of their analysis.

The term "pro-sex" is favored by lesbian sex radicals: Gayle Rubin employs the term "pro-sex feminism" in her groundbreaking essay "Thinking Sex" (302), while Pat Califia in a piece written in the nineties employs the kindred term "sex-positive" to designate the opposite camp to antiporn feminism ("Among Us, Against Us" 107). The term "anti-antiporn" seems to have been first introduced by Andrew Ross in his chapter on pornography in *No Respect* and appears to be favored by scholars surveying the debate from a purportedly "unbiased" point of view (cf. Modleski's chapter on pornography).

9. It is also important to note that the customary binary delineation of the debate—which I am replicating here—in fact covers over the existence of a whole range of feminist attitudes toward pornography that might be described more adequately as lying along a continuum. While women in the anti-antiporn camp oppose legal restrictions on pornography (whether in principle or out of fear that such restrictions will be aimed first and foremost against sexual minorities) many of them share antiporn feminists' concerns about mainstream pornography. On the other hand, while most spokeswomen of the antiporn camp extend their condemnation also to pornographic representations by women, some feminists who endorse the antiporn analysis regarding mainstream porn do see positive potential in alternative porn. In other words, the spectrum of feminist attitudes concerning pornography exceeds the binary structure of the debate, and many women who align themselves with rival positions do share similar concerns (I am indebted to Sarah Schulman for calling my attention to this point). It is important to recognize this in order to move the feminist discussion of pornography from the deadlock it has long ago reached. Unfortunately, within the limited scope of this overview, I cannot do justice to the multiplicity of voices and perspectives within each camp. However, I will highlight the divergent emphases of the two camps, in an attempt to show that their concerns are not necessarily incompatible.

10. Parts of the *Diary* were published in Carol Vance, ed., *Pleasure and Danger.*

11. These same two paragraphs recur in the article "Sexuality, Pornography, and Method: Pleasure under Patriarchy."

12. An antiporn feminist who does engage to some extent with the anti-antiporn stance is Sheila Jeffreys in the chapter "The Lesbian Sexual Revolution" of her book *The Lesbian Heresy*. Yet, she too relies mostly on her own formulations of pro-sex arguments and fails to quote her opponents. She also engages more with lesbian pornography itself rather than with theoretical defenses of it, and although her book was published in 1993, the only argument for lesbian pornography that she cites is by the British erotic author Barbara Smith.
13. This is the definition proposed in Dworkin and MacKinnon's civil rights ordinance, cited in *Only Words* (87).
14. For examples of such testimonies, see the records of the Minneapolis hearings collected in MacKinnon and Dworkin, *In Harm's Way*.
15. This claim and the quotation that follows it raise, of course, the question of the transparency or determinacy of the photographic and filmic image, as well as the question of levels of description. These issues will be elaborated in the section that discusses the problems in the antiporn position.
16. Note that her formulation does not specify that the violence reported is the violence shown on screen.
17. For example, discussing the definition of pornography proposed in the ordinance, MacKinnon says: "This definition is coterminous with the industry, from *Playboy*, in which women are objectified and presented dehumanized as sexual objects or things for use; through the torture of women and the sexualization of racism and the fetishization of women's body parts; to snuff films, in which actual murder is the ultimate sex act, the reduction to the thing form of a human being and the silence of women literal and complete" (*Only Words* 16).
18. For convenience sake (and since women often participate in more than one segment of the sex industry), I do not distinguish between porn magazine models, porn movie actors, and live show performers but employ the term "models" to designate all of the aforementioned.
19. For example, "With pornography, men masturbate to women being exposed, humiliated, violated, degraded, mutilated, dismembered, bound, gagged, tortured and killed" (*Only Words*, 12). There are also things to be said about the terms that MacKinnon employs

to describe what we see in pornography and what is done to the women in it, that is, not only about the grammar but also about the semantics of the descriptions, but this will be referred to later.

20. "In the case of other inequalities, it is sometimes understood that people do degrading work out of a lack of options.... With women, it just proves that this is what we are really for, this is our true nature" (*Feminism Unmodified* 180).

21. For Linda Marciano's testimony at the Minneapolis hearings, see *In Harm's Way* (60–68). The example of *Deep Throat* is a particularly poignant one, since the ethos of this film, which inaugurated the age of the hardcore feature film, embodies, as Linda Williams points out, the ideology of sexual liberation and, in particular, female sexual liberation. The story of *Deep Throat* is centered on a woman's quest for sexual fulfillment; that this fictional quest in fact covered a real tale of coercion and abuse seems to indict the ideology of sexual liberation as both a veil for and instrument of the actual exploitation of women (see Williams, *Hard Core* 110–114).

22. The view of visual representation, particularly cinematic representation as aggressive and violating, is not unique to MacKinnon. The sadism and phallicism of the cinematic "gaze" is a standard assumption of feminist film theory, originating in Laura Mulvey. Susan Sontag too offers a formulation that MacKinnon would have been glad to embrace: "To photograph people is to violate them ... to photograph someone is sublimated murder.... The act of taking pictures is a semblance of rape" (qtd. in Clover 177).

23. For a survey of the existing research on the perceptual and dispositional effects of exposure to (mostly visual) pornography, see Weaver. Weaver concludes that, on the whole, the existing body of research shows that exposure to erotica (his term) causes "enhanced sexual callousness toward women," and that there is also robust evidence for "adverse perceptual consequences resulting from exposure to coercive and/or violent erotica" (349). Interestingly, he finds that "idealized" or egalitarian portrayals of sexuality also have the same callousness-promoting effect. A previous survey (Donnerstein, Linz, and Penrod) reaches somewhat different conclusions, namely, that no definite conclusions could be drawn about nonviolent but degrading images of women, and that "the calloused attitudes to rape, which may in certain cases follow exposure to violent pornography, may not so much be *caused* by the exposure to pornography

as strengthened by it" (Segal, "Does Pornography Cause Violence?" 13). And in any case, many social scientists and media researchers question the soundness of the methodology, analytical categories, and data interpretation in such research (see McNair chap. 5; Christensen, esp. chap. 10). Further, they cast doubt over the very validity of the experimental approach to address the question of the effects of pornography. As Karen Boyle, following Robert Jensen, claims, this approach is deeply problematic for its reliance on a model of linear causality. To paraphrase Boyle: In a society saturated with sexist images of women, attempting to isolate any one representation as the "cause" of subsequent behavior, emotions, or attitudes is hopeless. Even establishing correlations between on-screen subordination of women and real-world subordination of women is problematic. (Cf. Segal, whose own conclusion from the "experimental muddle" is that *"it is never possible, whatever the image, to isolate it, to fix its meaning and predict some inevitable pattern of response, independently from assessing its wider representational context and the particular recreational, educational or social context in which it is received"* ["Does Pornography" 15]). And Jensen states: "It is not clear what the instruments that are used are actually measuring, and there is no way to devise an instrument to measure what we want to measure" ("Using Pornography" 103).

24. For example, "Pornography is a means through which sexuality is socially constructed, a site of construction. . . . It constructs women as things for sexual use . . ." (*Theory of the State* 139).

25. Judith Butler discusses in the introduction to *Bodies That Matter* the assumption that construction requires a subject and the deterministic understanding of construction as two common misunderstandings or reductions of the constructivist position (6–7).

26. For an elaborate analysis of MacKinnon's reliance on the Marxist model and a critique of her position based on this analysis, see Wendy Brown.

27. Drawing on Marxist epistemology, Nancy Hartsock's standpoint theory similarly assumes that the vision of the ruling class/gender is made real owing to its control of the means of mental as well as physical production, which gives it the power to define the terms for the community as a whole (288). However, since Hartsock sees women's standpoint as growing out of the kinds of work that women as a group perform under the sexual division of labor,

according to her description the male vision cannot shape social reality entirely. Under MacKinnon's description of male domination as all-encompassing, on the other hand, it is not clear what experience a dissenting feminist viewpoint could be grounded in.

28. In "Sexuality, Pornography, and Method" MacKinnon suggests that we can think of "women's sexuality as women's like Black culture is Blacks'—it is and it isn't" (343). By this she means that both should be understood as a response to powerlessness and cannot be regarded as expressions of agency and autonomy.

29. Examples given by Austin are the naming of a ship, the making of a promise or a bet, the pronouncement of the marriage vows, and so on.

30. This point has been made by Califia, "Among Us, Against Us"; Rubin, "Misguided, Dangerous, and Wrong"; Wicke; Williams, "Second Thoughts on Hard Core"; Echols; Modleski; and Ross, among others.

31. Rubin adds that even if we broaden the definition of pornography to encompass sexually explicit visual imagery in general, no systematic correlation could be found between cultures that produce such images and low status for women.

32. MacKinnon and Dworkin's antiporn ordinances include in their definition of pornography "the use of men, children or transsexuals in the place of women" (*Feminism Unmodified* 262n1).

33. The most famous example provided by Foucault in volume 1 of *The History of Sexuality* is the sexological discourse of the nineteenth century that defined homosexuals as a distinct species, thus giving institutional power a hold on the subjects it has constructed, while allowing them on the other hand to claim legitimacy on the ground of the naturalness of their sexuality (101).

34. "From the *testimony* of the pornography, what men want is: women bound, women battered, women tortured, women humiliated and defiled, women killed. Or, to be fair to the soft core, women sexually accessible . . ." (*Theory of the State* 138, my emphasis).

35. Mandy Merck, finding this ambiguity reflected in MacKinnon's metaphorization of men as dogs, asks: "But what should we fear most? The danger of male sexuality trained in sexism or the danger of it wild?" ("MacKinnon's Dog" 8).

36. Despite the fact that she identifies herself as a materialist or a post-Marxist, and despite her rejection of so-called feminine values and

of theories celebrating feminine difference, the assumption of an inherently predatory and sadistic male sexuality aligns MacKinnon with the theoretical paradigm of cultural feminism, which asserts precisely such difference and such values. On cultural feminism and the antiporn movement as its latter-day manifestation, see Alice Echols.

37. This point is made also by Stern and others.
38. "In practice, fucking is an act of possession—simultaneously an act of ownership, taking, force; it is conquering; it expresses in intimacy power over and against, body to body, person to thing" (Dworkin, *Pornography* 69, qtd. in MacKinnon, *Theory of the State* 282n38).
39. Cf. Rubin who remarks that Dworkin and MacKinnon's view of pornography as "a documentary of abuse" attests to "a fundamental confusion between the content of an image and the conditions of its production" ("Misguided" 266–268).
40. The same point of interpretive indeterminacy applies also to certain parts of the ordinance's definition of pornography. For instance, how does one determine what are "postures of sexual submission or servility"? As apparent from her discussion of *Deep Throat* in an amicus brief filed on behalf of Linda Marchiano in Indianapolis, MacKinnon defines oral sex performed by a woman on a man as a posture of sexual submission, but would she regard the opposite case in the same way? On this and other crucial points of definitional vagueness in the ordinance, see Duggan, Hunter, and Vance. For the ordinance's definition, see MacKinnon, *Feminism Unmodified* (176).
41. This criticism of the antiporn position is made by Rubin ("Misguided") among others.
42. For accounts of the latter sort, see the anthologies *Sex Work* and *Whores and Other Feminists*.
43. The former explanation is offered by Lynne Segal ("Sweet Sorrows, Painful Pleasures"), the latter by Judith Butler (*Excitable Speech* 68) and Wendy Brown (87), respectively.
44. "Where the cinema is seen to be structured by the Unconscious, in a simultaneous movement the viewer's unconscious is seen to be structured by the filmic work" (Stern 55).
45. This point is made by Snitow, Duggan ("Censorship"), Califia ("Among Us"), Rubin ("Misguided"), and others. Duggan provides a detailed case study of the passing of the Indianapolis ordinance, documenting the contribution of right-wing politicians and

Christian fundamentalists to the passing of this so-called feminist law. MacKinnon, who drafted the ordinance for the city council, is depicted as either ignorant of the nature of the political coalition behind it or turning a blind eye to it.

46. This is pointed out by lesbian sex radicals like Califia ("Among Us") and Rubin ("Thinking Sex") but reiterated also by Kipnis ("She-Male Fantasies"), Modleski, and Williams ("Second Thoughts").
47. MacKinnon ends her chapter on sexuality in *Theory of the State* with the following quote from Ti-Grace Atkinson: "I do not know any feminist worthy of the name who, if forced to choose between freedom and sex, would choose sex" (154); whereas Ann Snitow remarks of the same quote: "While women are forced to make such a choice we cannot consider ourselves free" (17).
48. This is true particularly of other lesbian sex radicals like Califia and many of the writers in Samois, ed., *Coming to Power*, but also of Willis and others.
49. For a more elaborate discussion of this point, see the introduction to the present volume.
50. Film, advertising, and mainstream media have probably a much more significant role in the cultural construction of sexuality than pornography, due to their larger volume and greater accessibility, yet none of these discourses is identified with "the sexual" in the same way as pornography.
51. This criticism is voiced by Teresa de Lauretis in relation to Judith Butler's polemic against Andrea Dworkin. De Lauretis criticizes reductive applications of Laplanche and Pontalis's theory of fantasy by cultural theorists and stresses the theoretical and political importance of retaining the threefold distinction between representation, action, and fantasy ("On the Subject of Fantasy").
52. For a broader discussion of Butler's theory of performativity, see chapter 5.
53. De Lauretis puts Dworkin's name in quotation marks to signal that she is not referring to Andrea Dworkin the author but to Dworkin as characterized by Judith Butler in her polemic against her.
54. "Much of what I heard was not just news; it was revelatory. There was a story about pornography that had not yet been told," writes Paul (3).
55. This dismissal of Dworkin and MacKinnon is, however, by no means universal. Karen Boyle, for instance, confesses her admiration

for their work, while asserting at the same time that they are not "the only word on anti-porn feminism," and that it's important to keep in mind the historical and disciplinary context of their work (Boyle "Introduction," 4).
56. As they note, the notion of "healthy sex" suggested in recent anti-porn writings pretty much fits into Rubin's description of the "charmed circle" of what is considered good sexuality, thus implying a very conservative sexual ideology. See Rubin, "Thinking Sex."
57. Paul adduces statistical evidence pointing to an increasing percentage of porn addiction in both adults and teenagers, in addition to some men's testimonies about their porn habit getting out of control, and then goes on to claim that there is no fundamental difference between regular users and those who are addicted, since "recovering pornography addicts describe their usage in very similar terms to those who continue to use pornography on a purportedly casual basis" (213–215).
58. See, for example, the following remark: "It's what all industrial products do, they kill creativity, they kill authenticity, and in their place they hand back to you a generic plasticized, formulaic version that hardly resembles the real thing" (Dines et al., "Arresting Images" 27).
59. As Smith and Attwood comment following Lynne Segal, this presentational style, which conjoins "shock cuts" with a narrative that invites horror and outrage as the appropriate reactions to the images, mimics the very qualities attributed to pornography, thereby reproducing what they consider a pornographic view of the world (48).
60. Similarly, Paul states: "To argue that pornography has no effect on the people who consume it would be like arguing that the multibillion-dollar advertising business is all for naught, that people aren't influenced by what they see, read or hear, and that all media are inconsequential" (72).
61. Mercer also points out the relative absence of black women from the antiporn movement and the fact that black feminism has not prioritized the issue of pornography.
62. "It's Easy Out Here for a Pimp: How a Porn Culture Grooms Kids for Sexual Exploitation," slide show, Stop Porn Culture, quoted in Smith and Attwood 42.
63. See Dines 98; Sabo 198–199.

64. Gagging refers to the insertion of a penis down a woman's throat until she gags. Unlike the practice of "deep throat" fellatio that emphasizes the expertise of the fellator, here the woman is usually passive, and the explicit objective is to induce gagging and retching. Ass To Mouth (ATM) refers to the practice of anal penetration immediately followed by oral penetration into the receptive partner's (or another person's) mouth without cleansing the penis. Both practices carry indisputable significations of domination and humiliation, the pleasure of the practice residing in the female performer's degradation. A study conducted in the mid-2000s that content-analyzed bestselling videos found that 41 percent of the scenes included ass to mouth and 28 percent included gagging (Bridges 46).
65. Interestingly, in the collection *Mainstreaming Sex*, edited by Feona Attwood, it is a male writer who expresses concern about the debasement of women and the treatment of female performers in the genre of extreme Gonzo and suggests that current academic porn studies do not sufficiently engage with the real conditions of the porn industry (Maddison).
66. For example, Duggan, Hunter, and Vance discuss the vagueness of the terms "subordination," "degradation, and "sex object" that appear in the definition of pornography in the Minneapolis ordinance ("False Promises").
67. *Adult Video News*, the porn industry magazine, defines Gonzo as "porno verité or reality-based porn, in which performers acknowledge the presence of the camera, frequently addressing viewers directly through it" (qtd. in Meagan Tyler 57).

Chapter 2. The Phantasmatic Gay Man

1. The reading of the *Beauty* trilogy is based in part on my "The Pervert's Progress."
2. Though, as befits fairy tales, no spatial and temporal coordinates are given, the queen's kingdom appears to be located in medieval Europe. This location serves to sever the trope of slavery from the colonial imaginary and especially from any paradigm of racial domination. When a phantasmatic "Orient" is drawn on in the third book, the colonial power relations are reversed as European

princes and princesses find themselves enslaved in the Sultan's court (though orientalist stereotypes are activated, notwithstanding). By severing slavery from a paradigm of racial domination, and imagining a system of erotic domination completely unfounded on any social power differentials, the text in effect refuses the harnessing of race, and of the trope of slavery in particular, by feminist antiporn discourse to describe the subordination of women in pornography.

3. Thus the male slaves are expected to maintain a constant erection even though they are rarely allowed to perform penetration.
4. The term "sex/gender system" was coined by Gayle Rubin in her essay "The Traffic in Women" to signify "the set of arrangements by which a society transforms biological sexuality into products of human activity, and in which these transformed sexual needs are satisfied" (159).
5. This shift is all the more apparent in the fact that it is Laurent's voice that ends the narrative, telling of his reunion with Beauty. In this narrative event, which concerns Beauty and Laurent equally, Rice chooses to adopt the male character's point of view, depriving us of any insight into Beauty's consciousness, to which we have been privy throughout the book. This choice corresponds to (and is made more poignant by) the fact that in this reunion Laurent assumes full command of the relationship, turning Beauty into his marital slave. And the decisive transfer of both sexual mastery and narrative focus to the male figure is reinforced by the weight of the closure.
6. Esther Newton writes of nineteenth-century sexual ideology: "The low status of working women and women of color, as well as their participation in the public sphere, deprived them of the feminine purity that protected bourgeois women from males and from deriving sexual pleasure" ("Mannish Lesbian" 284).
7. Thus, paradoxically, if Freud designates male sexual masochism "feminine masochism," since it places the subject "in a characteristically female situation," when women identify with the position of the (male) feminine masochist—rather than with a woman in a similar position—we get a further turn of the screw that prevents the construal of female masochistic desires as a simple extension of women's physiological or social "situation" ("Economic Problem" 277).
8. Of course, sexual agency does not exist independently of the actual power relations within which sexual interactions take place.

However, inasmuch as the notion of sexual agency is also an ideological construct, this kind of phantasmatic cross-gender identification can open the way for different interpretations and valuations of heterosexual female sexuality that circumvent its alleged incompatibility with sexual subjectivity.

9. The genre is known as "slash" because works that take as their premise an explicitly sexual relation between two of the main male characters of a TV series are designated in fan publications and websites by a slash, for example, K/S designates texts that feature a romantic and erotic relationship between Captain Kirk and Mr. Spock from the TV series *Star Trek*.

10. Anne Kustritz, whose article on slash fiction postdates Penley's by a decade, concurs with these demographics (Kustritz 371). However, these demographics may not be quite up to date, as in recent years there is an increased presence of queer-identified women and men in slash communities.

11. Camilla Decarnin makes a similar point concerning fag hags, that is, "women whose primary erotic objects are gay men." She suggests that fag hags "have consciously or otherwise recognized men's valued positioning in society and desired to be valued as men are valued, while retaining a wish to be erotic with men.... in other words, the woman recognizes in the faggot a socio-erotic position she herself would like to hold, as the recognized peer *and* lover of a male, a position impossible for women in sexist culture to secure" (10).

12. See Virginia Woolf, *A Room of One's Own*, chapter 5.

13. Cf. Lynne Segal's account of her readerly identification as a young heterosexual woman with James Baldwin and the "uncompromisingly unconventional passions of the homosexual/bisexual characters he depicted." Segal explains that narratives of gay male desire enable "the comforting doubling of identification, both with the desiring subject and the desired object" (*Straight Sex* 234).

14. On the other hand, perhaps writing their erotic fantasies "across the bodies of two men" enables women to write pornography without implicating their own bodies and their own sexuality, a strategy that is less self-revealing and therefore less threatening, especially bearing in mind that the authors are amateur writers.

15. When Decarnin's fag-hag interviewees are asked about the thing that attracts them most about gay men, they mention both gay

men's greater capacity for empathy and emotional expressiveness and the fact that "they tend to treat their bodies more as sexual objects and to present themselves as fuckable" (12).

16. In a similar vein, Leo Bersani suggests that male homosexual sex should be celebrated for its intrinsic potential to oppose phallocentrism: "Gay men's 'obsession' with sex . . . never stops re-presenting the internalized phallic male as an infinitely loved object of sacrifice." Hence, "The rectum is the grave in which the masculine ideal . . . of proud subjectivity is buried" and "it should be celebrated for its very potential for death" ("Is the Rectum a Grave?" 222).

17. On the other hand, the abundance of inanimate incarnations of the phallus still indicates a degree of abstraction that distinguishes the *Beauty* trilogy from more traditional heterosexual works such as Pauline Réage's *Story of O*, where the gaze of the female slaves is constantly directed at the actual male sex, which is unproblematically equated with the phallus.

18. Obviously, every lesbian community has a sexual culture. However, I am employing the term "sex culture" in a more specific sense, to designate explicit cultural preoccupation with sex, that includes the production of cultural artifacts such as pornographic literature, magazines, and films, as well as sex toys; the elaboration of sexual institutions such as sex parties and strip nights; and widespread discussion of sexuality in community forums.

19. Since the beginning of the 1990s, lesbian cross-identification with gay men has occurred increasingly under the auspices of the term "queer" as a joint identity category for men and women, as well as one that marks a distance from the supposedly monolithic identity category "lesbian" that has come to bear connotations of tameness, domesticity, and gender intransitivity. However, since I will be looking mostly at the early moments of this process of investment in gay male sexuality by those who today might identify as queer women or queer female-embodied persons—but who in the eighties or early nineties still identified mostly as lesbians or dykes—I will adhere to the category "lesbian" despite its somewhat dated feel.

20. A lesbian interviewee in Camilla Decarnin's article on fag hags expresses a similar connection between gender dysphoria and identification with gay men: "It's not a great distance to travel from being a butch dyke to being a butch faggot" (13). And as Gayle Rubin points out, gay male culture provided models for

butch-butch eroticism, which lesbian culture lacked ("Catamites and Kings" 472–473).
21. On butch masculinity as part of a range of alternative masculinities, see Halberstam. Since Halberstam's project is one of lending visibility to female masculinities, and asserting their independence of—even indifference to—male masculinity, she tends to naturalize female masculinity as given and irreducible. I, on the other hand, will often inquire into the *significance* of masculinity in its female manifestations, not to question its credibility in female-born persons but to underscore the equation between masculinity and sexual subjectivity.
22. This point will be elaborated in chapter 4.
23. These stories are "The Spoiler" in *Macho Sluts* and "Unsafe Sex" in *Melting Point*. Though some of her gay male fiction appeared in gay male publications, Califia has stated she believes that most of the readership of her gay male porn is lesbian ("Identity Sedition" 89). This is the point to acknowledge the challenge that reference to Califia's work presents to a contemporary critic. Currently known as Patrick Califia, Califia began living as a man in 2000, after being for over two decades an influential and controversial public figure in the lesbian community. As a prolific author of lesbian pornography and one of the pioneers and public spokespersons of lesbian sex culture, both Califia's fiction and her social and cultural commentary are central to this work. However, to adopt the accepted practice of retroactively using male pronouns to speak about texts Califia published when still identifying as female would be untrue both to the authorial position from which these texts were written and to their contexts of publication and reception. Califia himself in his 2002 book, *Speaking Sex to Power*, which includes essays written before his transition, decided to leave pieces written from a female perspective in their original voice and explains in the introduction that he has no intention to repudiate his life history as a woman, and that he believes that his current gender identity does not invalidate the positions he held and the work he did in his former identity as a dyke. He indicates that he does not wish to be erased from lesbian herstory and asserts that he did not understand himself in the past as a man. Since in this book I refer to stories and essays Califia published well before his transition, I chose to use the authorial name Pat Califia and employ female pronouns, a choice that should

in no way be construed as dismissive of his current gender identity but stems rather from the wish to remain faithful to the original point of view from which these texts were written and avoid turning Califia's later gender transition into a retrospective interpretive framework for these texts.

24. In recent years, a filmic equivalent of *Switch Hitters*, has emerged in the form of the international film project *Fucking Different*. The project began in 2005 in Berlin and was followed by sister films in New York, Sao Paulo, Tel Aviv, and San Francisco, all sharing the same concept: Gay men make films about lesbians and lesbians make films about gay men. The latest edition of the series, *Fucking Different XXX* (Germany 2011), features work by prominent international filmmakers.

25. Of course, gay men's relative lack of phantasmatic investment or interest in lesbian sexuality may also reflect the fact that in general men's experience is still constructed as the norm and as more valuable than women's experience. Further, inasmuch as male homosexuality is conceived under a gender-separatist topos (see the discussion of Sedgwick at the end of this chapter), this precludes identification with women, whether straight or lesbian.

26. *Herotica* is a collection of women's erotic fiction and includes both lesbian and straight stories.

27. Another clue that warns against a clear delimitation of fantasy from autobiography is the fact that the name of the gay male hero, Peter, echoes the name of the author, Roberta Stone (the narrator remains unnamed).

28. The function of leather or s/m as an identity-founding "orientation" that has the power to override gender boundaries will be discussed in chapter 6.

29. In a similar vein, Dorothy Allison writes about having untamed sex with women in tribute to the lost gay male sexual freedom obliterated by AIDS.

30. The significations of the dildo in lesbian representation and theorization will be discussed at length in chapter 4.

31. This point is made by Sheila Jeffreys (125–127). One need not share her negative valuation of the gay male influence on lesbian culture to agree with her observations regarding the identifications and discursive functions at stake in lesbian safe-sex discourse. At any rate, lesbian safe-sex discourse has largely died down since the

mid-nineties, though lesbian and queer video porn does occasionally feature latex gloves and condoms on dildos.
32. Jeffreys's critique of the changes in the lesbian community in the eighties and nineties may be related to her location in British and later Australian lesbian feminism. In these countries, lesbian feminism has maintained a stronger hold, and the convergence of lesbians and gay men has perhaps not been as marked as in the United States.
33. I am indebted to Gayle Rubin for her formulation of this point.
34. Such an argument would of course not be acceptable to lesbian feminist critics such as Jeffreys or Marilyn Frye, who view gay male culture as sharing "the same general principles of phallocracy" and gay men as loyal to male supremacy (Jeffreys 144–145). I will not argue here with their analysis, which conflates desire with class loyalty and disregards homophobia (cf. Earl Jackson's critique of Fry in *Strategies of Deviance* 8–11); my point is simply that *for* lesbians who form a phantasmatic identification with gay male sexuality, such identification may function to legitimate both passive and receptive desires and aggressive and sadistic ones by disrupting their equation with hetero-patriarchal femininity and masculinity, respectively.
35. In chapter 7 of *Group Psychology and the Analysis of the Ego* Freud formulates the distinction between identification and object choice as that between the wish *to be* and the wish *to have* (107). Throughout Freud's work these two wishes are always depicted as mutually exclusive. Even when in "The Ego and the Id," Freud discusses the "complete" (positive *and* negative) Oedipus complex, which entails taking both parents as objects of identification and object choice alike, the complex is described in terms of a double or compounded subject, with each component part maintaining a mutually exclusive relation between desire and identification (33–34).
36. Butler herself stresses that "cross-gendered identification is not the only paradigm for thinking about homosexuality, merely one among others" ("Melancholy Gender" 146).
37. It is also possible, and quite feasible, to see cross-gendered identifications as compensating for the loss of the man or woman one could never be, that is, for the need to renounce *being* the other sex. One might suggest that if a foreclosed desire can be transformed into melancholic identification, so too can the foreclosed ontological possibility of being the other sex. Because of the normative

assumption of sex-gender coherence, the loss of the man or woman one could never be is also an ungrievable one, hence, one that can lead to melancholic incorporation (this is one way to understand the butch's investment in masculinity or the drag queen's investment in femininity). However, this option too falls outside Freud's tradeoff paradigm that recognizes only the substitution of identification for object cathexis.

38. Cf. Diana Fuss: "The not inconsiderable achievement of Sedgwick's three influential books . . . is their collective challenge to the silent presumption that identities wholly correspond to identifications . . ." (6).
39. This notion of joint group membership is most evident in the identity category "queer" as a nongendered term subsuming lesbians and gay men.
40. Needless to say, in popular constructions of male homosexuality the inversion model is far from obsolete, and close relationships, both between gay men and straight women and between gay men and lesbians, are often predicated on the perceived "feminine" qualities of gay men—sensitivity, fashion sense, communicative skills, and so on. However, my focus here is on women's phantasmatic identifications with gay male *sexuality*, and it is in this particular context that gay men's *masculinity* acquires a new and previously unacknowledged significance.
41. Defining itself over against the categories "gay" and "lesbian," "queer" is an exceptional identity category in the sense that it calls into question essentialist constructions of identity. As Eve Sedgwick notes, "queer" as opposed to "gay" and "lesbian" is not an empirical category but hinges primarily on "performative acts of experimental self-perception and filiation," so that in important respects it is a term that "can signify only *when attached to the first person*" ("Queer and Now" 9, emphasis in the original).

Chapter 3. Refiguring Penetration

1. Note the rhetorical conflation of the man with his penis in this quote.
2. "Invasion" and "occupation" have specific military connotations. The female body is thus represented as a political entity, a metaphor

that inverts the "body politic" metaphor, which represents the nation as a body. (I am indebted to Mandy Merck for this observation.) The language of invasion, occupation, conquest, and ownership has also clear colonial overtones and draws on the implicit association of racial domination and slavery to bolster her argument that intercourse is incompatible with freedom.

3. In a similar vein, Judith Butler suggests that "pornography neither represents nor constitutes what women are, but offers an allegory of masculine willfulness and feminine submission." Butler is countering Catharine MacKinnon's claim that pornography constructs women's social reality and argues instead that it depicts "impossible and uninhabitable positions" and "compensatory fantasies." Thus, she in effect faults MacKinnon for taking pornography's "allegorical" representation at face value (*Excitable Speech* 68).

4. Tellingly, most of the chapter headings in her book invoke those cultural meanings and connotations of intercourse, for example, "Repulsion," "Communion," "Possession," "Occupation/Collaboration." These cultural meanings form the organizing axis of the book.

5. In the chapter entitled "Skinless," Dworkin uses language very reminiscent of Bataille to describe sexual experience: "Sometimes the skin comes off in sex. The people merge, skinless. The body loses its boundaries.... There is no physical distance, no self-consciousness.... Instead, there is necessity, nothing else—being driven, physical immersion in each other but with no experience of 'each other' as separate entities coming together" (*Intercourse* 21–22). That Dworkin is familiar with Bataille's work on eroticism is indicated by a short and dismissive reference to it in which she defines eroticism as "classy sex" and reduces Bataille's notion of the affinity between sex and death to a "convergence of sadism and sex on the woman's body" (*Intercourse* 190–191).

6. The parameters he mentions as relevant to this phantasmatic potential are penetration, physical position (top/bottom), and penile thrusting, as well as the high store that men set on the penis itself.

7. This assertion begs the question of what qualifies as a relationship and where does one draw the line between sex and a relationship; for example, doesn't an anonymous sexual encounter also qualify as a relationship of sorts, and might not power differentials play a role even in such a minimal relationship?

8. Cf. Lynda Hart, who notes that while "the 'woman' in Bersani's imaginary must be either a heterosexual female or a gay male, who presumably share the 'self-shattering' experience of being penetrated . . . the ecstasy of that self-shattering . . . is in the becoming of woman, which the heterosexual female does not share with the gay male. Not because she already is a woman but because she has already become one (in most cases)" (106).
9. It might be worthwhile to consider the possibility that on this point the feminist project may entail different political agendas for women and men.
10. Indeed, some representations of heterosexual sex turn the tables completely and figure women penetrating their male lovers. This is the theme of the video *Bend Over Boyfriend 2* by S.I.R. Productions, which features several episodes of heterosexual sex in which women anally penetrate their male partners with a dildo. It is probably no coincidence, however, that the video was produced by a company owned and managed by a lesbian couple that produces mostly lesbian porn; and that both *BOB 2* and its predecessor, the instructional film *Bend Over Boyfriend*, star bisexual author and educator Carol Queen. Cf. Heather Butler, who incorporates *BOB* in her history of lesbian video porn. Butler notes that the sexual techniques and practices advocated in the film are primary components of queer sex and concludes that we can see it as an example of lesbians instructing heterosexuals on new ways of sexual expression. Similarly, Michelle Carnes notes that though the *BOB* films are addressed to heterosexual couples, they transgress normative understandings of "normal" heterosexuality (Butler 190–191; Carnes 158).
11. John Boswell notes that the active/passive division current in the modern West has displaced the donor/recipient distinction, that is, the giving versus receiving of semen, which predominated in classical antiquity. Boswell speculates that it is this shift of paradigm that has made the Christian West more tolerant of fellatio than the ancients, since while the fellator occupies the ignoble pole of the donor/recipient divide, he escapes the charge of passivity (33–34). In contemporary pornography, the practice of face-fucking (as opposed to regular fellatio) and the increasingly popular practice of "gagging" seem to be intended to realign active/passive with donor/recipient.

12. See especially the prominent role of anal sex in the Marquis de Sade's novels or its depiction as violent and violating in Pauline Réage's *Histoire d'O*. The transgressive status of anal sex has of course a lot to do with the Christian prohibition on sodomy and its status as mortal sin. Many nonreligious discourses also reject anal sex owing both to its nongenerativity and scatological associations.
13. Cf. Ann Cvetkovich who, comparing the status of penetration in lesbian and in gay male culture, proposes that "the penetration of the anus is perhaps even more culturally freighted as a signifier of power than the penetration of the vagina" (136).
14. It may be objected that the fantasy positions associated with penetration are unrelated to the anatomy of the participants, hence, that the meanings of penetration in a lesbian context are not radically affected by the absence of genital pleasure for the penetrator. While I agree that sexual pleasure cannot be reduced to genital pleasure, and that the phantasmatic component is central to sexuality, nevertheless one mustn't lose sight of the character of sexual experience as embodied experience. The presence or absence of genital pleasure for the penetrator cannot but have some kind of psychic registration. Such a psychic registration does not rule out the phantasmatic inscription of the act in phallic terms; indeed, since lesbian sexuality is inflected by the heterosexual imaginary, penetration is bound to carry phallic connotations. However, while the phantasmatic dimension of a sexual exchange need not correspond to its corporeal actuality, it would be wrong to assume that the significations of the exchange are wholly determined by the phantasmatic stratum to the exclusion of the embodied dimension.
15. Thus, penetration may still be equated with power and domination, but the latter come to signify the power to gratify one's partner, and to dominate her through controlling her pleasure, rather than the power to use one's partner for one's own gratification.
16. There can, of course, be exceptions to this rule. Even between two women, sexual penetration might manifest a desire to overpower, humiliate, or hurt the bottom rather than pleasure her, yet even sadistic gratification of this kind remains distinct from genital gratification.
17. In their history of the butch/femme bar community in Buffalo, New York, Davis and Kennedy define image (i.e., dress and mannerism) and sexuality as the two determinants of butch/femme roles.

18. I am using here the terms "fucked" and "penetrated" more or less interchangeably, though of course the former term is far more figuratively charged than the latter, and furthermore, in lesbian usage, getting fucked does not necessarily signify being penetrated and may refer to other forms of receiving sexual gratification. This refusal of lesbian discourse to distinguish penetration from non-penetrative sexual practices on the linguistic plane itself contests the diacritic status of penetration in dominant culture. However, most of the femme accounts under discussion do refer to penetrative sex.
19. Cvetkovich comments on this linguistic strategy: "Ultimately the exchange of power seems more important than the actual physical acts . . . what is more important than the actual body parts is the 'appropriation of the body' (to use David Halperin's term) to signify the intersubjective dynamics of giving and taking. Given the complex interdependence of the physical and the psychic, a more explicit naming of the body would not help to represent the sexual act more accurately" (140).
20. As Gayle Rubin points out, the term "leather" carries in gay male culture a whole set of diverse significations: "Leather can connote brotherhood, masculinity, and independence, as well as certain sexual specializations. It may signal merely a passion for motorcycles. It may indicate an interest in sexual and social interactions among men with masculine personal styles, or announce a preference for some variety of 'kinky sex.'" Yet, as she stresses, all these desires, practices, and symbols are colored by masculinity when expressed through the key symbol of gay male leather ("Elegy" 102–103).
21. Male-male sex as a male initiation rite has, of course, a long and venerable history. The institution of paederastic love in ancient Greece is one of its more sublimated manifestations, while initiation rites for young warriors in New Guinea included daily oral insemination by older warriors, the ingestion of semen being thought to counter the feminizing influences of birth and rearing by women (Herdt). For a discussion of Greek paederasty as initiation and comparisons to other initiation rites involving male-male sex, see David Halperin.
22. In chapter 6 I will address the problem that this equation poses for the lesbian adoption of the gay male model of sexual subjectivity.
23. Needless to say, however, not all gay encounters take place between partners of equal status; same-sex interactions may be inflected by

other social power differentials, such as race, class, and so on. Indeed, in the sexual encounter depicted in the story, the neutralization of the gender hierarchy depends to a large extent on its replacement by the postcolonial power relations that obtain between the (presumably white) American couple and their Mexican and Chicano partners. The narrator herself situates the encounter within the frame of global economic exploitation and US cultural hegemony. At the end of the story, after blithely noting how shockingly cheap the transaction has been, she muses: "I wondered if this was how Japanese businessmen in Thailand felt. Was I contributing to the decline of the Third World?" (Queen, "Sweating Profusely" 195). But this thought does not mar the jubilant note of the closure, and moreover, the comparison to Japanese sex tourists only serves to reinforce her masculine positioning by marking her as a sexual consumer rather than a sexual commodity.
24. See, for instance, Angela Brown, ed., *Set in Stone: Butch-on-Butch Erotica*.
25. In anal fisting the heteronormative model of sexual penetration, that is, penis in vagina, is doubly displaced; the penis is demoted from its status as the privileged agent of penetration by the hand, and the vagina is displaced by the anus from its naturalized position as the orifice "made to be entered."
26. Cf. Rubin: "Many butches who lust after other butches have looked to gay male literature and behavior as sources of imagery and language. The erotic dynamics of butch-butch sex sometimes resemble those of gay men, who have developed many patterns for sexual relations between different kinds of men. Gay men also have role models for men who are passive or subordinate in sexual encounters yet retain their masculinity" ("Of Catamites and Kings" 472–473).
27. I will discuss the ways in which penetration figures in FTM porn in chapter 6.

Chapter 4. The Phallus and Its Vicissitudes

1. See also Chris Straayer's account of the emergence of lesbian pornography: "By the 1990s, artful interventions by both independent and commercial sex-tape producers displayed a signature aesthetic: the ideological collapse of commodity fetish and psychological

fetish was exploited in the sex toy" (216). Similarly, Colleen Lamos notes not only the increased representational and discursive prominence of the dildo but also a marked and steady increase in the sale of dildoes in shops and mail-order catalogues that serve lesbians (101).
2. Case seems to share this opinion, as she cites the argument that "masquerading lesbians, oppressed, finally, by codes of invisibility, had little choice but to appropriate the phallus in order to appear" ("The Student" 39). It is the phallus as signifier of desire and sexual agency whose appropriation allows the lesbian to appear, to inscribe her difference visually.
3. Colleen Lamos's essay "Taking On the Phallus" undertakes a somewhat similar critical project in its juxtaposition of feminist readings of the phallus and lesbian discourse on the dildo, though the scope of her theoretical inquiry is more restricted and her textual examples are different.
4. Lacanians, however, normally assert the autonomy of the symbolic order in relation to the social and posit a distinction between sexual difference and gender, regarding the latter as socially constructed and the former as a structural and constitutive aspect of the human subject. From the perspective of Lacanian psychoanalysis, social construction theory is seen to engage with second-order phenomena, for example, "the role of society in legitimizing and regulating particular forms of subjectivity," while psychoanalysis asks about the more foundational "role of the unconscious in the formation of subjectivity" (Elliot and Roen 246). However, much of the attraction of psychoanalysis for feminist and queer theorists depends on an understanding of the symbolic as, precisely, culturally constructed, that is, as the registration of social norms in the individual psyche.
5. The phallus is both the agent of castration (signifier of the father's imaginary attributes) and the object of the mother's desire, hence, that which the child desires but is forbidden to be; it is the lost object of desire and the signifier of the desire of the other; it is also the privileged signifier, representing the being sacrificed in subjectivation; and, as that which one can either have or be, it is the mark of sexual difference.
6. In Eve Sedgwick's felicitous phrase, psychoanalysis is "the modular science of the phallus, complete with a transformational grammar

for translating every organ, every behavior, every role and desire into a calculus of phallic presence or absence" ("Is the Rectum Straight?" 95). As Sedgwick notes, the resulting theoretical elegance is the source of "the intense intellectual appeal of psychoanalysis," but this elegance comes at the price of tautological slipperiness.
7. As Rubin points out, "One can read Freud's essays on femininity as descriptions of how a group is prepared psychologically, at a tender age, to live with its oppression" ("Traffic" 196).
8. Jacqueline Rose, writing from an orthodox Lacanian perspective, criticizes Rubin's account for "losing sight ... of the concept of the unconscious and the whole problem of sexual identity, reducing the relations described to a quite literal set of acts of exchange" (69n55).
9. An example for a term having both an ordinary usage and a specialized technical usage would be the two denotations of "mouse." According to *Webster's Ninth New Collegiate Dictionary*, "mouse" refers both to "any of numerous small rodents with pointed snout, rather small ears, elongated body, and slender tail" and to "a small mobile manual device that controls movement of the cursor in a computer display." The two referents exist independently in spite of the metaphorical link that grounds their homonymy.
10. Since, obviously, every linguistic expression is a signifier, Lacan seems to be referring not to the term "phallus" but to the object this term refers to, an object that he defines as a signifier.
11. This understanding is similar to the one offered by Laplanche and Pontalis in their definition of "phallus": "In psychoanalysis, the use of this term underlines the symbolic function taken on by the penis in the intra- and inter-subjective dialectic" ("Phallus" 312).
12. In "Splitting of the Ego in the Process of Defence," Freud further complicates his understanding of the process by positing two events that need to take place simultaneously for fetishistic disavowal to occur: the sight of the female genitals and a threat of castration. The sight alone, when unaccompanied by a threat, can be defended against and need not induce a fetishistic reaction.
13. In "Fetishism," Freud uses "phallus" and "penis" interchangeably; hence, I will not attempt a rigorous distinction between the two either.
14. As Laqueur shows, the one-sex model dominated biology and medicine until the eighteenth century, when it gave way to the two-sex

model. However, if we heed Eve Sedgwick's reminder that paradigm changes are never entirely clear-cut, it shouldn't surprise us to find a premodern sexual theory springing up in an early twentieth-century discipline (*Epistemology* 44–48).

15. It might also be objected that according to Freud, an attraction to shoes—or any other fetish object or trait—does not necessarily displace an attraction to women entirely. Freud distinguishes two classes of cases: one "in which the sexual object is required to fulfill a fetishistic condition" (i.e., the shoe remains attached to the woman), and the more pathological one in which the fetish "becomes the *sole* sexual object" (Freud, "Three Essays" 153–154). And while in the first class of cases the fetish serves to buttress heterosexual attraction by "endowing women with the characteristic which makes them tolerable as sexual objects" (Freud, "Fetishism" 155), the distinction between the fetish and the woman who bears it remains intact.

16. Gayle Rubin suggests some of the material and cultural factors that need to be taken into account in a historically informed study of fetishism ("Sexual Traffic" 52).

17. Relying on the psychoanalytic understanding of castration as a threat to the subject's narcissism, de Lauretis reinflects the notion of castration, assigning it the more general sense of "narcissistic wound," a sense that is only secondarily refigured in terms of sexual difference.

18. Not surprisingly, Judith Halberstam rejects both de Lauretis's reading of the character of Stephen Gordon and her theory of lesbian desire in general. Clearly, de Lauretis's understanding of lesbian masculinity in terms of fetishism is at odds with the primacy and irreducibility that Halberstam accords female masculinity. However, while as I noted, de Lauretis's model is problematic on several counts, I doubt that there is ground for accusing her of "butchphobia" as Halberstam does. Surely, rejecting a character's self-understanding or even an author's understanding of her character is a legitimate critical move, and moreover, in stressing Stephen Gordon's sense of lack and dispossession de Lauretis is merely following Radclyffe Hall's text rather than condemning masculine women to "the pathos of male mimicry" (Halberstam 102). The pathos is already inherent in the novel, and the charge of reducing lesbian masculinity to male

mimicry clearly does not do justice to de Lauretis's far more complex theorization and cannot be reconciled with her rejection of Freud's notion of the masculinity complex.
19. Please note that this survey is not organized chronologically. Butler's essay predates de Lauretis's book, and de Lauretis alludes to it and distinguishes her notion of lesbian fetishism from Butler's trope of the lesbian phallus, though as she points out, both the term "phallus" and the term "fetish" function to signify desire.
20. Butler's implicit definition of the lesbian phallus is in line with Pat Califia's characterization of the butch phallus and its dependence on the femme's response: "If the butch phallus does not succeed in giving the femme sexual pleasure, it does not exist" ("Genderbending" 180).
21. Merck claims that the physical and instrumental specificity of Butler's catalogue runs counter to her definition of the phallus as "an idealization, a phantasm" ("Lesbian Hand" 133). Yet, while obviously a pelvic bone cannot enjoy in our culture the same degree of idealization as a penis, it is not merely instrumental either, since in a lesbian context it becomes charged with the valence of sexual agency.
22. Lamos makes a useful distinction between three "meanings" assigned to the dildo or three foci of lesbian popular discourse on the dildo: 1. the dildo as "unnatural": an artificial commodity or prosthesis, incompatible with "natural" lesbian sexuality; 2. the dildo as a fetish object aligned with other fetishistic practices, such as s/m; 3. and the dildo as an assertion of male identification (103).
23. Other lesbian production companies that emerged in the 1980s, such as Tigress, Tri-Image, and Lavender Blue, did not survive as long as Fatale.
24. The images she watches seem to be taken from old Hollywood films and represent the normative ways of looking at women constructed by classical Hollywood cinema. These images include a woman hitching rides, another woman escaping down stairs, and a burlesque dancer performing on a stage, namely, women as either glamorous erotic objects or potential sexual prey.
25. Cf. Lamos, who also cites the dildo in lesbian pornography and sexual practice as evidence for female fetishism and women's share in the perverse visual pleasures that Mulvey designated as male (Lamos 116–117).

26. Cf. Lamos: "The simultaneous avowal and disavowal of sexual difference inherent in the dildo renders it a fetish in the psychoanalytic sense" (111).
27. Cf. Straayer: "Just as the presence of the penis marks hardcore pornography, the dildo's presence heightened the level of sexual energy in lesbian porn" ("Discourse Intercourse" 215).
28. Thus, for example, she says of *Deep Throat*, the film that inaugurated the genre of feature-length hardcore pornography: "In just about every sense, *Deep Throat* can be said . . . visually to fetishize the penis" (*Hard Core* 112).
29. This insight finds expression in the popular adage that the penis is a dildo substitute. Lesbian folk wisdom often extols the advantages of the dildo over the penis: With a dildo you can change size and shape according to the preferences of your partner, stay hard for as long as you like, and remove it at will.

    The dildo falls short, however, in one respect: it does not ejaculate, whereas it's the ejaculating penis that has become the central fetish of hardcore porn. This shortcoming is remedied in *Clips* by the female cum shot, discussed later, a solution that splits off ejaculation from the image of the phallus.
30. Cf. Lamos: "The dildo exposes the penis as a deceptive, nonidentical double of the phallus" (111).
31. One is reminded here of Althusser's tenet that obviousness is an ideological effect.
32. Screening the film to various audiences, I have noticed that male spectators often failed to note her orgasm.
33. Similarly, Lamos asserts that lesbian representations of the dildo "offer the opportunity of displacing and delegitimating phallic authority and sexual agency at the same moment as they claim such authority and agency for the dildo" (118).
34. Cf. note 4 in this chapter regarding lesbians' need to appropriate the phallus in order to overcome their cultural invisibility.
35. However, heterosexual porn too occasionally has recourse to the figure of the phallus to signify female sexual agency. In Magenta Michaels's short story "Taking Him on a Sunday Afternoon" (already mentioned in the previous chapter), the narrator initiates sex with her lover, taking the aggressor's role, and while fellating him imagines having a dick and penetrating him. In that fantasy she is still a woman, but having a dick is associated with domination,

the power to initiate and orchestrate the sex, unlimited access to her lover's body, and complete control of both his pleasure and her own. The fantasy arises when she tries to insert a finger into his anus and he resists, and she reflects that if she had a dick he would not be able to rebuff her. In the actual situation depicted in the story the narrator does exert sexual agency—within the bounds acceptable in the protocols of heterosexual sex—but this agentic stance, culturally coded as masculine, spontaneously gives rise to the phantasmatic figure of the phallus as its ultimate manifestation and culmination, implying that as a woman she is barred from full exercise of such agency.

36. This is not to suggest that there is *a single* lesbian feminist project and *a single* heterosexual feminist project, or that Gallop should be regarded as representing heterosexual feminism and a film like *Clips* as representing lesbian feminism. The two do, however, testify to the existence of divergent goals and divergent strategies in the two constituencies.

Chapter 5. Sexuality beyond Gender

1. My discussion of the notion of performance relies in large part on Marvin Carlson.
2. See especially the work of Erving Goffman, for example, *The Presentation of Self in Everyday Life*.
3. See the work of Victor Turner (e.g., *From Ritual to Theatre* and *Dramas, Fields, and Metaphors*) and Richard Schechner (e.g., *Between Theater and Anthropology*).
4. Schechner calls performance "restored behavior" (qtd. in Carlson 15).
5. Many common usages of the notion simply assume the theatrical frame heedless of Butler's objections; I, however, would like to argue for reintroducing it to the concept of gender performativity based on a careful exegesis of Butler's thought.
6. Cf. also: "If gender attributes, however, are not expressive but performative, then these attributes effectively constitute the identity they are said to express or reveal" (*Gender Trouble* 141).
7. "Consider gender, for instance, as *a corporeal style*, an 'act,' as it were, which is both intentional and performative, where '*performative*'

suggests a *dramatic* and contingent construction of meaning" (*Gender Trouble* 139, last emphasis mine).
8. For example, Butler employs (though in a loose sense) the term "social drama," coined by the anthropologist Victor Turner to convey an understanding of social situations, especially ones of conflict, in terms of dramatic structure (*Gender Trouble*, 140; Burke 784).
9. Derrida asks: "Could a performative utterance succeed if its formulation did not repeat a 'coded' or iterable utterance, or in other words, if the formula I pronounce in order to open a meeting, launch a ship or a marriage were not identifiable as *conforming* with an iterable model, if it were not then identifiable in some way as a 'citation'" (Derrida 191–192).
10. *Paris Is Burning*, which documents a subculture of black and Hispanic gay men and drag queens in New York City of the 1980s, a subculture that revolves around drag balls, demonstrates the expansion of the notion of drag to other dimensions of identity, most notably race and class. In these balls contestants compete in a wide array of categories that involve the performance not only of femininity or straight masculinity but also of whiteness, or more accurately white-marked statuses and roles, such as "opulence," "executive," "high-fashion model," among others. The film collaborates in highlighting the performativity of race and class by cross-cutting from these performances of white upper-class femininity and masculinity by poor blacks and Latinos to real-life professional and affluent white women and men on the streets of uptown Manhattan. The construction of an alternative kinship system, which Butler upholds as this culture's main achievement, is of particular importance for queers of color, who as members of underprivileged ethnic groups are rendered even more vulnerable by the break with their families and communities of origin.
11. Butler also addresses in this text the shortcomings of the theatrical trope for describing gender constitution. Chief among them is the very definition of the theatrical in contradistinction to the real (as that which is "just an act," "only a play"), whereas gender performance constitutes the real.
12. It is possible that the term "gender fuck" had its inception even earlier, in the early seventies.
13. Two exceptions are Butler's reference to anal sex between men as reinscribing the boundaries of the male body (*Gender Trouble*

132–133) and her comments on the recirculation of the phallus within the context of lesbian sexual exchange, where "having" the phallus can be symbolized by "an array of purposefully instrumentalized body-like things" (*Bodies That Matter* 88–89). I am indebted to Mandy Merck for pointing out this latter example to me.

14. Cf. Califia: "Modern butch/femme lesbians talk more about how these roles can be used to provide sexual pleasure and less about their springing from intrinsic differences in people's personalities or hormones" ("Genderbending" 181). However, since the mid-1990s there is also a notable process of resolidification of butch (and to a lesser degree femme) identity, set in motion partly by the publication of Leslie Feinberg's *Stone Butch Blues*.

15. The observation about the need for a validating audience fits in with Jacob Hale's notion of the relationality of gender (and, hence, the possibility of multiple, context-specific gendered statuses), which will be discussed in greater detail later on. Hale suggests that two people can constitute a gender culture, and that in this culture of two, one person can ratify the other's gender performance (or performativity in Hale's terms) by reading it correctly and reinforcing it. Such an ad hoc culture of two is what we find in the scene Califia depicts (Hale, "Leatherdyke Boys").

16. See, however, Staci Newmahr's objection to this trope in a recent study. Based on ethnographic research conducted in a Northeastern pansexual s/m community, she claims: "Real-life SM, at least in this community, is rarely role play. Scenes do not typically involve the adoption of alternate personae or plotlines. . . . SM scenes are unscripted and unrehearsed, and participants experience them as interpersonal adventures rather than performances." Newmahr stresses the bodily aspect of s/m and asserts that "for most players, SM is about constructing experiences of imbalanced power relationships at least in part through actions on the body." Her own formulation is that SM "occup[ies] an ambiguous space between role play and reality" (60–65). While I do not contest her observations concerning the community she studied, one must make allowance for changes in the modes in which s/m is practiced over time and across different subcultural settings and traditions. Newmahr does, for instance, note that role play is crucial to the interactions between professional dominatrixes and their clients.

17. And even in a public space, as Newmahr notes, onlookers do not exactly function as an audience in the sense that the participants are not playing *to* them (62).
18. Butler, then, does not equivocate or waver, as it might seem, when she states that "parody by itself is not subversive" (*Gender Trouble* 139). For the subversive potential latent in her "structural" notion of parody to be realized, the parody needs to be perceived as such rather than as a failed imitation, for instance.
19. Cf. Anne McClintock's account of the relationship of Arthur Munby and Hannah Cullwick, a Victorian s/m relationship between an upper-class gentleman and a working-class maid. McClintock's analysis reveals the relationship, which seems at first glance like a mere extension of class oppression, to be a far more complex negotiation of power and pleasure that provides Cullwick with a "means of gaining ritual control over her own very real social empowerment" (159).
20. That such performativity is unauthorized is evident from the fact that while real policemen can exercise violence with relative immunity, an s/m top playing a violent cop could risk arrest and criminal indictment. In general, s/m identity, while not conferring any real privileges, may serve as ground for discrimination. Cf. Califia: "Those feminists who accuse sadomasochists of mocking the oppressed by playing with dominance and submission forget that *we* are oppressed. We suffer police harassment, violence in the street, and discrimination in housing and employment. We are not treated the way our system treats its collaborators and supporters" ("Feminism and Sadomasochism" 170). Gayle Rubin makes a similar point in "Thinking Sex" when she describes sadomasochists as occupying the bottom of the erotic pyramid and subject to both legal persecution and psychiatric pathologization.
21. Cf. Hart: "It seems that the antitheatrical prejudice . . . is an operative paradox in such [s/m] performances. For, on the one hand, by virtue of the very fact of their theatricality these practices occupy a denigrated space in our cultural imaginary. On the other hand, practitioners of s/m sexuality have found some means of defense against the onslaught of both the New Right and some feminists by appealing precisely to that theatricality that is otherwise demeaned" (148).

22. Straight s/m is invested either in the image of feminine submission or in the image of feminine coldness and cruelty.
23. Rubin actually uses the words "male and female."
24. The topos of cross-gender queer sex will be discussed separately in the next chapter.
25. The author, Carol Queen, identifies as bisexual, and her protagonist, Randy, is identified as bisexual on the book's back cover, though the text itself avoids affixing any identity labels to her. The novel does make clear, however, that like her gay male partners, Randy is embedded in a same-sex social context even as she strays away from it.
26. In terms of her sexual repertoire, later chapters of the novel, which I will not discuss here, reinforce Randy's exemplary queer credentials through reference to her past relationships with transgendered partners: one of her ex-lovers is an MTF transsexual and another is a butch-turned-FTM. The use of transgender as a marker for "queer" is noted—and problematized—by Jay Prosser in the first chapter of *Second Skins*.
27. On traditional butch/femme roles, see Kennedy and Davis's excellent book, *Boots of Leather, Slippers of Gold: The History of a Lesbian Community*. The notion of butch and femme as categories of lesbian gender is derived from Gayle Rubin, "Of Catamites and Kings."
28. Thus, "femme" acquires unorthodox meanings in Randy's utterance: "I love these impeccable daddies. They appeal to the femme in me" (Queen, *Leather Daddy* 25).
29. It is worth noting that the erotically charged gay male imagery invoked is highly racially coded; both Randy's effete young Cambridge faggot and Jack's Tom-of-Finland hypermasculinity are clearly marked as white. The novel does contain the character of an African American s/m top, Jack's buddy and part-time lover Demetrius, introduced at the end of the third chapter. Yet while figuring him as both desirable and sexually dominant, the text also draws on several stereotypes concerning black men in general and black gay men in particular: His cock is described as exceptionally large and thick (Randy passes out when giving head to him); he is bisexual, having been married for many years before finding his way to the gay scene; and he is described as the embodiment of queer elegance.
30. I will address the move from a performative understanding of gender to a desire for gendered embodiment in the next chapter.

Chapter 6. Female Sexual Subjectivity in a Queer World

1. It would of course be correct to describe the kind of sex these works portray as bisexual, hence, behaviorally at least the characters who engage in it might be regarded as bisexual, while Randy in *Leather Daddy* is even identified by the text as bisexual. However, I would contend that a reading of the topos of cross-gender queer sex merely in terms of bisexuality glosses over some crucial aspects, notably the sense of transgressiveness that attends the cross-gender sex due to the fact that the characters are mostly embedded in a same-sex social context. The readings of "The Surprise Party" and *The Leather Daddy and the Femme*, and the ensuing discussion of the topos of cross-gender queer sex are based on my "Girl Meets Boy: Cross-gender Queer Sex and the Promise of Pornography."
2. I have encountered the topos of cross-gender queer sex only in fiction by women and not in gay male texts. One exception is the story "Dress Pinks" by M. Christian, a male author. Yet interestingly, the volume this story appears in is a collection of "lesbian erotica," albeit by a male writer, so that, while the author is male, the fantasy is presumably geared toward a lesbian readership. In this story there is also a final twist, when the handsome young leatherman the female protagonist has sex with is eventually revealed to be a woman after all. The absence of fantasies of cross-gender queer sex in porn by men demonstrates once more the slant I have noted in chapter 2, of lesbians making a phantasmatic investment in gay men and gay male sexuality that does not quite have a counterpart on the other side of the gender divide.
3. In this story, homosexuality, both male and female, is clearly identified with a gender separatist rather than a gender integrative position, to use Sedgwick's terms (*Epistemology* 88–90). Though, significantly, while the three leathermen are unambiguously aligned with masculinity, the protagonist, as butch, occupies a gender-liminal position, that is, her female masculinity signifies a distance both from males and maleness and from femininity. However, as the plot unfolds, the balance between alienation and identification shifts, with the latter, which is covert at first, gaining the upper hand. And consequently, the separatist definition of gender yields before a minoritizing definition of sexuality that unites leathermen and s/m dykes.
4. Sexual proficiency and self-control are what distinguish the

competent s/m practitioner from the amateur, but they are also, as Don implies, what distinguish the man from the adolescent, thus revealing the masculine coding of s/m.

5. Don tells his two friends: "Maybe it will help if you don't think of her as a girl. After all, she doesn't want to be a woman. She wants to be a man. She dresses like one, talks like one, walks like one. She's a queer, like you boys. Queers have sex with other queers, right?" (231).
6. See note 3.
7. I have argued earlier that even in those cases when s/m roles do reflect and refer to actual status or power differentials between the participants, the hyperbolic character of s/m and its status as unauthorized performativity still work to denaturalize social roles and the power vested in them. In the story, however, the slippage in the ontological status of the fictional reality—that is, between the construction of the narrative as depicting a rape and its construction as depicting consensual s/m play between friends—undercuts the parodic effect by drawing dangerously close to the violent phantasmatic script that underlies the performance.
8. The masculine coding of anal receptivity recurs in several places in the text: Lane asks Jack to teach her to "take it like a man," and during their first sexual encounter, he is described as "fuck[ing] her arse as if she was a man" (Sandler 16, 21).
9. In fact, the first two chapters of the novel were published separately in 1994, and the fourth in 1996, so the transition I am tracing was even more rapid.
10. I'm indebted to David Halperin for bringing this article to my attention.
11. In the essay "Shameful Fantasies: Cross-Gender Queer Sex in Lesbian Erotic Fiction" I suggest also another, complementary, explanation for the fantasy of sex with gay men as a modified version of more disturbing and identity-threatening unconscious wishes.
12. This cross-cultural influence is thematized explicitly in *Leather Daddy*, when the text notes that Randy enjoyed reading and masturbating to *Mr. Benson*, the gay s/m classic.
13. Cf. Feona Attwood's assertion, drawing on Anthony Giddens, that "sex is often now seen as central to the creation and expression of an individual's self" (xv).

14. Prosser cites Roland Barthes's assertion that reference is the founding order of photography (210).
15. Cf. Noble, who observes in relation to different texts of transgender porn: "[The] gendered space of 'fag' masculinity is available to trans men as a productive trope of gendered sexual receptivity" (316).
17. Other instances include Émilie Jouvet's *Too Much Pussy!* (2010), released in 2011 in a hardcore version under the title *Much More Pussy!* Her *One Night Stand* (2006) too opens with a preface in which all the performers talk about their motivations for participating in the film and their experience in making it. In transgender porn one of the earliest works in the genre is Annie Sprinkle's *Linda/Les and Annie* (1989), and a more contemporary one is Luke Woodward's *Enough Man* (2004).
18. Even the interview format is carried to a limited degree into the masturbation sequences, with Angel occasionally interposing with questions or remarks.
19. See Boyd; Califia, *Sex Changes*; Hale, "Consuming the Living."
20. See Halberstam's chapter "Transgender Butch" and Hale, "Consuming the Living."
21. The most notorious example is the former policy of the Michigan Womyn's Festival of admitting only womyn-born womyn. On the history of transwomen's exclusion from the festival and the struggle against it, see Boyd, and Califia, *Sex Changes*.
22. To avoid misunderstandings, my comments should in no way be construed as proposing a view of female-to-male transgenderism as a politically regressive phenomenon. First of all, my comments concern the FTM movement as a cultural phenomenon rather than gender transition as a personal choice; second, this cultural phenomenon, which has many radical political implications (e.g., its contribution to the pluralization and demystification of masculinity), is discussed here solely from one particular angle: its relation to the feminist project of articulating female sexual subjectivity.
23. Noble claims: "Trans, butch, and FTM bodies become extremely significant hinge points within the complex nexus of feminist porn and its masculinities. Recent portrayals of FTM trans masculinities . . . have *transed* or deterritorialized both masculinities and porn from the heteronormative male phallic body and the visual spectacle of the money shot" (304).

24. See Rubin, "The Traffic in Women."
25. *Alley of the Tranny Boys* exemplifies such an attitude in the last episode that features a sexual interaction between two of the transmen, Guy and Angel, and Jade Blue, an Asian-looking, feminine cisgendered woman. In this episode Jade is clearly in a submissive role: She sucks Angel's toes as Guy first finger-fucks and then fists her. During the entire interaction the two men converse with each other over her head, commenting on her performance and referring to her by epithets such as a "tranny fag hag" and a "foot slut." They do not address her, except when instructing her to do something, and the toe-sucking is clearly a practice of humiliation and an allusion to cock-sucking (she fits as much as three toes in her mouth and is instructed to move her head up and down). The men's amused self-possession contrasts with her inarticulate cries, and their male bonding clearly takes place at her expense. While this is not the only episode in the film to feature an s/m dynamics, there is no fantasy script being enacted, as in the episode with the cop, and the bottom's role is not constructed as masculine. Rather, the episode figures a common dynamic in straight porn where a sexually active woman is labeled a slut and "put in her place" through sexual humiliation and heterosexual intimacy is displaced by male bonding. In the episode in question, Jade's sexual submissiveness is also racially overdetermined by the pornographic trope of Asian women as obedient and eager to please.
26. Émilie Jouvet's *One Night Stand* is a case in point. The film contains a diverse range of performers, including one FTM, and the sexual couplings it portrays include femme-on-femme, transman and femme, leather fags having rough sex, among others. The popular *Crash Pad* series also presents a wide array of bodies and couplings including genderqueer, FTM bear sex, and recently also sex between transwomen. And the website queerporntube.com features an especially high percentage of trans and genderqueer representations.
27. The latter variation is represented by the story "Walt" in *Best Transgender Erotica*.
28. Gayle Rubin is one of the few to attend to the divergent meanings of masculinity in lesbian gender expression. In her essay on the category "butch" she notes that masculine gender codes may signal, among other things, desire to engage in active or initiatory sexual behaviors or signify a claim to privileges or deference

usually reserved for men (Rubin, "Catamites" 467). In other words, an investment in masculinity should not always be construed in identitarian terms, and it might be instructive to interrogate its significations.
29. In this respect, the fact that a relatively large percent of FTMs identify as gay men seems meaningful.

Coda

1. While I never ask students if they found certain representations arousing, they sometimes feel comfortable enough to share their less cerebral responses or at least hint at them obliquely.
2. Linda Williams records similar displacements in her description of the first class she taught on pornography, where upon exposure to gay male porn male students channeled their homophobic anxiety into condemnation of unsafe sex practices or critiques of silly plots ("Porn Studies" 16–18). In my classes I did not encounter such instances of displaced homosexual panic, probably owing to a very low percent of heterosexual male students. One instance I do recall occurred following a screening of *Bend Over Boyfriend 2* (which portrays women anally penetrating men), when a presumably heterosexual man vehemently protested that "this is NOT heterosexual sex" and was passionately opposed by the rest of the class.
3. For example, my experience is that most people who encounter images of anal fisting for the first time perceive them as violent. It has to be pointed out to them that the anal sphincter needs to be coaxed gently and patiently in order to accommodate a whole hand, and that this cannot be achieved without the active cooperation of the insertee.

Works Cited

Adams, Parveen. "Of Female Bondage." *Between Feminism and Psychoanalysis*. Ed. Teresa Brennan. London: Routledge, 1989. 247–265. Print.

Adams, Parveen, and Jeff Minson. "The Subject of Feminism." *The Woman in Question: M/f*. Ed. Parveen Adams and Elizabeth Cowie. Cambridge: MIT, 1990. 81–101. Print.

Alexander, Martha. "Passion Play." *Coming to Power*. Ed. Samois. Boston: Alyson, 1981. 230–244. Print.

Alley of the Tranny Boys. Dir. Christopher Lee. San Francisco, 1998. Film.

Allison, Dorothy. "Her Body, Mine, and His." *Pomosexuals*. Ed. Carol Queen and Lawrence Schimel. San Francisco: Cleis, 1996. 107–112. Print.

Austin, J. L. *How to Do Things with Words*. 1962. Oxford: Oxford UP, 1975. Print.

Althusser, Louis. "Ideology and Ideological State Apparatuses." *Lenin and Philosophy*. Trans. Ben Brewster. New York: Monthly Review, 1971. 127–186. Print.

Angel, Buck. "The Power of My Vagina." *The Feminist Porn Book*. Ed. Tristan Taormino et al. New York: Feminist Press, 2013. 284–286. Print.

Attwood, Feona. "Introduction: The Sexualization of Culture." *Mainstreaming Sex*. xiii–xxiv.

Attwood, Feona, ed. *Mainstreaming Sex: The Sexualization of Western Culture*. London: I. B. Tauris, 2009. Print.

Balibar, Étienne. "Subjection and Subjectivation." *Supposing the Subject.* Ed. Joan Copjec. London: Verso, 1994. 1–15. Print.

Bataille, Georges. *Erotism: Death and Sensuality.* Trans. Mary Dalwood. San Francisco: City Lights, 1986. Print.

The Sluts and Goddesses Video Workshop. Dir. Annie Sprinkle & Maria Beatty. 1992.

Beggan, James K., and Scott T. Allison. "Reflexivity in the Pornographic Films of Candida Royalle." *Sexualities* 6.3–4 (2003): 301–324. Print.

Bend Over Boyfriend 2. Dir. Shar Rednour and Jackie Strano. S.I.R. Productions, 2003. Film.

Benjamin, Jessica. *The Bonds of Love: Psychoanalysis, Feminism, and the Problem of Domination.* New York: Pantheon, 1988. Print.

Bersani, Leo. *The Freudian Body: Psychoanalysis and Art.* New York: Columbia UP, 1986. Print.

———. *Homos.* Cambridge: Harvard UP, 1995. Print.

———. "Is the Rectum a Grave?" *October* 43 (1987): 197–222. Print.

Bersani, Leo, and Ulysse Dutoit. *The Forms of Violence: Narrative in Assyrian Art and Modern Culture.* New York: Schocken, 1995. Print.

Blake, Nayland. "Tom of Finland: An Appreciation." *Out in Culture: Gay, Lesbian, and Queer Essays on Popular Culture.* Ed. Corey K. Creekmur and Alexander Dotey. London: Cassel, 1995. Print.

Booth, Wayne C. *The Rhetoric of Fiction.* Harmondsworth: Peregrine, 1987. Print.

Boswell, John. "Revolutions, Universals, and Sexual Categories." *Hidden from History: Reclaiming the Gay and Lesbian Past.* Ed. Martin Duberman, Martha Vicinus, and George Chauncey Jr. New York: NAL, 1989. 17–36. Print.

Boyd, Nan Alamilla. "Bodies in Motion: Lesbian and Transsexual Histories." *The Transgender Studies Reader.* Ed. Susan Stryker and Stephen Whittle. New York: Routledge, 2006. 420–433. Print.

Boyle, Karen. "Introduction." *Everyday Pornography.* Ed. Karen Boyle. New York: Routledge, 2010. 1–13. Print.

Boyle, Karen. "Screening Violence: A Feminist Critique of the Screen Violence Debate." Women's Worlds 99: 7th International Interdisciplinary Congress on Women. Tromso. June 1999. Address.

———, ed. *Everyday Pornography.* New York: Routledge, 2010. Print.

Bridges, Ana J. "Methodological Considerations in Mapping Pornography Content." *Everyday Pornography.* Ed. Karen Boyle. New York: Routledge, 2010. 34–49. Print.

Bright, Susie. "Introduction." *Herotica*. Ed. Susie Bright and Joani Blank. New York: Plume, 1992. ix–xvii. Print.

Brown, Angela, ed. *Set in Stone: Butch-on-Butch Erotica*. Los Angeles: Alyson, 2001. Print.

Brown, Wendy. "The Mirror of Pornography: MacKinnon's Social Theory of Gender." *States of Injury: Power and Freedom in Late Modernity*. Princeton: Princeton UP, 1995. 77–95. Print.

Burke, Peter. "Social Drama." *The Fontana Dictionary of Modern Thought*. 2nd ed. 1988. Print.

Butler, Heather. "What Do You Call a Lesbian with Long Fingers? The Development of Lesbian and Dyke Pornography." *Porn Studies*. Ed. Linda Williams. Durham: Duke UP, 2004. 167–197. Print.

Butler, Judith. *Bodies That Matter: On the Discursive Limits of "Sex."* New York: Routledge, 1993. Print.

———. "Critically Queer." *GLQ* 1 (1993): 17–32. Print.

———. *Excitable Speech: A Politics of the Performative*. New York: Routledge, 1997. Print.

———. "Gender as Performance: An Interview with Judith Butler." *Radical Philosophy* 67 (Summer 1994): 32–39. Print.

———. "The Force of Fantasy: Feminism, Mapplethorpe, and Discursive Excess." *Feminism and Pornography*. Ed. Cornell. 487–507.

———. *Gender Trouble: Feminism and the Subversion of Identity*. New York: Routledge, 1990. Print.

———. "Imitation and Gender Insubordination." *The Lesbian and Gay Studies Reader*. Ed. Henry Abelove, Michel Aine Barale, and David Halperin. New York: Routledge, 1993. 307–320. Print.

———. "Melancholy Gender/Refused Identification." *The Psychic Life of Power*. Stanford: Stanford UP, 1997. 132–150. Print.

———. "Performative Acts and Gender Constitution." *Performing Feminisms: Feminist Critical Theory and Theater*. Ed. Sue-Ellen Case. Baltimore: Johns Hopkins UP, 1990. 270–282. Print.

———. Preface. 1999. *Gender Trouble: Feminism and the Subversion of Identity*. vii–xxvi.

———. "The Lesbian Phallus and the Morphological Imaginary." *Bodies That Matter: On the Discursive Limits of "Sex."* 57–91.

Califia, Pat. "Among Us, Against Us: Right Wing Feminism." *Public Sex: The Culture of Radical Sex*. Pittsburgh: Cleis, 1994. 113–122. Print.

———. "Among Us, Against Us: The New Puritans." *Public Sex*. 107–112.

———. "The Calyx of Isis." *Macho Sluts*. Boston: Alyson, 1988. 84–176. Print.

———. "Daddy." *Melting Point*. Boston: Alyson, 1993. 62–90. Print.

———. "Feminism and Sadomasochism." *Public Sex*. 165–174.

———. "Gay Men, Lesbians, and Sex: Doing It Together." *Advocate* (July 1983). Rpt. in *Public Sex*. 183–189.

———. "Genderbending: Playing with Roles and Reversals." 1983. *Public Sex*. 175–189.

———. "Identity Sedition and Pornography." *Pomosexuals*. Ed. Queen and Schimel. 87–106.

———. "See No Evil: An Update on the Feminist Antipornography Movement." *Public Sex*. 123–135.

———. *Speaking Sex to Power: The Politics of Queer Sex*. San Francisco: Cleis Press, 2002. Print.

———. "The Surprise Party." *Macho Sluts*. 211–248.

———, ed. *Doing It for Daddy*. Boston: Alyson, 1994. Print.

Califia, Patrick. *Sex Changes: Transgender Politics*. 2nd ed. San Francisco: Cleis Press, 2003. Print.

Carlson, Marvin. *Performance: A Critical Introduction*. London: Routledge, 1996. Print.

Carnes, Michelle. "Bend Over Boyfriend: Anal Sex Instructional Videos for Women." *Pornification: Sex and Sexuality in Media Culture*. Ed. Susanna Paasonen, Kaarina Nikunen, and Laura Saarenmaa. Oxford: Berg, 2007. 151–170. Print.

Case, Sue-Ellen. "The Student and the Strap: Authority and Seduction in the Class(room)." *Professions of Desire*. Ed. George E. Haggerty and Bonnie Zimmerman. New York: MLA, 1995. 38–46. Print.

———. "Toward a Butch-Femme Aesthetics." *Making a Spectacle*. Ed. Lynda Hart. Ann Arbor: U of Michigan P, 1989. 282–299. Print.

Caught Looking Inc., ed. *Caught Looking: Feminism, Pornography, Censorship*. 1986. East Haven: Long River, 1992. Print.

Chodorow, Nancy. "Being and Doing: A Cross-Cultural Examination of the Socialization of Males and Females." *Women in Sexist Society*. Ed. Vivian Gornick and B. K. Moran. New York: Basic Books, 1971. 259–291. Print.

Christensen, F. M. *Pornography: The Other Side*. New York: Praeger, 1990. Print.

Christian, M. "Dress Pinks." *Speaking Parts*. Los Angeles: Alyson, 2002. Print.

Clips. Fatale Videos, 1985. Film.

Clover, Carol J. *Men, Women, and Chain Saws*. Princeton: Princeton UP, 1992. Print.

Comella, Lynn. "From Text to Context: Feminist Porn and the Making of a Market." *The Feminist Porn Book*. Ed. Tristan Taormino et al. 79–93. Print.

Coopersmith, Jonathan. "Pornography, Videotape, and the Internet." *CyberPorn and Society*. Ed. Alexander C. Halavais. Dubuque: Kendall Hunt, 2006. 3–15. Print.

Cornell, Drucilla. "Feminism Always Modified: The Affirmation of Feminine Difference Rethought." *Beyond Accommodation*. New York: Routledge, 1991. 119–164. Print.

———, ed. *Feminism and Pornography*. New York: Oxford UP, 2000. Print.

Cowie, Elizabeth. "Fantasia." *The Woman in Question*. Ed. Parveen Adams and Elizabeth Cowie. Cambridge: MIT, 1990. 149–196. Print.

———. "Pornography and Fantasy: Psychoanalytic Perspectives." *Sex Exposed*. Ed. Lynne Segal and Mary McIntosh. London: Virago, 1992. 132–152. Print.

Creet, Julia. "Lesbian Sex/Gay Sex: What's the Difference?" *Out/Look* (Winter 1991): 29–34. Print.

Cvetkovich, Ann. "Recasting Receptivity: Femme Sexualities." *Lesbian Erotics*. Ed. Karla Jay. New York: New York UP, 1995. 125–146. Print.

Davis, Madeline D., and Elizabeth Lapovsky Kennedy. *Boots of Leather, Slippers of Gold: The History of a Lesbian Community*. New York: Penguin, 1994. Print.

Decarnin, Camilla. "Interviews with Five Faghagging Women." *Heresies* 3.12 (1981): 10–14. Print.

Delacoste, Frédérique, and Priscilla Alexander, eds. *Sex Work: Writings by Women in the Sex Industry*. Pittsburgh: Cleis, 1987. Print.

de Lauretis, Teresa. "On the Subject of Fantasy." *Feminisms in the Cinema*. Ed. Laura Pietropaolo and Ada Testaferri. Bloomington: Indiana UP, 1995. 63–85. Print.

———. "Popular Culture, Public and Private Fantasies: Femininity and Fetishism in David Cronenberg's *M. Butterfly*." *Signs* 24.2 (1999): 303–334. Print.

———. *Practice of Love: Lesbian Sexuality and Perverse Desire*. Bloomington: Indiana UP, 1994. Print.

Dines, Gail. *Pornland: How Porn Has Hijacked Our Sexuality*. Boston: Beacon Press, 2010. Print.

Dines, Gail, Linda Thompson, Rebecca Whisnant, and Karen Boyle.

"Arresting Images: Anti-Pornography Slide Shows, Activism, and the Academy." *Everyday Pornography*. Ed. Boyle. 17–33.

Derrida, Jacques. "Signature Event Context." Trans. Samuel Weber and Jeffrey Mehlman. *Glyph* 1 (1977): 172–197. Print.

Donnerstein, Edward, Daniel Linz, and Steven Penrod. *The Question of Pornography: Research Findings and Policy Implications*. London: Collier Macmillan, 1987. Print.

Duggan, Lisa. "Censorship in the Name of Feminism." *Caught Looking*. 1986. Ed. Caught Looking Inc. 62–69.

———. "The New Homonormativity: The Sexual Politics of Neoliberalism." *Materializing Democracy: Toward a Revitalized Cultural Politics*. Ed. Russ Custronovo and Dana D. Nelson. Durham: Duke UP, 2002. 175–194. Print.

Duggan, Lisa, Nan D. Hunter, and Carol S. Vance. "False Promises: Feminist Antipornography Legislation." *Sex Wars: Sexual Dissent and Political Culture*. Ed. Duggan and Hunter. 43–63.

Duggan, Lisa, and Nan D. Hunter, eds. *Sex Wars: Sexual Dissent and Political Culture*. New York: Routledge, 1995. Print.

Dworkin, Andrea. *Intercourse*. New York: The Free Press, 1987. Print.

———. *Pornography: Men Possessing Women*. New York: Perigee, 1979. Print.

Dyer, Richard. "Male Gay Porn: Coming to Terms." *Jump Cut* 30 (1985): 27–29. Print.

Easton, Susan. *The Problem of Pornography: Regulation and the Right to Free Speech*. London: Routledge, 1994. Print.

Echols, Alice. "The New Feminism of Yin and Yang." *Powers of Desire: The Politics of Sexuality*. Ed. Ann Snitow, Christine Stansell, and Sharon Thompson. New York: Monthly Review, 1983. 439–459. Print.

Elliot, Patricia, and Katrina Roen. "Transgenderism and the Question of Embodiment: Promising Queer Politics?" *GLQ* 4.2 (1998): 231–261. Print.

Findlay, Heather. "Freud's 'Fetishism' and the Lesbian Dildo Debates." *Out in Culture: Gay, Lesbian, and Queer Essays on Popular Culture*. Ed. Corey K. Creekmur and Alexander Doty. London: Cassel, 1995. 328–342. Print.

Foucault, Michel. *The History of Sexuality: An Introduction*. 1976. Trans. Robert Hurley. New York: Vintage, 1990. Print.

Fraser, Nancy. "Rethinking the Public Sphere: A Contribution to the

Critique of Actually Existing Democracy." *Habermas and the Public Sphere.* Ed. Craig Calhoun. Boston: MIT Press, 1992. 109–142. Print.

Freud, Sigmund. *The Standard Edition of the Complete Psychological Works.* Trans. and ed. James Strachey. 24 vols. London: Hogarth, 1953–1974. Print.

———. "A Child Is Being Beaten." 1919. *Standard Edition.* Vol. 17. 179–204.

———. "Creative Writers and Day-Dreaming." 1908. *Standard Edition.* Vol. 9. 141–153.

———. "The Economic Problem of Masochism." 1924. *Essential Papers on Masochism.* Ed. M. A. Fitzpatrick-Hanly. New York: New York UP, 1995. 274–285. Print.

———. "Fetishism." 1927. *Standard Edition.* Vol. 21. 147–157.

———. "Group Psychology and the Analysis of the Ego." 1921. *Standard Edition.* Vol. 18. 105–116.

———. "Mourning and Melancholia." 1917. *Standard Edition.* Vol. 14. 237–258.

———. "Splitting of the Ego in the Process of Defence." 1940. *Standard Edition.* Vol. 23. 271–278.

———. "The Ego and the Id." 1923. *Standard Edition.* Vol. 19. 13–59.

———. "The Sexual Theories of Children." 1908. *Standard Edition.* Vol. 9. 209–226.

———. "Three Essays on the Theory of Sexuality." 1905. *Standard Edition.* Vol. 7. 123–243.

Frye, Marilyn. "Lesbian 'Sex'" *Sinister Wisdom* 35 (Summer–Fall 1988). Print.

Fung, Richard. "Looking for My Penis: The Eroticized Asian in Gay Video Porn." *How Do I Look? Queer Film and Video.* Ed. Bad Object Choices. Seattle: Bay Press, 1991. 145–168. Print.

Fuss, Diana. *Identification Papers.* New York: Routledge, 1995. Print.

Gallop, Jane. "Beyond the Phallus." *Thinking Through the Body.* New York: Columbia UP, 1988. 119–133. Print.

Gino, Alex. "Becoming." *Best Transgender Erotica.* Ed. Hanne Blank and Raven Kaldera. Cambridge, MA: Circlet, 2002. 189–194. Print.

Goffman, Erving. *The Presentation of Self in Everyday Life.* Garden City: Doubleday, 1959. Print.

Griffin, Susan. *Pornography and Silence: Culture's Revenge against Nature.* New York: Harper & Row, 1981. Print.

Grosz, Elizabeth. "The Labors of Love, Analyzing Perverse Desire: Interrogation of Teresa de Lauretis' *The Practice of Love.*" *Differences* 6.2–3 (1994): 274–295. Print.

———. "Lesbian Fetishism?" *Differences* 3.2 (1991): 39–54. Print.

———. "Phallus: Feminist Implications." *Feminism and Psychoanalysis: A Critical Dictionary.* Ed. Elizabeth Wright. Oxford: Blackwell, 1992. Print.

Halberstam, Judith. *Female Masculinity.* Durham: Duke UP, 1998. Print.

Hale, C. Jacob. "Consuming the Living, Dis(re)membering the Dead in the Butch/FTM Borderlands." *GLQ* 4.2 (1998): 311–348. Print.

———. "Leatherdyke Boys and Their Daddies: How to Have Sex without Women or Men." *Social Text* 15.52–53 (Fall/Winter 1997): 223–236. Print.

Halperin, David. *One Hundred Years of Homosexuality.* New York: Routledge, 1990. Print.

Halavais, Alexander C. "Small Pornographies." *CyberPorn and Society.* Ed. Alexander C. Halavais. Dubuque: Kendall Hunt, 2006. 32–37. Print.

Hardy, Simon. "More Black Lace: Women, Eroticism and Subjecthood." *Sexualities* 4.4 (20001): 435–453. Print.

Hart, Lynda. *Between the Body and the Flesh: Performing Sadomasochism.* New York: Columbia UP, 1998. Print.

Hartsock, Nancy. "The Feminist Standpoint: Developing the Ground for a Specifically Feminist Historical Materialism." *Discovering Reality: Feminist Perspectives on Epistemology, Metaphysics, Methodology, and Philosophy of Science.* Ed. Sandra Harding and Merrill B. Hintikka. Dordrecht: Kluwer, 2003. Print.

Herdt, Gilbert H. *Guardians of the Flutes: Idioms of Masculinity.* New York: Columbia UP, 1981. Print.

Hunt, Lynn. "Obscenity and the Origins of Modernity." *The Invention of Pornography: Obscenity and the Origins of Modernity, 1500–1800.* Ed. Lynn Hunt. New York: Zone, 1993. 9–45. Print.

Hunter, Nan D. "Contextualizing the Sexuality Debates: A Chronology." *Sex Wars: Sexual Dissent and Political Culture.* Ed. Duggan and Hunter. 16–29. Print.

Jackson, Earl. *Strategies of Deviance: Studies in Gay Male Representation.* Bloomington and Indianapolis: Indiana UP, 1995. Print.

Jacobs, Katrien. *Netporn: DIY Web Culture and Sexual Politics.* Lanham: Rowman & Littlefield, 2007. Print.

Jeffreys, Sheila. *The Lesbian Heresy*. London: The Women's Press, 1994. Print.

Jenkins, Henry. *Textual Poachers: Television Fans and Participatory Culture*. New York: Routledge, 1992. Print.

Jensen, Robert. "Using Pornography." In Gail Dines, Robert Jensen, and Ann Russo, *Pornography: The Production and Consumption of Inequality*. New York: Routledge, 1999. 101–146. Print.

Johnson, Mykel. "Butchy Femme." *The Persistent Desire A Femme-Butch Reader*. Ed. Joan Nestle. Boston: Alyson, 1992. 395–398. Print.

Joshi, Sam. "'Watcha Gonna Do When They Cum All Over You?' What Police Themes in Male Erotic Video Reveal about (Leather)sexual Subjectivity." *Sexualities* 6.3–4 (2003): 325–342. Print.

Juffer, Jane. *At Home with Pornography: Women, Sex, and Everyday Life*. New York: New York UP, 1998. Print.

Kaldera, Raven. "As the Sparks Fly Upward." *Best Transgender Erotica*. Ed. Hanne Blank and Raven Kaldera. Cambridge: Circlet, 2002. 207–222. Print.

Kendrick, Walter. *The Secret Museum: Pornography in Modern Culture*. New York: Penguin, 1988. Print.

Kipnis, Laura. "(Male) Desire and (Female) Disgust: Reading Hustler." *Cultural Studies*. Ed. Lawrence Grossberg, Cary Nelson, and Paula Treicher. New York: Routledge, 1992. 373–391. Print.

———. "She-Male Fantasies and the Aesthetics of Pornography." *Dirty Looks: Women, Pornography, Power*. Ed. Pamela Church Gibson and Roma Gibson. London: British Film Institute, 1993. 124–143. Print.

Kustritz, Anne. "Slashing the Romance Narrative." *The Journal of American Culture* 26.3 (2003): 371–384. Print.

Lacan, Jacques. *The Four Fundamental Concepts of Psychoanalysis*. Trans. Alan Sheridan. New York: Norton, 1978. Print.

———. "The Function of Language in Psychoanalysis." *The Language of the Self*. Ed. Anthony Wilden. Baltimore: Johns Hopkins UP, 1968. 1–87. Print.

———. "The Signification of the Phallus." *Écrits: A Selection*. Trans. Alan Sheridan. London: Tavistock, 1980. 281–291. Print.

Lamos, Colleen. "Taking On the Phallus." *Lesbian Erotics*. Ed. Karla Jay. New York: New York UP. 101–124. Print.

Laplanche, Jean, and Jean-Bertrand Pontalis. "Fantasy and the Origins of Sexuality." *Formations of Fantasy*. Ed. Victor Burgin, James Donald, and Cora Kaplan. London: Methuen, 1986. 5–34. Print.

———. "Identification." *The Language of Psychoanalysis*. Trans. Donald Nicholson Smith. London: Karnac, 1988. 314–319. Print.
———. "Phallus." *The Language of Psychoanalysis*. 312–314.
———. "Phantasy." *The Language of Psychoanalysis*. 205–208.
Laqueur, Thomas. *Making Sex: Body and Gender from the Greeks to Freud*. Cambridge: Harvard UP, 1990. Print.
Levy, Ariel. *Female Chauvinist Pigs: Women and the Rise of Raunch Culture*. New York: Free Press, 2005. Print.
Macey, David. "Phallus." *Feminism and Psychoanalysis: A Critical Dictionary*. Ed. Elizabeth Wright. Oxford: Blackwell, 1992. Print.
McHale, Brian. "Free Indirect Discourse: A Survey of Recent Accounts." *PTL* 3 (1978): 249–287. Print.
MacKinnon, Catharine. *Feminism Unmodified: Discourses on Life and Law*. Cambridge: Harvard UP, 1987. Print.
———. *Only Words*. London: HarperCollins, 1994. Print.
———. "Sexuality, Pornography, and Method: Pleasure under Patriarchy." *Ethics* 99.2 (1989): 314–346. Print.
———. *Toward a Feminist Theory of the State*. Cambridge: Harvard UP, 1989. Print.
MacKinnon, Catharine, and Andrea Dworkin, eds. *In Harm's Way*. Cambridge: Harvard UP, 1997. Print.
Maddison, Stephen. "'Choke on It, Bitch!' Porn Studies, Extreme Gonzo, and the Mainstreaming of Hardcore." *Mainstreaming Sex: The Sexualization of Western Culture*. Ed. Attwood.
Marcus, Steven. *The Other Victorians: A Study of Sexuality and Pornography in Mid-Nineteenth-Century England*. New York: New American Library, 1974. Print.
Martin, Biddy. "Feminism, Criticism, and Foucault." *Feminism and Foucault*. Ed. Diamond Irene and Lee Quinby. Boston: Northeastern UP, 1988. 3–19. Print.
———. "Sexualities without Gender and Other Queer Utopias." *Coming Out of Feminism?* Ed. Mandy Merck, Naomi Segal, and Elizabeth Wright. Oxford: Blackwell, 1988. 11–35. Print.
McClintock, Anne. *Imperial Leather: Race, Gender, and Sexuality in the Colonial Context*. New York: Routledge, 1995. Print.
McNair, Brian. *Mediated Sex: Pornography and Postmodern Culture*. London: Arnold, 1996. Print.
Mercer, Kobena. "Just Looking for Trouble: Robert Mapplethorpe and Fantasies of Race." *Sex Exposed: Sexuality and the Pornography Debate*.

Ed. Lynne Segal and Mary McIntosh. Virago, 1993. 92–110. Rpt. in *Feminism and Pornography*. Ed. Drucilla Cornell. New York: Oxford UP, 2000. 460–476. Print

Merck, Mandy. "The Lesbian Hand." *In Your Face*. 124–147.

———. "MacKinnon's Dog: Antiporn's Canine Conditioning." *In Your Face: Nine Sexual Studies*. New York: New York UP, 2000. 89–107. Print.

———. "*More of a Man*: Gay Porn Cruises Gay Politics." *Perversions: Deviant Readings*. New York: Routledge, 1993. 217–235. Print.

———. "Savage Nights." *Coming Out of Feminism?* Ed. Mandy Merck, Naomi Segal, and Elizabeth Wright. Oxford: Blackwell, 1988. 214–243. Print.

Michaels, Magenta. "Taking Him on a Sunday Afternoon." *Herotica 2*. Ed. Susie Bright and Joani Blank. New York: Plume, 1992. 18–19. Print.

Millet, Kate. *Sexual Politics*. New York: Avon, 1971. Print.

Modleski, Tania. *Feminism without Women: Culture and Criticism in a "Postfeminist" Age*. New York: Routledge, 1991. Print.

Mulvey, Laura. "Visual Pleasure and Narrative Cinema." *The Sexual Subject: A Screen Reader in Sexuality*. London: Routledge, 1992. 22-34. Print.

Muñoz, José Esteban. *Cruising Utopia: The Then and There of Queer Futurity*. New York: NYU Press, 2009. Print.

Nagle, Jill, ed. *Whores and Other Feminists*. New York: Routledge, 1997. Print.

Nestle, Joan. "The Gift of Taking." *A Restricted Country*. London: Pandora, 1996. 117–120. Print.

———, ed. *The Persistent Desire: A Femme-Butch Reader*. Boston: Alyson, 1992. Print.

Newmahr, Staci. *Playing on the Edge: Sadomasochism, Risk, and Intimacy*. Bloomington and Indianapolis: Indiana UP, 2011. Print.

Newton, Esther. "'Dickless Tracy' and the Homecoming Queen: Lesbian Power and Representation in Gay Male Cherry Grove." *Margaret Mead Made Me Gay*. Durham: Duke UP, 2000. 63–89. Print.

———. "The Mythic Mannish Lesbian: Radclyffe Hall and the New Woman." *Hidden from History: Reclaiming the Gay and Lesbian Past*. Ed. Martin Duberman, Martha Vicinus, and George Chauncey Jr. New York: NAL, 1989. 281–293. Print.

Noble, Bobby. "Knowing Dick: Penetration and the Pleasures of Feminist

Porn's Trans Men." *The Feminist Porn Book.* Ed. Tristan Taormino et al. 303–319.

Nussbaum, Martha. "The Professor of Parody." *The New Republic.* 22 Feb. 1999. Print.

Paasonen, Susanna. *Carnal Resonance: Affect and Online Pornography.* Cambridge: MIT Press, 2011. Print.

Patton, Cindy. "Safe Sex and the Pornographic Vernacular." *How Do I Look? Queer Film and Video.* Ed. Bad Object Choices. Seattle: Bay Press, 1991. Print.

Paul, Pamela. *Pornified: How Pornography Is Damaging Our Lives, Our Relationships, and Our Families.* New York: Times Books, 2005. Print.

Penley, Constance. "Feminism, Psychoanalysis, and the Study of Popular Culture." *Cultural Studies.* Ed. Lawrence Grossberg, Cary Nelson, and Paula Treichler. New York: Routledge, 1992. 479–500. Print.

Penley, Constance, Celine Parrenas Shimizu, Mireille Miller-Young, and Tristan Taormino. "The Politics of Producing Pleasure." Introduction. *The Feminist Porn Book.* Ed. Tristan Taormino et al. 9–20.

Philips, Ian. "Walt." *Best Transgender Erotica.* Ed. Hanne Blank and Raven Kaldera. Cambridge, MA: Circlet Press. 241–257. Print.

Preston, John. *Mr. Benson.* New York: Badboy, 1992. Print.

Prosser, Jay. *Second Skins: The Body Narratives of Transsexuality.* New York: Columbia UP, 1998. Print.

Queen, Carol. "Ganged." *Best Gay Erotica 1996.* Ed. Michael Ford. San Francisco: Cleis, 1996. 38–50. Print.

———. *The Leather Daddy and the Femme.* San Francisco: Cleis, 1998. Print.

———. "Sweating Profusely in Mérida: A Memoir." *Herotica 3.* Ed. Susie Bright. New York: Penguin, 1994. 190–195. Print.

Queen, Carol, and Lawrence Schimel. Introduction. *Switch Hitters.* Eds. Carol Queen and Lawrence Schimel. Pittsburgh: Cleis, 1996. 9–15. Print.

Ramsland, Katherine. *The Roquelaure Reader: A Companion to Anne Rice's Erotica.* New York: Plume/Penguin, 1996. Print.

Réage, Pauline. *Story of O.* Trans. S. d'Estree. New York: Ballantine, 1973. Print.

Renarde, Giselle. "The Therapist and the Whore." *Take Me There: Trans and Genderqueer Erotica.* Ed. Tristan Taormino. San Francisco: Cleis, 2011. 28–39. Print.

Rice, Anne [A. N. Roquelaure]. *The Claiming of Sleeping Beauty*. London: Futura, 1987. Print.
———. *Beauty's Punishment*. New York: E. P. Dutton, 1984. Print.
———. *Beauty's Release*. New York: E. P. Dutton, 1985. Print.
Richardson, Diane. *Rethinking Sexuality*. London: Sage, 2000. Print.
Roche, Charlotte. *Wetlands*. Grove, 2010. Print.
Rose, Jacqueline. *Sexuality in the Field of Vision*. London: Verso, 1986. Print.
Ross, Andrew. *No Respect: Intellectuals and Popular Culture*. New York: Routledge, 1989. Print.
Rubin, Gayle. "The Catacombs: A Temple of the Butthole." *Leatherfolk*. Ed. Mark Thompson. Boston: Alyson, 1991. 119–141. Print.
———. "Elegy for the Valley of the Kings: AIDS and the Leather Community in San Francisco, 1981–1996." *Changing Times*. Ed. Martin Levine, Peter Nardi, and John Gagnon. Chicago: U of Chicago P, 1997. 101–144. Print.
———. "Misguided, Dangerous, and Wrong: An Analysis of Antipornography Politics. *Deviations: A Gayle Rubin Reader*. Durham: Duke UP, 2011. 254–275. Print.
———. "Of Catamites and Kings: Reflections on Butch, Gender, and Boundaries." *The Persistent Desire*. Ed. Joan Nestle. Boston: Alyson, 1992. 466–482. Print.
———. "Sexual Traffic." Interview with Judith Butler. *Coming Out of Feminism?* Ed. Mandy Merck, Naomi Segal, and Elizabeth Wright. Oxford: Blackwell, 1998. 36–73. Print.
———. "Thinking Sex: Notes for a Radical Theory of the Politics of Sexuality." *Pleasure and Danger*. Ed. Carole S. Vance. Boston: Routledge & Kegan Paul, 1984. 267–319. Print.
———. "The Traffic in Women: Notes on the 'Political Economy' of Sex." *Toward an Anthropology of Women*. Ed. Rayna R. Reiter. New York: Monthly Review Press, 1975. 157–210. Print. Russell, D. E. H. "Pornography and Rape: A Causal Model." *Making Violence Sexy: Feminist Views on Pornography*. Ed. D. E. H. Russell. Buckingham: Open UP, 1993. 120–150. Print.
———. "Pornography and Violence: What Does the Research Say?" *Take Back the Night: Women on Pornography*. Ed. L. Lederer. New York: William Morrow and Company, 1980. 218–238. Print.
Ryberg, Ingrid. "Imagining Safe Space: The Politics of Queer, Feminist,

and Lesbian Pornography." Diss. in Cinema Studies at Stockholm U, Sweden, 2012. Print.

Sabo, Anne G. *After Pornified: How Women Are Transforming Pornography and Why It Really Matters.* Winchester, UK: Zero Books, 2011. Print.

Sadownick, Doug. "The Birth of Queer Nation and the Death of 'Gay' and 'Lesbian.'" *LA Weekly.* 17–23 May 1991. Print.

Samois, ed. *Coming to Power: Writings and Graphics on Lesbian S/M.* Boston: Alyson, 1981. Print.

Sandler, Helen. *Big Deal.* London: Sapphire, 1999. Print.

Sara, Lady. "The Triangle." *Leather Women.* Ed. Laura Antoniou. New York: Rosebud, 1993. 167–201. Print.

Sarracino, Carmine, and Kevin M. Scott. *The Porning of America: The Rise of Porn Culture, What It Means, and Where We Go from Here.* Boston: Beacon Press, 2008. Print.

Schechner, Richard. *Between Theater and Anthropology.* Philadelphia: U of Penn P, 1985. Print.

Sedgwick, Eve Kosofsky. *Epistemology of the Closet.* Berkeley: U of California P, 1990. Print.

———. "Is the Rectum Straight?" *Tendencies.* Durham: Duke UP, 1993. 73–103. Print.

———. "Queer and Now." *Tendencies.* 1–20.

Segal, Lynne. "Sweet Sorrows, Painful Pleasures: Pornography and the Perils of Heterosexual Desire." *Sex Exposed.* Ed. Lynne Segal and Mary McIntosh. London: Virago, 1992. 65–91. Print.

———. "Does Pornography Cause Violence? The Search for Evidence." *Dirty Looks: Women, Pornography, Power.* Ed. Pamela Church Gibson and Roma Gibson. London: British Film Institute, 1993. 5–21. Print.

———. *Straight Sex: Rethinking the Politics of Pleasure.* Berkeley: U of California Press, 1994. Print.

Silverman, Kaja. "Masochism and Male Subjectivity." *Camera Obscura* 17 (1988): 31–66. Print.

———. "The Lacanian Phallus." *Differences* 4.1 (1992): 84–115. Print.

Simpson, Mark. "A World of Penises." *Male Impersonators: Men Performing Masculinity.* New York: Routledge, 1994. Print.

Smith, Clarissa. *One for the Girls: The Pleasures and Practices of Reading Women's Porn.* Bristol, UK: Intellect, 2007. Print.

Smith, Clarissa, and Feona Attwood. "Emotional Truths and Thrilling Slide Shows: The Resurgence of Antiporn Feminism." *The Feminist Porn Book.* Ed. Taormino et al. 41–57.

Smyth, Cherry. "The Pleasure Threshold: Looking at Lesbian Pornography on Film." *Feminist Review* 34 (Spring 1990): 152–159. Print.

Snitow, Ann. "Retrenchment vs. Transformation: The Politics of the Antipornography Movement." *Caught Looking*. 1986. Ed. Caught Looking Inc. 10–17.

Sontag, Susan. "The Pornographic Imagination." *Styles of Radical Will*. New York: Farrar, Straus and Giroux, 1969. 35–73. Print.

Sonnet, Esther. "'Erotic Fiction by Women for Women': The Pleasures of Post-Feminist Heterosexuality." *Sexualities* 2.2 (1999): 167–187. Print.

Stern, Lesley. "The Body as Evidence: A Critical Review of the Pornography Problematic." *Screen* 23.5 (1982): 38–60. Print.

Stone, Roberta. "The Journal." *Herotica 2*. Ed. Susie Bright and Joani Blank. New York: Plume, 1992. 29–42. Print.

Straayer, Chris. "Discourse Intercourse: A Compendium of Sexual Scripts." *Deviant Eyes, Deviant Bodies*. New York: Columbia UP, 1996. 184–232. Print.

———. "The Seduction of Boundaries: Feminist Fluidity in Annie Sprinkle's Art/Life." *Deviant Eyes, Deviant Bodies*. 233–252. Print.

Stryker, Susan. "The Transgender Issue: An Introduction." *GLQ* 4.2 (1998): 145–158. Print.

Sweeney, Robin. "Daddy." *Doing It for Daddy*. Ed. Califia. 89–100.

Tankard Reist, Melinda, ed. *Getting Real: Challenging the Sexualisation of Girls*. Melbourne: Spinifex Press, 2010. Print.

Taormino, Tristan, Celine Parrenas Shimizu, Constance Penley, and Mireille Miller-Young, eds. *The Feminist Porn Book: The Politics of Producing Pleasure*. New York: The Feminist Press, 2013. Print.

Tavel, Catherine. "About Penetration." *Herotica 3*. Ed. Susie Bright. New York: Plume, 1994. 56–69. Print.

———. "Claudia's Cheeks." *Herotica 2*. Ed. Susie Bright and Joani Blank. New York: Plume, 1991. 171–181. Print.

Turner, Victor. *Dramas, Fields, and Metaphors*. Ithaca, NY: Cornell UP, 1974. Print.

———. *From Ritual to Theatre*. Cambridge, MA: Performing Arts Journal Publications, 1982. Print.

Tyler, Carole-Anne. "Boys Will Be Girls: The Politics of Gay Drag." *Inside/Out*. Ed. Diana Fuss. New York: Routledge, 1991. 32–70. Print.

Tyler, Meagan. "'Now, That's Pornography!' Violence and Domination in Adult Video News." *Everyday Pornography*. Ed. Boyle. 50–62.

Valentine, David. *Imagining Transgender: An Ethnography of a Category.* Durham: Duke UP, 2007. Print.

Vance, Carol S., ed. *Pleasure and Danger: Exploring Female Sexuality.* London: Routledge & Kegan Paul, 1984. Print.

Wagner, Peter. *Eros Revived: Erotica of the Enlightenment in England and America.* London: Secker & Warburg, 1988. Print.

Warner, Michael. *Publics and Counterpublics.* New York: Zone, 2002. Print.

———. *The Trouble with Normal: Sex, Politics, and the Ethics of Queer Life.* Cambridge: Harvard UP, 2000. Print.

Waugh, Tom. "Men's Pornography: Gay vs. Straight." *Jump Cut* 30 (1985): 30–34. Print.

Weaver, James. "Responding to Erotica: Perceptual Processes and Dispositional Implications." *Responding to the Screen: Reception and Reaction Processes.* Ed. Jennings Bryant and Dolf Zillmann. Hillsdale: Lawrence Erlbaum, 1991. 329–354. Print.

Whatling, Clare. "Who's Read *Macho Sluts*?" *Feminism and Cultural Studies.* Ed. Morag Shiach. Oxford: Oxford UP, 1999. 417–430. Print.

"When Girls Look at Boys." *On Our Backs* (July–August 1989): 29–31, 42–43. Print.

Wicke, Jennifer. "Through a Gaze Darkly: Pornography's Academic Market." *Dirty Looks: Women, Pornography, Power.* Ed. Pamela Church Gibson and Roma Gibson. London: British Film Institute, 1993. 62–80. Print.

Wilden, Anthony, ed. *The Language of the Self.* Baltimore: Johns Hopkins UP, 1968. Print.

Williams, Linda. *Hard Core: Power, Pleasure, and the "Frenzy of the Visible."* Berkeley: U of California P, 1989. Print.

———. "Porn Studies: Proliferating Pornographies On/Scene: An Introduction." *Porn Studies.* Ed. Williams. 1–23.

———. "Pornographies On/Scene or *Diff'rent strokes for Diff'rent folks.*" *Sex Exposed.* Ed. Lynne Segal and Mary McIntosh. London: Virago, 1992. 233–265. Print.

———. "A Provoking Agent: The Pornography and Performance Art of Annie Sprinkle." *Dirty Looks: Women, Pornography, Power.* Ed. Pamela Church Gibson and Roma Gibson. London: British Film Institute, 1993. 176–191. Print.

———. "Second Thoughts on Hard Core: American Obscenity Law and the Scapegoating of Deviance." *Dirty Looks: Women, Pornography,*

Power. Ed. Pamela Church Gibson and Roma Gibson. London: British Film Institute, 1993. 176–191. Print.

Williams, Linda, ed. *Porn Studies*. Durham: Duke UP, 2004. Print.

Willis, Ellen. "Feminism, Moralism, and Pornography." *Powers of Desire: The Politics of Sexuality*. Ed. Ann Snitow, Christine Stansell, and Sharon Thompson. New York: Monthly Review, 1983. 460–467. Print.

Woolf, Virginia. *A Room of One's Own*. London: Hogarth, 1949. Print.

Zealand, Steven. *The Masculine Marine: Homoeroticism in the U.S. Marine Corps*. New York: Harrington Park, 1996. Print.

Ziv, Amalia. "Girl Meets Boy: Cross-gender Queer Sex and the Promise of Pornography." *Sexualities* 17 (2014): 885–905. Print.

———. "Shameful Fantasies: Cross-Gender Queer Sex in Lesbian Erotic Fiction." *Gay Shame*. Ed. David M. Halperin and Valerie Traub. Chicago: U of Chicago P, 2009. 165–175. Print.

———. "The Pervert's Progress: An Analysis of *Story of O* and the Beauty Trilogy." *Feminist Review* 46 (Spring 1994): 61–75. Print.

Index

ACT UP, 189
Adams, Parveen, 188
AIDS, 89, 91, 92, 112
Alley of the Tranny Boys, 207, 212–13
alternative masculinities, 85
anal receptivity, 115–16, 119. See also Bersini, Leo
Angel, Buck, 4, 209, 217, 240. See also FTM porn
anti-antiporn position, 2, 8, 28–30, 48–53, 69, 237n8. See also Califa, Pat; Rubin, Gayle; Williams, Linda; Willis, Ellen
antiporn movement, 1, 6, 230; campaigns, 26, 58–66; flaws of, 41–48. See also Dines, Gail; Dworkin, Andrea; Levy, Ariel; MacKinnon, Catharine; Paul, Pamela
Aretino, Pietro, 11
Attwood, Feona, 60, 67
Austin, J. L., 40, 54, 173
"authentic sexuality," 60–62. See also Paul, Pamela

Balibar, Etienne, 15
Barnard College Conference on Women and Sexuality, 26
Bashevis Singer, Isaac, 105
Bataille, Georges, 109–11, 112, 114
Beatty, Maria, 4, 134
Beauty Trilogy, The, 22, 72–83. See also Rice, Anne
Benjamin, Jessica, 96
Bersani, Leo, 111–17, 185, 186
Big Deal, 201–202, 205. See also Sandler, Helen
Bloch, Ernst, 9
Booth, Wayne, 75
Boswell, John, 113, 255n11
Boyle, Karen, 241n23
Bridges, Ana, 67
Bright, Susie, 8
Brown, Wendy, 37, 43–44, 45
Butler, Judith, 17, 178–79; *Bodies That Matter*, 54; "Critically Queer," 194; *Excitable Speech*, 40–41, 54–56; "Force of Fantasy," 19; *Gender Trouble*, 190; "Melancholy Gender/Refused Identification," 94; "The Lesbian Phallus," 155–57, 166–67; theory of gender performativity, 173–78
Califa, Pat, 8, 26, 50, 86, 250n23; "Daddy," 168, 188; "Feminism and Sadomasochism," 184; "Genderbending," 179, 181; "Identity Sedition,"

Califa, Pat (*continued*)
89–91; *Sex Changes*, 215–16; "The Calyx of Isis," 132–33; "The Surprise Party," 198–201
Califa, Patrick. *See* Califa, Pat
Case, Sue-Ellen, 163, 165, 180
castration complex, 140, 142, 149–51, 154, 161
Catacombs (San Francisco), 90–91
Clips, 22, 158, 165, 167, 263n29. *See also* Fatale Video; cum shot
Comella, Lynn, 5–6
Coming To Power, 184, 223–34. *See also* Samois
Cornell, Drucilla, 45, 46, 106–107
Cowie, Elizabeth, 17–18, 47
Creet, Julia, 89–90
cross-gender identification, 93–99, 195–96. *See also* Sedgwick, Eve Kosofsky
cross-gender queer sex, 197–206, 224. *See also* FTM porn
cum shot, the, 163–65. *See also Clips*
Cvetkovich, Ann, 123–25, 256n13, 257n19

de Lauretis, Teresa, 18, 56–57, 150, 152–55
Derrida, Jacques, 54, 265n9
dildo, 139–49, 262n22; as fetish, 161–62; in lesbian pornography, 92–94, 139. *See also* phallus
Dines, Gail, 17, 27, 58–66
docu-porn, 209. *See also* Buck, Angel
Duggan, Lisa, 49
Dworkin, Andrea 26, 32, 57, 113–14; *Intercourse*, 101–9. *See also* intercourse (heterosexual); penetration
Dyer, Richard, 126–27

Engberg, Mia, 4
Equal Rights Amendment, the, 48

fantasy, 10, 17–19, 47–48, 57. *See also* gay male sexuality
female sexual subjectivity, 14–16, 51, 107–108, 226. *See also* gender performativity; lesbian sex culture

Fatale Video, 4, 158, 174, 178. *See also Clips*
Feminist Anti-Censorship Taskforce (FACT), 26. *See also* anti-antiporn
feminist film theory, 51–52, 240n22
Feminist Porn Awards, 5
Feminist Porn Book, The, 5, 6, 66–67, 211
fetishism, 149–57, 158–62, 163, 166. *See also Clips*; dildo; Freud, Sigmund; phallus
Findlay, Heather, 139, 161
First Amendment, the, 40
Foucault, Michel, 8, 11, 14, 42, 51, 113
Freud, Sigmund, 94, 95, 99, 112, 149–51; and female castration, 140–42; and identification, 94–95; and the phallic stage 141–42. *See also* phallus
Frye, Marilyn, 89, 93
FTM, 169, 206–17, 226; FTM identity, 212–14, 216–18, 222, 226; FTM porn 4, 23, 206–209, 212. *See also* Buck, Angel; gender performativity
Fuss, Diana, 98–99

Gallop, Jane, 145–47, 167, 264n36
gay male sexuality, 71; as fantasy, 86–89; gay male sex culture, 88–94, 131
gender performativity, 171–73; and gender-bending, 178–80; and sexual subjectivity, 193–94; in lesbian pornography, 180–82; pitfalls of, 194–196; S/M and performativity, 182–88. *See also* Butler, Judith: theory of gender performativity; *The Leather Daddy and the Femme*
Grosz, Elizabeth, 142, 143, 150–52, 155

Halavais, Alexander, 231
Halberstam, Judith, 213–14, 225
Hale, Jacob, 169, 187, 192, 212, 216
Halperin, David, 14
Hartsock, Nancy, 241n27
Hart, Lynda, 183, 186–87
Heresies, 26
History of Sexuality, The, 14, 36. *See also* Foucault, Michel

Hite, Shere, 108
HIV. *See* AIDS
Horney, Karen, 141
Houston, Shine Louise, 4
Hunt, Lynn, 11, 12

impotence, 47, 118
intercourse (heterosexual), 44–45, 82, 113; and anal receptivity, 115–18; 118–22; *Intercourse*, 101–109; masculinist interpretation of, 108–109; political dimensions of, 102–1055; privileged position of, 118–22. *See also* Dworkin, Andrea; penetration
inversion paradigm, 93

Jeffreys, Sheila, 92–93, 216, 239n12
Jones, Ernst, 141
Jouevet, Emilie, 4
Joy, Petra, 4

Kendrick, Walter, 12
Kinney, Nan. *See* Fatale Video
Kustritz, Anne, 82

Lacan, Jacques, 141–44, 146, 147. *See also* phallus
Language of Psychoanalysis, The, 18, 72
Leather Daddy and the Femme, The, 23, 189–93, 197. *See also* gender performativity; Queen, Carol
Levy, Ariel, 27, 221–22
lesbian sex culture: and AIDS, 91–92; gay male intertext, 84–94; phallicization of, 92, 93. *See also* gender performativity; lesbian S/M
lesbian S/M, 90, 92–93, 169, 182–88, 203–204, 212, 216, 266n16; S/M fiction 4, 128, 132–33, 192, 198–201, 218–33. *See also* Califia, Pat; gender performativity; Hale, Jacob; lesbian sex culture; Samois
Lovelace, Linda. *See* Marchiano, Linda
Lust, Erika, 4

MacCowen, Lyndall, 123
MacKinnon, Catharine, 1, 26–27, 63, 108; critique of pornography, 30–41; *Feminism Unmodified*, 34–35, 37–38; *On Collaboration*, 29; *Only Words*, 32, 33, 34, 38; *Towards a Feminist Theory of the State*, 29, 36, 42–48. *See also* antiporn movement
male homoeroticism, 72–73, 74. *See also Beauty Trilogy, The*
Marchiano, Linda, 33, 35
Marcus, Steven, 8
Martin, Biddy, 194–96, 206
Marx, Karl, 43
Meese Commission on Pornography, the, 27
Mercer, Kobena, 63
Merck, Mandy, 39, 40, 116, 156–57
Minneapolis and Indianapolis antiporn ordinances, 26–27, 243n40, 251n5, 240n21, 246n66
Millet, Kate, 74
Modleski, Tania, 184, 235n13. *See also Coming to Power*
Mulvey, Laura, 51–52, 160, 161
Muñoz, José Esteban, 9

Nestle, Joan, 124–25
Newton, Esther, 15, 93, 247n6

oedipality, 93, 94, 95, 144–45, 161. *See also* Freud, Sigmund
On Our Backs, 4, 84

Paul, Pamela, 2, 17, 27, 60, 62, 65
Pavlov, Ivan, 39
penetration, 104–6, 113; anal penetration, 118–20, 122; in gay male pornography, 125–30; in lesbian sexuality, 122–25; in lesbian S/M porn, 132–33; vaginal penetration, 116, 210, 211. *See also* Dworkin, Andrea; intercourse (heterosexual)
penis, 45, 103, 260n13; as synecdoche of masculinity, 127–28; occupation by, 105; penis envy, 168–69. *See also* phallus
Penley, Constance, 81, 82–83
performance, 171–73

phallus, 16, 22, 85, 140; and the fetish, 149–57; and the Oedipus complex, 144–45; as a Lacanian signifier, 146–47, 162; feminist readings of, 144–49; in lesbian pornography 157–68; phallic power, 80, 115; phallocentricism, 115, 117; "splitting" the phallus, 165, 167; uses of, 140–44. *See also* Butler, Judith; *The Lesbian Phallus*

phantasmic strategies, 19, 117–25, 133–37, 194, 197. *See also* cross-gender queer sex; FTM; queer intertextuality

pornography: alternative, 6, 19–20; and behavioral conditioning, 38–39; arguments in support of, 40–53; "definition," 10–14; feminist, 5, 6, 20, 64, 66–68; feminist critique of, 2, 13, 27; history of, 11–13; linguistic performativity and, 39–41, 173; social construction of, 36–37, 42, 51; teaching pornography, 227–30. *See also* Steinem, Gloria

"Pornotopia." *See* Marcus, Steven

Preston, John, 128

Prosser, Jay, 196, 207, 225

Queen, Carol, 23, 86, 90, 130, 131. *See also Leather Daddy and the Femme, The*

queer intertextuality, 218–26

Queer Nation, 20, 189

Queer theory, 194, 196, 225, 228

Ramsland, Katherine, 75–77, 79

rape, 45, 106

Rednour, Shar, 4

Rice, Anne, 8, 22, 75, 97. *See also Beauty Trilogy, The*

Roquelaure, A. N. *See* Rice, Anne

Roquelaure Reader, The, 75–76. *See also Beauty Trilogy, The*

Rose, Jacqueline, 143, 260n8

Ross, Andrew, 13

Royalle, Candida, 4, 66

Rubin, Gayle, 41, 50–51, 60, 90, 126, 129, 133, 144–45, 188, 257n20

Ryberg, Ingrid, 5

Sabo, Anne, 66–67

Sade, Marquis de, 12

Samois, 26, 223. *See also* lesbian S/M

Sandler, Helen, 198, 201, 203. *See also Big Deal*

Schimel, Lawrence, 86, 90

sex education, 62

Sedgwick, Eve Kosofsky, 9, 96–98, 253n38, 259n6. *See also* cross-gender identification

Sexing the Transman, 209–11

Silverman, Kaja, 79–81, 147–49

Simpson, Mark, 126

S.I.R. Productions, 4, 255n10

Sluts and Goddesses Video Workshop, The, 134–36

Smith, Clarissa, 67

Smyth, Cherry, 164

Social Purity Movement, the, 49

Sontag, Susan, 13, 240n22

Span, Anna, 4, 69

Sprinkle, Annie, 4, 134–36

Steinem, Gloria, 236n18

Stern, Lesley, 26, 47, 52

Stone, Roberta, 86

Stonewall, 9

Stop Porn Culture, 27. *See also* Dines, Gail

Sundahl, Debbie. *See* Fatale Video

Sweeney, Robin, 169

Switch Hitters, 86, 251n24

Take Back The Night, 26

Taormino, Tristan, 4

Tavel, Catherine, 119, 120

Tom of Finland, 126, 190

Tyler, Carole-Anne, 116

utopia, 9, 10; "concrete utopia," 10

vagina, 105, 107, 108, 116, 226; deterritorialization of, 212. *See also* penetration

Valentine, David, 217

Waugh, Tom, 127
Williams, Linda, 1, 2, 20, 52, 162–63, 168
Willis, Ellen, 26, 49, 50
Women Against Pornography (WAP), 25, 61

Women Against Violence In Pornography and the Media (WAVPM), 25

Zealand, Steve, 129